Surviving and Thriving
THE ESSENTIAL Teacher's Guide

OUT SOON!

Surviving and Thriving:
Educating Children With Additional Needs In The Mainstream Classroom

Surviving and Thriving:
Assisting Your Child With Additional Needs In The Mainstream Classroom

Surviving and Thriving: The Essential Teacher's Guide

First published in Australia in 2015 by Burst Creative

Copyright © Nadine King 2015

All rights reserved. This publication is copyright. Other than for the purposes of and subject to the conditions prescribed under the Copyright Act, no part of it may in any form or by any means (electronic, mechanical, micro copying, photocopying, recording or otherwise) be reproduced, stored in a retrieval system or transmitted without prior written permission. The Australian Copyright Act 1968 (the Act) allows a maximum of one chapter or 10 percent of this book, whichever is the greater, to be photocopied by any educational institution for its educational purposes provided that the educational institution (or body that administers it) has given a remuneration notice to the Copyright Agency (Australia) under the Act. Enquiries should be addressed to the publisher.

Publisher
Burst Creative
PO Box 4019 Ringwood Victoria 3134 Australia
Email: info@burstcreative.com.au
Web: www.burstcreative.com.au

Design and Typesetting
Burst Creative
PO Box 4019 Ringwood Victoria 3134 Australia
Email: info@burstcreative.com.au
Web: www.burstcreative.com.au

Printed and bound in Australia by Burst Creative

Cataloguing-in-Publication details are available from the National Library of Australia
www.trove.nla.gov.au

ISBN 978-0-99431-301-0

Although every precaution has been taken in the preparation of this book, the publisher and author assume no responsibility for errors or omissions. Neither is any liability assumed for damages resulting from the use of this information contained herein.

This book is dedicated to:

P

Gentle hearts are counted down
The queue is out of sight and out of sounds
Me, I'm out of breath, but not quite doubting
I've found a door which lets me out!
(David Bowie, Rock 'n 'Roll With Me, Diamond Dogs, 1974)

C

Fox: Should we take the short cut or the scenic route?
Mrs Fox: Let's take the short cut.
Fox: But the scenic route is so much prettier.
Mrs Fox: Okay, let's take the scenic route.
Fox: Great. It's actually slightly quicker, anyway.
(Wes Anderson (2009) & Roald Dahl (1970), Fantastic Mr Fox

J

'I should wake you up more often, little duck'
(Katniss Everdeen, Mockingjay by Suzanne Collins, 2010)

'Close your eyes, tap your heels three times and think to yourself, "There's No Place Like Home."
(Glinda, The Good Witch of the South, The Wizard of Oz, 1939)

About The Author

After completing a Bachelor of Arts in Disability Studies I realised it wasn't quite right for me. Needing a job, I ended up as a storeperson at a hardware wholesalers and worked my way up to Assistant Manager. Perhaps administration/secretarial work was a better match, so I completed an Advanced Diploma of Business at night whilst working as Production Manager of a textiles company. Daughter number one was born then so for the next ten years waitressing became my casual job that fitted around children. When daughter number two came along I continued to waitress four nights a week at a local motel restaurant, eventually becoming relief manager of the motel.

Around this time my eldest started school and I loved being a parent helper in the classroom and volunteered as much as I could. I began to realise my skills and personality fitted really well with teaching. Back to university I went, this time studying for a Masters in Education (Primary), cramming in my study around when the girls were at school and childcare.

In 2008 I was lucky to gain my first teaching position at the local primary school where my girls attended. I've had a very varied career so far, never teaching the same grade level two years in a row! In 2014 I took twelve months leave to write this book and worked as a Casual Relief Teacher for the first time ever, averaging 3-4 days per week for most of the year. In 2015 I am enjoying teaching Visual Art.

Contents

1	Application	5
2	Interview	13
3	Enjoying Teaching	23
4	First Few Days	31
5	Classroom Management	41
6	Resource Organisation	59
7	Behaviour Management	67
8	Planning	85
9	Differentiation	93
10	Aides	101
11	Disabilities	109
12	Student Hygiene	127
13	Poo Wee Vomit	135
14	Technology	143
15	Partnering Positively With Parents	161
16	Working Effectively With Colleagues	185
17	Homework	203
18	Displays	211
19	Boundaries	215
20	The Bits That Don't Fit Into Another Chapter Neatly!	223
21	Five Minute Fillers	233
22	Report Writing	241
23	Parent Teacher Interviews	255
24	Casual Relief Teaching	263
25	Specialists	271
26	Templates	279
	Acknowlegements	281

Introduction

The purpose of this book is to support pre-service and graduate teachers by providing them with tools that will facilitate a long and rewarding career in the classroom. Studies show that between five and seven years after graduating, many teachers leave the education field for a completely different industry. The reasons are many – lack of support, disillusion with the system, difficult parents, challenging children, to name a few. At this point teachers have developed valuable knowledge and skills through their experiences and it's such a shame knowing the knowledge and skills of experienced teachers is lost to the education field. It's important also to continue your journey. Practising teachers are continually adding to the cumulative asset of teacher knowledge and contributing invaluable skills and relationships to future generations.

During my first year of teaching I found little enjoyment and experienced a lot of stress. I wanted to give it away many times. My class was really difficult, mentoring was poor and I felt overwhelmed frequently. The only thing preventing me from chucking in the towel was the amount of money I'd spent on gaining my Masters Degree!

Too many times to count I would have appreciated being able to pick up a 'how to' book, find a quick fix, or at least a suggested way forward, and then implement a change to help my problem. Talking to colleagues helped, however there's a limit to how many questions you can ask before you become super annoying.

Sometimes as you begin teaching, you can feel like you are in survival mode. The purpose of this book is to support you through your teaching journey from 'surviving' to 'thriving.' The more proficient, relaxed and organised teachers we have, the better the educational outcomes for our children and the better you will handle yourself and enjoy your job.

How To Use This Book

This book is written in stand-alone chapters. That means you can choose to read specific chapters to get the help you are looking for. References to other chapters are made, simply so you can refer to them if you want more information on a particular topic.

When you undertake any professional development, it's always a good sign if you are inspired to make changes as soon as possible in your own classroom. Attempting to make too many large and labour intensive changes is not recommended, as it can become too burdensome or difficult. The same applies for this book; work out what your most pressing concerns are and tackle those. Once you experience some success, start to take on more.

Not all of the ideas presented will be relevant or applicable to your personal situation. They are a guide only and based on successful personal experience. I fully intend for you to take my suggestions and mould them into your own effective strategies.

I love to hear from my readers. Please let me know about your successes after reading my book, information you would've liked but was missing, and to suggest alternative strategies. I can be contacted on twitter https://twitter.com/thrivingteach, via my website www.survivingandthriving.com.au, Instagram http://instagram.com/survivingandthriving and on the Facebook page, https://www.facebook.com/survivingandthrivingteaching. Your feedback helps me write professional development and to inspire my Surviving and Thriving members!

Are you looking for some regular, practical and helpful classroom and teaching tips? Why not sign up as a Surviving and Thriving member? You'll enjoy receiving fortnightly emails on all of the topics covered in the chapters, plus a few more.

Follow this link to subscribe www.survivingandthriving.com.au/members

Finally, congratulations on choosing teaching as a career. It's exciting, busy, independent, ever changing and rewarding. May you **SURVIVE** and **THRIVE!**

Application

Chapter Overview

- Curriculum Vitae
- Written application
- Proofreading and editing
- Addressing Key Selection Criteria

Your written application is the only chance to impress a panel enough to offer you an interview. Sometimes there may be upwards of fifty applications for a single position and an interview might be offered to approximately five applicants. If you are applying for many jobs and not getting an interview then your written application is letting you down. If you are getting interviews but not cracking a job offer, better read the chapter on Interviews.

Curriculum Vitae

You will be required to submit a Curriculum Vitae (C.V.) with your application. This should be succinct, not longer than two pages, and include all relevant experience and qualifications. It's a good idea to spend a fair bit of time on both the content and the layout. Using design software, if you are able to, will help to give your C.V. an edge. Perhaps ask a friend to help if you are stuck here. I always have! Remember when designing the layout - less is more. It has to be very easy to read and not fussy. If I am reading your C.V., I need to scan down it to see all the relevant points easily.

C.V. Subheadings

BACKGROUND INFORMATION

Name, email address and phone number are the obvious starting points here. Unless requested, I would leave it at that. No photo, location or date of birth. Omit these as they are irrelevant to your application. All humans make judgements, even when we try not to. If you are asked to include a photo, ensure it is a good headshot taken for this purpose. Don't just crop one from one of your social media accounts. The lighting must be good, hair and makeup neat and subtle, minimal jewellery and a smart shirt. It's your decision about how far you wish to travel for a job, not the panel's decision that it's too far to travel; leave your address off. A panel can probably work out how old you are approximately by your experience and qualifications so there's no need to spoon-feed it to them. Your age is irrelevant to your ability to be a teacher.

QUALIFICATIONS

MAJOR

Here you need to include your Year 12 qualification, university degrees and any other further education. Set them out in order from earliest to most recent. All you need to state is the qualification, venue you gained it from and year you graduated. If you gained honours or any other award, go you! Include them here. These are the little things that help us stand out from all the other applicants.

MINOR

Over the years we do many short courses. Only include these on your C.V. if they are relevant. A barista qualification means you can make great coffee (hopefully) and Food Safety means you won't give anyone food poisoning (fingers crossed), but are they going to help you be a good teacher? Sadly, no, (unless you are teaching Food Technology!), although maybe colleagues might benefit!

List all the short courses you have completed and think about whether they might help your application. Things like a mini bus licence, ladder licence (laughable but helpful), first aid, Bronze Medallion or balloon tying. Just kidding, but you get the drift. A colleague read an application where the applicant's ice skating achievements were all listed!

Employment History

This needs to be listed from more recent to most distant. Set it out something like this:

> **2014**   **Best Ever Primary School**
> **Pre-Service Teacher in 5/6, 8 week placement.**
>
> Responsibilities included: lesson sequence planning, contributing to team planning, attending staff meetings, behaviour management, full control in the classroom, administering assessment both formative and summative, planning for an excursion.

Try to include as many responsibilities as possible. If this is your first teacher position then you will definitely need to include previous jobs outside education. Perhaps if you have cafe experience at a few venues you can lump them together and make a general listing. For example, 2009-2012, Various Cafes. Add a general overview of responsibilities included. Don't forget to add any volunteering, particularly if it's in the education field.

RECENT PROFESSIONAL DEVELOPMENT

On student placement you may have had the opportunity to participate in some professional development (P.D). Universities also provide P.D. at times. Make sure you keep a list, as you will also need this for your registration. Details aren't necessary, just a date and title.

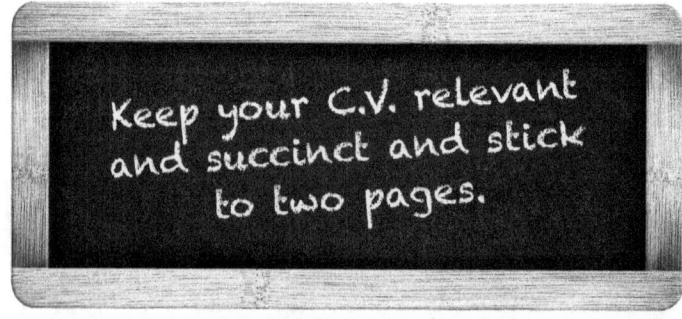

Keep your C.V. relevant and succinct and stick to two pages.

REFEREES

These are fairly crucial. In some cases, if there have been a lot of applications for a position, the panel may ring referees prior to offering an interview, as a way of culling applicants. Generally however, referees are rung after an interview. Listing three would be ideal, in case they have trouble contacting one. Choose people who are able to speak well on your behalf and can respond to questioning about your teaching abilities. The more recently they have had interactions with you the better. If you are already a graduate teacher then it's pretty important to have your current or recent principal or assistant principal listed. Ask your mentor also. If you are just finishing uni then ask your supervisors where you had placement. Possibly a boss or mentor outside of teaching who can talk up your character could be a referee too.

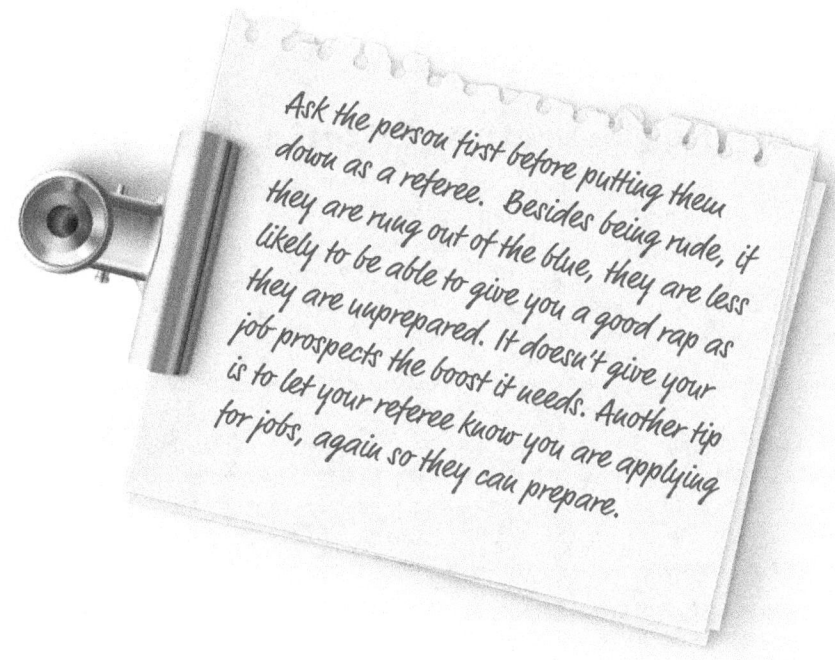

Ask the person first before putting them down as a referee. Besides being rude, if they are rung out of the blue, they are less likely to be able to give you a good rap as they are unprepared. It doesn't give your job prospects the boost it needs. Another tip is to let your referee know you are applying for jobs, again so they can prepare.

Some school systems allow you to include personal references. If this is a possibility, then by all means include it, especially if it's a ripper. Ensure it is recent and relevant to teaching. You may have had a part time job as a cleaner, but a panel don't really want to read a reference from a job like this, unless it is a personal reference testifying to your outstanding character. A good reference may tip the panel's opinion of you, enough to offer an interview.

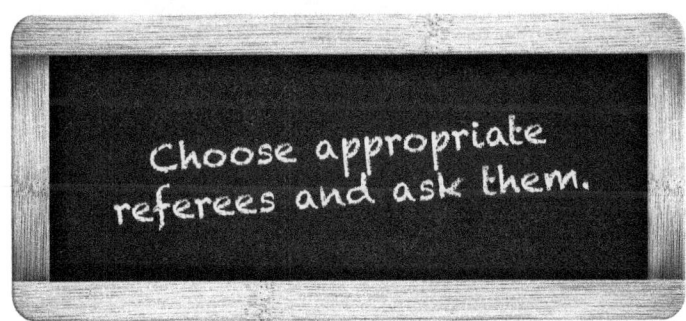

Choose appropriate referees and ask them.

Keep it Relevant

Depending on the job you are applying for, your C.V. may need to be amended for each application. For example, if you have extra experience or qualifications in equestrian, these are most likely irrelevant for an application to a government school. Don't take up space in your C.V. if it isn't needed. Some independent schools would jump at these extra skills. This is where research is your best friend. Besides reading a school's website thoroughly, ask your friends and colleagues if they have any extra information relevant to that school.

Written Application

This is the section a panel will look at most closely. It will take you hours and hours to write your first application, but after this you should only need to make minor amendments depending upon the individual school's requirements. To get an interview your written application really needs to stand out as there are so many applicants for each position. So, how do you stand out?

Addressing Key Selection Criteria (K.S.C.)

This is the biggy. Generally, new graduate positions have between five-seven K.S.C. for you to respond to. Start by making notes for each criteria until you can begin to pad it out more. You MUST say what you CAN do or WILL do. I can't state this more strongly. Don't fill your page with theory - the panel know all this stuff - tell them what you can do in relation to the criteria. Each K.S.C. usually has multiple components to it and you must address all parts of it. It's just like writing an essay. All aspects must be addressed for you to get a good mark!

Let's look at this sample K.S.C. and pull it apart: *Demonstrate an understanding of how students learn and effective classroom teaching strategies and the capacity to work with colleagues to continually improve teaching and learning.* Gee, they don't want much from one K.S.C. do they? This needs three separate responses: how students learn, effective teaching strategies and working with colleges to improve. It's important not to miss any of them and to give each of them an equal weighting. Remember to include what you have done already by using words like created, built, planned, utilised, catered and enabled. Use those action verbs!

When you are just starting out you most likely won't have a lot of experience to draw upon to state what you do. Panels understand this. It's okay in this situation to include some quotes from your supervising teachers on placement that they wrote on your reports. Only use one to two per K.S.C. however, and keep them relevant to the criteria. Don't include them if they aren't exactly right and don't worry if you don't have any. They aren't necessary, just a helpful addition. One application I have read was full of them and therefore they gave me nothing of substance. They didn't get an interview.

Keep it real. A written application isn't a forum for dramatics. I have read an actual application with this statement on it. "On an excursion I helped supervise I was able to keep the students safe from extreme danger when we were out in public." Full marks for telling me what they can do, but extreme danger? You will just make yourself look silly. Perhaps if the excursion was scuba diving in the open ocean in shark infested waters. And the sharks are hungry.

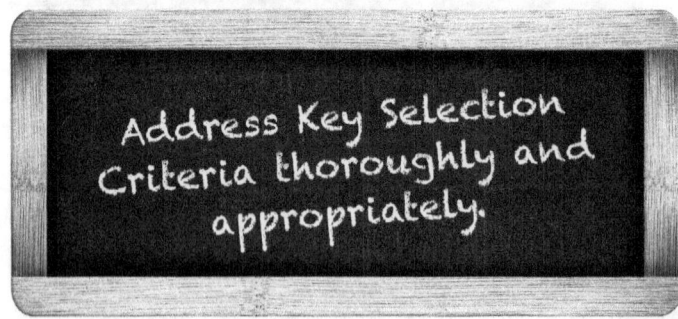

Address Key Selection Criteria thoroughly and appropriately.

Make it your own work

Teachers or leaders who read applications have to read a lot of them. It's pretty easy to spot one that you didn't write yourself. If it gets past them and they offer you an interview, it's usually obvious if your responses don't match the application. Don't be lazy and give them someone else's work. It won't benefit you in the long run. From K.S.C. one to K.S.C. six, your writing style and responses must be consistent and flow. Try to keep your comments to a page per criteria, or just a little over. You need to be able to answer the criteria within this limit, otherwise it becomes too much for a panel to read.

Proofreading and Editing

As a teacher you will be teaching the skills of editing and proofreading. You may as well work on your own skills via your application. Don't make corrections at the sentence and word level if you still need to work on the content. Set your application aside for a day and come back to read through it with fresh eyes. Have you answered all aspects of each K.S.C.? Does it make sense? Have you used enough action verbs to show what you can do? Can you cut waffle, repetition or sentences that don't really add to your application? Be brutal. Ask someone you trust to read through it for their opinion. Once you have done this then you can proofread for typos, grammar and spelling errors. I have read many mistake laden applications for teacher positions. Really? This is your core business and you haven't bothered to edit and proofread properly? This is your only chance to impress a panel and be offered an interview. Don't let them slide your application to the bottom of the pile due to a lack of proofreading. I know everyone's forte is not spelling and grammar, so ask someone who is good at it.

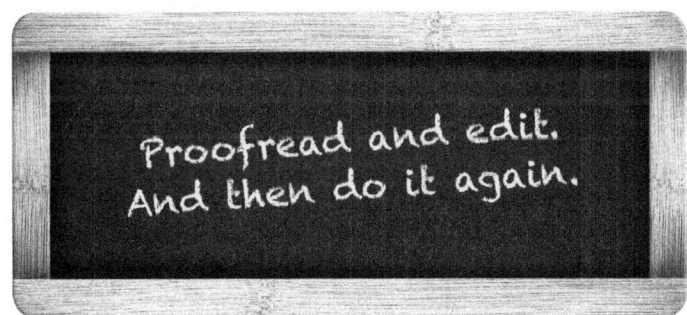

Inspiring quotes

"Tell me and I forget. Teach me and I remember. Involve me and I learn."
Chinese proverb

'Those that know, do. Those that understand, teach."
Aristotle

"While we teach, we learn."
Seneca

All admirable and inspiring quotes. Don't use them!

Leaving university your head is full of theory and knowledge, you are enthusiastic and not jaded, so it's understandable you want to throw a bit of that into your written application via a quote or two. But guess what? You are not the first person to use a quote. In fact, I think the number of beginning teachers who have included a learned quote or two by a wise philosopher must be in the millions by now. Just in Australia. It's not an original idea. If a panel have to read that in your application their eyes are going to glaze over. Don't waste space on quotes, instead use this space to tell me what YOU can do. I already know what Aristotle stood for.

Use this page to document any changes you may like to make on your application.

Interview

Chapter Overview

- Personal presentation
- Getting there
- Articulation
- What to say
- Asking questions
- Dazzling the panel

Congratulations on getting to the next step - The Interview!

I have separated the interview process into six distinct steps. Pull off all six and the job should be yours! The key is preparation and this requires you to put in some effort and time. You cannot expect to get a job easily in the current market without research and planning. An interview panel only have about thirty minutes with you to judge your suitability to work in their school. Looking good, feeling assured about your appearance and walking in confidently are all excellent ways to begin.

Personal Presentation

Your attire plays a supporting role in your interview. There are plenty of easily accessible tips around regarding how to dress for an interview, however time after time I have seen people get it wrong. When you get it wrong, some interviewers may be a little distracted from giving you their full attention and YOU may be a little distracted trying to cover up or have to sit in an awkward position so as to feel comfortable. I have seen a young girl with a VERY generous bust wear a dress that revealed too much cleavage and another wear a too tight dress that unfortunately revealed every lump and bump. I can't imagine they were comfortable - I know I felt a little uncomfortable for them! You don't want to be remembered for allowing your outfit to take centre stage. It's important to plan your outfit and appearance carefully and trial it. You want to be able to stride into the interview room with confidence, dressing in an outfit that makes you feel professional. Always aim for comfortable, well fitting, clean and stylish. Never aim for too tight, too short, too low, see through, shabby or grubby. It's a good idea to select an interview outfit and reuse it if it ticks all of the criteria.

Ladies

Put your chosen outfit on and lean forward. Showing a bit too much of your girls, girls?? Or a little see through anywhere? Change your outfit! Sit down. Does your skirt ride up a little too high? Pants ride up your butt? Change your outfit! Walk around. Are your shoes too high, too loose, too tight, too worn or scuffed? Any tears in your hosiery? Put a spare pair of stockings in your car or bag. Long skirt get caught anywhere as you walk? Change your outfit! Look in the mirror. Makeup and your hairstyle shouldn't be O.T.T. Aim for subtle and enhancing of your features.

Lads

A tip for guys is to check whether the school interviewing you has a dress policy. If you can't find it on the school's website, just ring reception and ask. A suit and tie may be overkill in a government school but essential in a private setting. Generally, don't wear denim.

Important in all this advice is to not lose your own sense of style. Who you are should shine through. That being said, when you walk into the interview room, the panel's eyes should not be drawn to any one feature or item.

> You are not dressing for a nightclub or party. Plan your outfit and trial it. Go conservative with makeup, hair and jewellery. Check the interviewing school's dress code and maintain your own sense of style.

Getting There

Arriving late to your interview shows a lack of planning and consideration. This will also increase your nerves and stress dramatically. The panel only have a short time to make judgements about you so if you are late, perhaps they may assume this is a habit for you. To avoid this you need to prepare in a few ways. How will you get there? If you are driving, is your car reliable and does it have a full tank of petrol? Running out of fuel or having your car break down on the way is stressful. Is there a reliable car you can borrow from someone for a few hours? Could someone give you a lift? Could you book a taxi? When choosing to drive yourself, it is imperative that you plot your route.

Alternatively, you may need to rely on public transport. Look up the school's location and the nearest transport network and plan the trip. How will you get from the station or stop to the school? How long will it take? Are you wearing shoes you can walk comfortably in? Sort this out the day before so on the day of the interview your sole focus is on excellent responses to the questions.

Occasionally there are unavoidable incidents that will cause you to be late, such as road works, car accidents or public transport incidents. If this is the case, then you MUST ring the school to inform them or reschedule. You can kiss your chances goodbye if you don't do this. Have the school's phone number handy in case you need it while travelling. It's much better to arrive early and will really lower your tension levels. Sit in your car or find a bench seat in the schoolyard and go through your notes then head into reception around five minutes prior to your interview time.

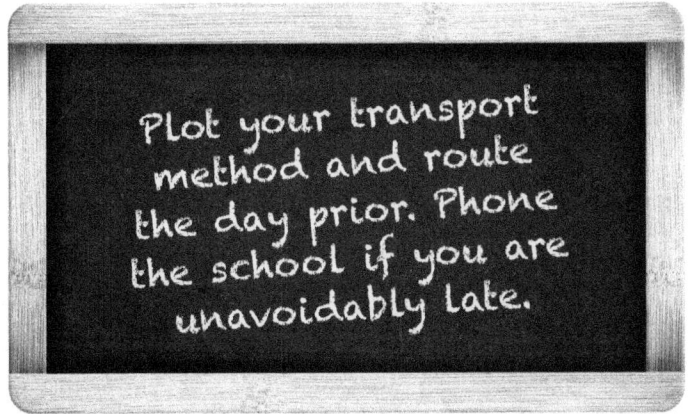

Plot your transport method and route the day prior. Phone the school if you are unavoidably late.

Articulation

Ohmygoditssotemptingtospeakfasttogeteverythingout. Huh? Yeah, that's what seems to happen in a lot of interviews. Many of us tend to speak quickly when we are nervous. Speaking rapidly puts us under stress, not allowing our thoughts time to catch up. Slowing down gives our brain time to formulate an optimal response and effectively communicate it.

An interviewer will need to take notes as you speak and it's far easier for them if you are speaking clearly and slowly. One of the easiest interviews for note taking I have ever conducted was when the pre-service teacher spoke quite slowly. The best bit though, was that she paused after each concept, to gather her thoughts, and was then able to make another comment to further support her response. I was able to jot down many of her points comprehensively and that made it far easier later on to compare her responses to the other applicants. Another bonus to this approach was it allowed her to feel like she had really gotten out all the points she wanted to make. Your ability to talk to the panel will be an indication to them of how you speak in front of your class.

Speaking slowly really does require practise. If you are at university they will usually conduct mock interviews towards the end of your degree where you can get some helpful feedback. Those of you who want more practise might like to pair up with a friend and have them ask some questions, observe your response and comment on how you responded. At this stage, don't worry about the content of your response too much. Your focus is on a clear and slow paced response with good pausing. An excellent tool for feedback is to record your speech via a desktop, laptop or other portable device. It's always a little confronting to hear how we sound. All those umms, aahs and yeah nahs we didn't even know we did! Take heart though, practise really does help.

Volume and strength of voice are also important. Too loud or too soft are both a little annoying and can convey messages of a dominating or too timid personality. Teachers need strong voices and to be able to project them.

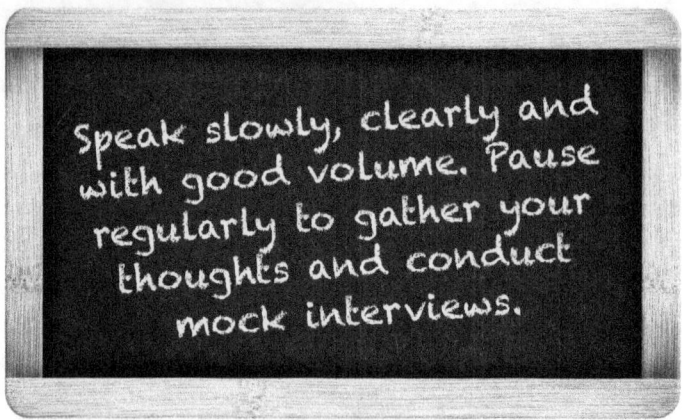

What To Say

When you are directed to enter the room, shake hands with all panel members and introduce yourself. This is very important as it portrays manners, confidence and warmth. On a recent panel I was on, only one of the eight applicants did this and it was very appreciated by my fellow interviewers.

It's usually obvious which seat is the 'Hot Seat' but if it's not, don't assume, ask! When you sit down, make sure you find a comfortable position where you have good posture and your knees can stay together. It's not a time to allow your legs to loll open, for you to slump, or to recline back too far so you look like you are watching your favourite T.V. show. Nor should you perch too stiffly on the edge of your chair. You are aiming for relaxed alertness.

Finally, put any bags on the floor at the side of your chair and if you have a folio, book or tech device you wish to use in the interview, place it on your knee or the table in front of you. NO GUM AND PUT YOUR PHONE ON SILENT BEFORE YOU ENTER THE ROOM!

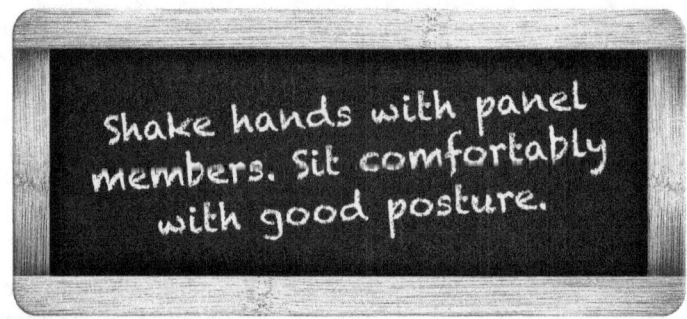

Responding to questions is the most nerve racking part of an interview - making sure you answer the questions correctly, with enough detail, to ensure the panel know you know what you are talking about. The key here is preparation again. In your written application that was good enough to get you the interview, you responded to a series of questions. These points should form the basis of the questions the interviewers ask you. The panel members understand you possibly haven't had much experience and will take that into account, however they really need to know what knowledge you have and how you intend to teach.

Prior to an interview, it's an excellent idea to revisit the key selection criteria and formulate some notes of the major ideas you wish to convey for each concept. Make some dot points. Some schools will kindly give you access to the questions the panel will ask you for a fifteen minute window immediately prior to your interview. If you have made dot points, now is the time to compare them to the questions and use them to make some more notes on the question sheet. You will be allowed to take those notes into the interview to refer to. The interviewers will probably be impressed that you cared enough to come prepared.

> Make notes based on the written application questions and access the school's website and policy documents prior to interview. Make notes on the interview questions during reading time.

Every part of the question is important. These have been well thought out in order to ensure you are giving them the most comprehensive picture they can get of you in a short space of time. If you were asked this question, *'Describe different student learning styles and how you adjust lessons to benefit those differing learning styles,'* you MUST respond to both parts of that statement. You will need to draw on your knowledge of learning styles gained at university, plus point out an example or two of how you have adjusted or planned for those differences, either on placement or as a qualified teacher.

Often in an interview we can feel very nervous. Panel members can usually pick this by your body language and voice. It's okay to admit you are nervous; it can help to break the ice and relax you. When you are asked a question it can sometimes be quite long or have several parts you need to respond to. This is hard to keep in our mind as we answer. It's perfectly feasible to ask for the question to be repeated or to check if you answered all parts of the question adequately. Interviewers would prefer your response is complete and reflects you, rather than an incomplete or incorrect answer.

Most schools will want to know about your knowledge and experience in the following:

Curriculum

- » Your state or nation's official curriculum
- » Experience in using the documents to plan
- » Assessment and reporting documents/software
- » How assessment informs your teaching

Learning

See chapters on Differentiation (9) and Disabilities (11)

- » Differing learning styles
- » Your own self-reflection and evaluation
- » Differentiation
- » Disabilities

Instructional Skills

- » Effective classroom teaching strategies or techniques

Teams

See chapters on Planning (8) and Working Effectively with Colleagues (16)

- » Ability to work and plan with others effectively
- » An occasion things went well and how you contributed
- » An occasion of discord and how you coped
- » Contributing to broader school activities
- » Capacity to develop constructive relationships

Behaviour Management

See chapter on Behaviour Management (7)

- » Your philosophy
- » Techniques
- » Approach to social and emotional development
- » Strategies for handling difficult children

Technology

See chapter on Technology (14)

- » Software and hardware you are familiar with
- » Incorporating technology in lessons
- » Connect, collaborate, contribute and create

Miscellaneous

- » Classroom culture
- » Personal strengths and weaknesses both as a teacher and a person. (Prepare some appropriate examples for this one. Make your strengths shine and choose a weakness that is not too weak and talk also how you work on the weakness. Just had to share this example, not from the teaching industry luckily! A friend's father was on an interview panel and asked the weaknesses question. The interviewee replied with, "I have a masturbation problem and usually masturbate several times a day at work, in the bathroom." Think he got the job?)

This is not an exhaustive list, however, preparing a response to all of these points, that reflects both your experience and knowledge, should cover 90% of the questions asked of beginning teachers in interviews.

Asking Questions

After the main part of the interview, many panels offer you the opportunity to ask questions. Often any questions you came with are answered through your discussions, however it's a good idea to have a question or two up your sleeve. Looking through a school's website, strategic plan and policy documents prior to the day may prompt a question or two. Bring them with you and jot them on your question sheet. It's very easy to forget what they are when you are concentrating on responding to the interviewers so intelligently! A wise word though - now is not the time to ask about money.

Sample questions you may ask:

(If they are not already addressed via your research on their website or via the interview).

- » Does the school have an official mentoring program? If so, what does it look like?
- » Is there an induction program for new graduates and what does it involve?
- » How many extra responsibilities are expected for a beginning teacher? What types?
- » What are the meeting expectations per week?
- » Are the teaching areas open and shared or individual?
- » Do any opportunities exist for team teaching?
- » How is technology integrated into the curriculum?
- » Can you outline the school's wellbeing policy?
- » Can you give me details regarding the school's discipline policy?
- » What are your expectations for teachers at this school?
- » What are the class sizes across the school?

The interviewers may give you a few minutes to leave the room after the main part of the interview is over. This is so they can quickly check if they want you to expand more in any particular area. You also have some quick breathing space to look back at your key points and decide whether anything needs to be added or clarified. This may be the time you think of some more questions. If a panel has no further questions for you, then it's safe to say you have conveyed your message adequately.

The interview is your final opportunity to sell your ability to be an effective and awesome teacher. There's no room for self-doubt or self-consciousness. No one else is there to extol your virtues and rave about you. That's your job. Don't end up kicking yourself for not being more convincing. Make it clear you are keen to learn as much as you can and are willing to teach any level or specialist area.

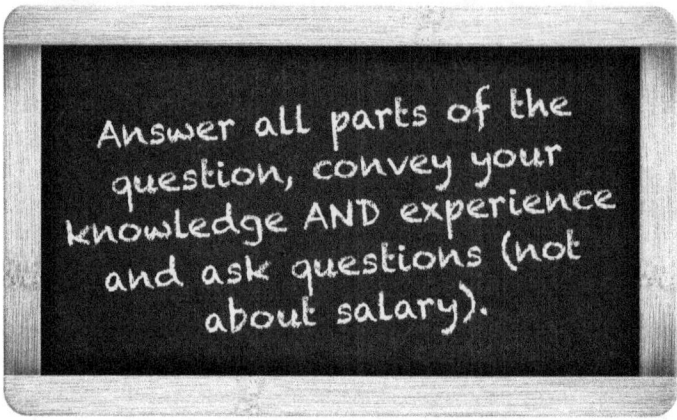

Dazzling the Panel

Ways to dazzle a panel go in and out of fashion. Recently, folios have made way for digital presentations. This is where putting in extra effort prior to an interview should reap you some reward. The point to razzle and dazzle is to SUPPORT your responses to the criteria. It's not just glitz and gloss for the sake of it. You definitely need substance.

The key here is brevity. In an interview of thirty or forty minutes, much of that time needs to be taken up with talking. A panel of three or four doesn't have time to individually look at or process much extra, whilst still concentrating on what you have to say. Personally, I find a tablet device to be the most user friendly and portable. It fits easily into most bags and is easy to pass around for a closer look, including zooming in. You can update your resources easily, including photographing hard copies of documents or work samples to access.

What should you present?

Throughout university, placements and beginning teaching positions, you will have created and gathered a fair amount of resources and experience. Look carefully at how you have responded to the key selection criteria, in particular, the examples you used. Hopefully you have some digital resources that illustrate and support this. For example, showing a unit or term planner that you developed may support a question about curriculum planning, differentiation, planning for different learning styles or working in teams. Think creatively about how you can use what you have done to illustrate your point.

What platform?

This is entirely up to you and the apps or software you are most comfortable using. My suggestion is to have grouped any resources you intend to use in an easily accessible place and have tested them a few times. It looks pretty unprofessional if you spend time searching and can't find what you want. This also distracts you and puts unnecessary stress upon you. I also suggest any presentations are not Internet reliant and are very easy for panel members to scroll through or navigate. Not everyone is tech savvy!

> A digital presentation should support your responses. Choose resources that can potentially support several question areas and make it user friendly.

Final Word

Finally, panel members are human too. At some stage they have had to be in your position, newly graduated and enthusiastic. Their aim will be to make you feel comfortable and to be compassionate.

This chapter has detailed four distinct steps in the interview process. Don't disregard any of them as less important than another. All four should be given equal weighting. If you prepare thoroughly and focus on the right things then acing your interview is possible.

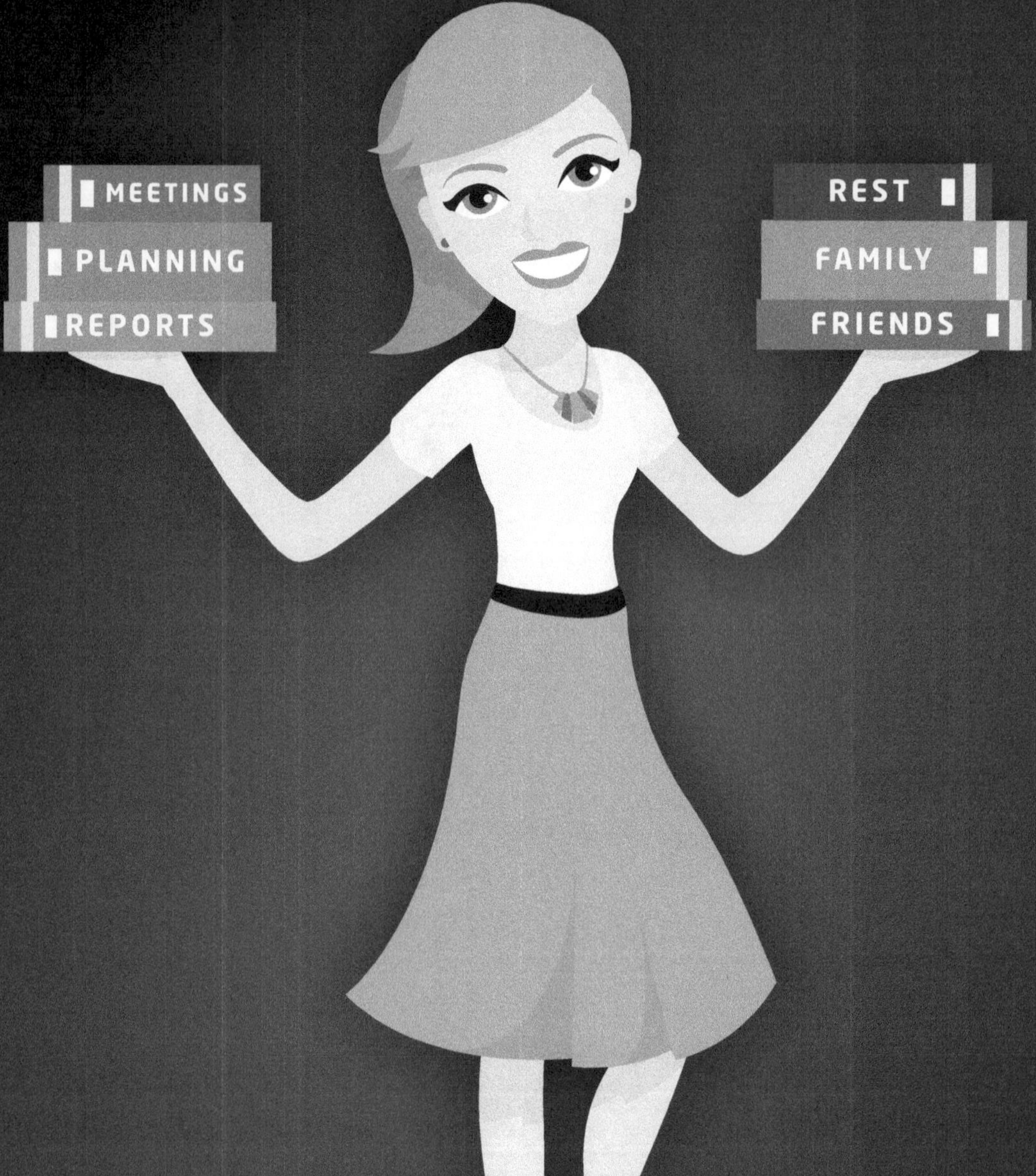
MEETINGS
PLANNING
REPORTS
REST
FAMILY
FRIENDS

Enjoying Teaching

Chapter Overview

- » Finding joy in your teaching
- » Being organised
- » Rest
- » Balance
- » Planning
- » Connections
- » Support
- » Reflection

Finding Joy In Your Teaching

Teaching is an awesome profession and I absolutely love being a teacher. No two days are the same; actually no two hours are the same! It's a privilege to have an influence during a child's formative years and we should always strive to remember how our input affects children.

During the early days of your teaching career, sometimes it's hard to appreciate that you could ever end up enjoying teaching. Many factors have an impact on your ability to enjoy your career and there are ways to adjust your approach to make improvements. I was hard pressed to enjoy much of my first year - no mentor, little support and a third of my class had special needs or behavioural issues. I had to make a mandatory report for suspected abuse three times for three different students! At one stage we were holed up in the classroom with the police on their way, trying to stay safe from a very angry person. I worked at school from 8a.m. to 6p.m. every single day and then spent many hours in the evenings and on weekends still working. What I experienced most in my first year of teaching was numbing exhaustion and frustration.

Finding joy in your teaching career is something we should all strive to experience for longevity and mental health. This is relevant no matter how many years you have been teaching. Some years are more challenging than others and the key to a thriving career is knowing how to cope in an emotionally healthy way with the difficult times, without becoming cynical and jaded.

Organisation

Being well planned and organised really minimises stress. So how do you do this?

Make a list. I always have a list or two going. Whenever something pops into my head that I need to follow up on, I add it to the list, and delete it when I am done! That's a good feeling. In the early days it may be a common feeling that many things are swimming around in your head. Making lists reduces the drowning swimmers and helps you feel more relaxed and calm. It's your choice where you keep your lists. I use the sticky note app on my laptop, as it's my preferred device for both work and home. Therefore I see the lists frequently.

Use your in school hours planning time effectively. A chat at the photocopier is nice but do this consistently and you are wasting time. Refer to your list and start to tick things off. Generally, I plan at home as it works better for me, and I use school planning time to create displays, prepare resources, mark homework and other work, tidy up, rearrange my classroom, find resources for planning later, filing, make contact with parents or to follow up my extra responsibilities.

It's virtually impossible to do everything you need to do during school hours. Even if you tried, there are too many interruptions and meetings. Prioritise what needs to be done that day or that week and postpone the non-essentials. If you do find yourself with a spare hour, use it well by selecting the most urgent thing needing to be done. Try to see a task to completion, rather than dipping your toe into a few and getting none finished.

Use a calendar or diary religiously. Enter into it all yard duty, meetings and other work related requirements and refer to it daily. Forgetting your duties, especially ones that effect others, can cause friction or possible reprimand. Knowing what's on for the day, or for tomorrow, reduces last minute stress. As a teacher we need to be best friends with the concept of 'flexibility'. If this is an attribute you struggle with, ensure that the things you cannot be flexible about are accounted for via a calendar. Setting an alert will also help you remember.

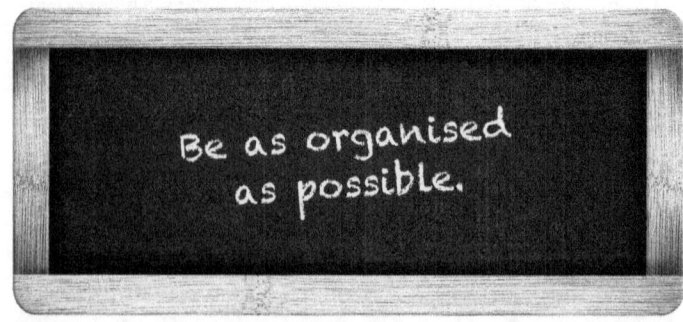

Rest

Get plenty of sleep and rest. Are you an early riser or night owl? I'm an early riser so I have to remember to not get tricked by the night owl into staying up too late. When the night owl does dupe me then I'm a bit tired at work the next day. That translates into being slightly less patient with children. It's not easy to enjoy your job when you are tired or cranky. Perhaps that might mean a nana nap after school in the early days, or saying no to school night outings for a while, until you can work out how much sleep and rest you need. Teaching really is exhausting so we need to rest when we can.

Prioritise rest.

Balance

After the first few weeks or term is behind you, it may be time to reintroduce some social activities. Your head isn't spinning with schoolwork so much and you find you have room to think about non-school things. It's important to always maintain a healthy work-life balance. Too much of either and some things will suffer. This balance is one key to enjoying your job long term. Teaching requires a lot of energy and thought, especially if you want to be a good one, so you need to feed yourself with some fun stuff when you are not thinking about work.

Balance within the classroom is important too. Try to be purposeful about noticing the good things that happen every day. Praising and encouraging children for the little things is a positive step towards more self-motivated improvement from them. The child who has been noticed and rewarded for their learning or behaviour, is more likely to want to keep earning that praise, leading towards a happier child and happier teacher. Sometimes it really is hard to find anything positive about some children but it's these kids who respond best to praise. You'll be surprised at the turn around you will see if you begin to praise the kids who cause you the most hair pulling! (See Behaviour Management chapter (7) for more tips).

Strive for a healthy work/life balance.

Planning

Lesson planning is one of the most enjoyable and important parts of the job. Knowing you are well planned and with all resources ready each day, really reduces stress and anxiety. This allows you to be more relaxed, hopefully leading to more enjoyment.

The way you plan is highly personal and may be dependent on the structure of your team. In your beginning years, aim for as much team planning as you can organise. Don't be afraid to speak up within your team to ask for pointers or assistance with regards to planning. Some schools isolate staff by insisting on individual planning. This also has a detrimental effect on students, as it's extremely difficult to plan engaging, relevant and appropriate lessons, day in and day out, when you are working by yourself. If this is the case in your school, see if someone within your team is willing to give planning together a go. (See chapter on Planning (8) for more advice).

I have operated in many teams over the years and they all plan slightly differently. I think best practice model is where all team members take responsibility for a curriculum area (or two) each term and plan all lessons and prepare/source all required resources. In a weekly team meeting you share the lessons you have planned for the week, via a communal document, and then listen to what others have planned for you to teach within their planning area. That way you get to focus on a specific curriculum area and plan sequential and scaffolded lessons effectively in depth. Your time and brain isn't being too stretched then! Switch around what you plan each term, to develop your knowledge and skills in all areas of the curriculum.

Connections

Making strong connections with students and colleagues is a good basis towards finding long-term enjoyment of your career. Children love to share what's happening in their lives but they also love hearing about your own life. No matter what grade you are teaching, make some time to allow them to share, and entertain them with stories from your own life. Listen to them whenever possible. Connected students feel happier and safer and in turn you will be happier. It's always lovely coming to work when the students call out to you or rush over because they have a good relationship with you. Who doesn't like being welcomed and appreciated?

Share happy, exciting or funny stories from your life. Avoid talking or moaning about the negative things that happen to you. Children don't really understand how to process the negativity and definitely aren't going to connect with you on this. Once you know your class, try to remember something individual about each student that you can connect with them about occasionally. Knowing how a particular sports team is travelling, asking how a party went, asking if they won at their sport on the weekend or quietly checking something more personal are all easy ways to connect. Children also love being able to tease you. If they are doing this in a polite way then they are probably feeling quite connected to you!

Feeling a connectedness to the workplace and colleagues is also a great way to enjoy your work. Make an effort to go to staff drinks or social events, help out a colleague occasionally or even instigate some social activities yourself. Seek out like-minded people at work, even better if they are in your team. Share ideas and thoughts.

One way to make your self feel disconnected is to gossip, moan or be negative. We all need to let off steam but strive to avoid that being your prime modus operandi. If this is the way you choose to behave then you are likely to attract other negative people and that is certainly not uplifting. Continually looking at the negatives feeds more negativity and you will find yourself in a downward spiral and hard pressed to find any joy. Be polite and friendly to everyone and you will experience a cheerful and relaxed work environment.

Sadly, there are still some teachers out there who choose to destabilise and even sabotage other staff or leadership. Handling these people is very tricky. (See chapter on Working Effectively with Colleagues for more ideas). Often they will give with one hand, blinding you with their understanding or generosity, whilst taking with the other hand. These people are not good people to make connections with and will really put a dint in your enjoyment of work. Your aim should be to be pleasant at all times, show gratitude when they offer you something and to avoid getting drawn into gossiping or slandering of other staff. They are immature and damaged individuals with low self esteem, who desire to bring others down to make themselves look good and thereby bolstering their self esteem. If this person is your immediate superior, I really feel for you. Speak to other like-minded people or upper leadership to put forward your plight and ask for suggestions on managing them if needed. Good luck!

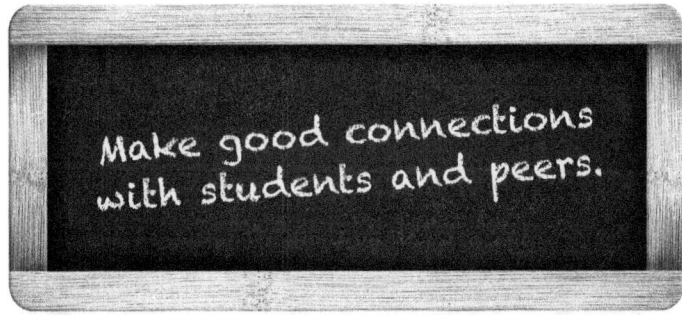

Support

It's imperative that you seek out or are provided with appropriate support networks in the early days of your teaching career. This can be difficult to obtain, particularly if you don't know anyone at your new school.

Good mentors are worth their weight in gold. I floundered in my first year, as my assigned mentor wasn't really willing to play that role. Instead, some kind teachers within the school provided support and guidance where possible. The principal recognised the situation I was in and moved me in my second year to a level where I would receive much more support. She was concerned that I would quit teaching if I didn't have better guidance and input. I wouldn't have resigned that quickly but I certainly wasn't enjoying teaching very much. The move to a new mentor made all the difference.

The mentor relationship works both ways. They cannot be expected to know every area you need support. You need to tell them the things you are struggling with and ask for guidance. Be as specific as you can. Perhaps even ask them to observe you whilst teaching and choose a time when you are likely to be experiencing the area you want to improve in. Be open to all feedback. This is crucial.

If there is no formal mentor assigned to you, ask your principal for an appropriate person to assist you. If this is not forthcoming, seek out someone within the school, preferably in your team. A number of mentors in your early teaching years can be of benefit. Don't limit yourself to colleagues just within your school. Cultivate relationships with teachers at other schools that you may know, or ask your university mates how they handled some situations. Advice and assistance is available in many places, you just have to look and ask. Don't struggle on with thinking things will get better by themselves. It really does help to ask for assistance.

It's not enough to just request help. You need to take responsibility for making improvements. Listen to their feedback with an open mind and really reflect on what you are doing now that is ineffective. It's not always an easy process emotionally, but the sooner you choose to heed feedback and acknowledge your input, the quicker you will feel happier as a teacher.

Unforeseen issues crop up all the time in our classrooms. Perhaps you have quite a few students with special needs that have no aide time allocated, or there are some problematic behavioural issues. If this is the case, and you have been unable to come up with a management plan yourself, definitely speak up. Letting these problems continue will really affect your mood and enjoyment in the classroom. Ask for suggestions or extra help. Sometimes leadership don't know that a particular mix of students is toxic or negative, or that some students require a lot of extra assistance.

Reflection

Being mindful of all of these points is a great start to achieving enjoyment in your teaching. There will be other areas that contribute to your happiness and longevity as a teacher. The key is to recognise what's not working or causing some angst, seek solutions and feedback, be open and reflective, and implement some changes. The first solution is not always the right one. Keep searching. I hope that you can get the balance right to enjoy a long and fulfilling teaching career.

Use this page to document what you currently enjoy about teaching and ways you might like to make changes to improve your enjoyment.

First Few Days

Chapter Overview

- » Preparation before the first day
- » Student resources you will need
- » The first day/week
- » End of the first day (there's wine involved)
- » Teacher resources you will need
- » The day before the first day
- » Activities

CHAPTER 4

Prepare for exhaustion! Your first few days as a professional teacher are exhilarating, exhausting, rewarding and overwhelming. No matter how many years teachers get under their belt, there are always first day nerves. In my first year of teaching I taught a Prep class. I was very happy about this, as my youngest child had just completed Prep so I felt quite aware of the things they had to learn and what the children were interested in at this age. I also figured the curriculum wasn't too demanding and that I'd cope. Plus, I was teaching in the school I'd done my last placement in and knew my way around and the staff reasonably well. And yet, I closed those double doors at 12p.m. (I know, I know, I only had to last three hours), threw the bolt, leaned my back against them and thought to myself, "What the hell have I done?"

No matter how much preparation you do or how well prepared you feel, the first few days of teaching are exhausting. Actually, the whole first term is pretty exhausting. Sometimes a little nap after work helps, or having cooked some meals on the weekend ready for you to just zap in the microwave is a lifesaver.

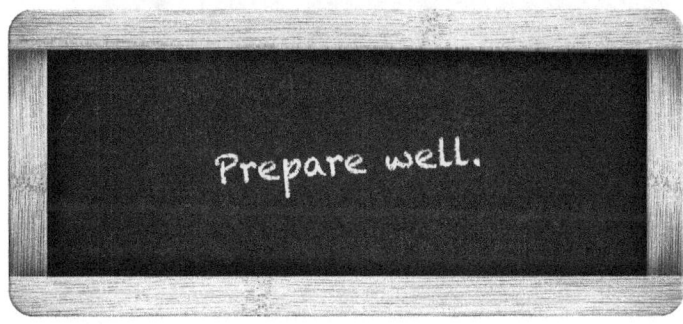

Preparation Before The First Day

Before the school year starts it is helpful to meet your new team and mentor and ask as many questions as you can. Familiarise yourself with the curriculum you will be teaching. Share planning with team members, if possible. All teachers have had a first day so should understand your nerves or the need to ask copious amounts of questions.

Setting your room up is fun and really helps cement in your mind that you are a teacher! Don't worry about putting up too many displays or posters, you and your class will make plenty throughout the year. It's nice to make a communal one in the first week though. Ask your team or mentor for room set up tips. As a rough guide you will need enough floor sitting space near the main area you will be using for whole class teaching, perhaps a comfortable reading area, and desks in groups. Desk groupings are fluid, depending on how children interact with one another. Just make sure there's enough room for chairs and for you to walk behind those chairs once there are students in them. Also ensure the walkway from the classroom door is clear and easily accessed. Once the term starts you might like to ask your students if they have any old beanbags or cushions they can donate. I've found children always love sitting on these on the floor, often preferring to work there rather than at desks. (See Classroom Management chapter (5) for more tips).

Some schools allow you to post home letters of introduction to the students. The children love receiving mail and it helps some students feel more comfortable about the new year, especially if you are new to the school and they don't know you. Make it light and fun, talk a little about yourself and a little about what the year might hold. If they are junior students, perhaps include a few stickers!

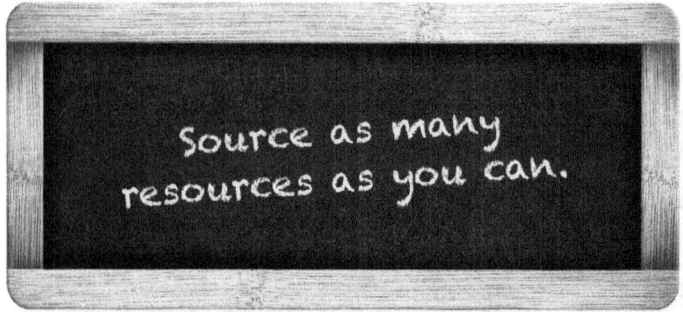

Each classroom needs a large amount of resources. Teachers build up a bank of these throughout their careers. The school should provide all teacher supplies such as pens, tape and staplers, but you may need to ask for more specific resources. If you purchase anything out of your own money, as we have all done, keep your receipts handy for tax time. When you are just starting out it may feel like you don't have enough supplies for the students in your room. Here are some tips:

- Visit garage sales and second hand shops to buy books, textas, dress ups and games
- Think about what you have at home you can repurpose
- Borrow a big box of books from the school library to put in your room
- Ask your team leader for your share of numeracy and literacy equipment or find out where it is stored
- Find out from your team what resources are appropriate for the level you are teaching
- The internet is your best friend for locating posters, templates and ideas
- Laminate supplies where possible so you have them for years to come

Teacher Resources You Will Need

- Pens - red, blue and black
- Greylead pencils
- Erasers
- White board markers
- White board eraser
- Stapler and staples
- Wall stapler and staples
- Sticky tape
- Masking tape
- Ruler
- Timers
- White out
- Paper clips
- Bulldog clips
- Magnets
- Pins for display boards
- Blue-tak
- String
- Pegs
- Plastic pockets
- Display books
- Colour card paper in A3 & A4
- White card paper in A3 & A4
- Lined paper
- Textas
- Black permanent markers
- Glue sticks
- Glue pots
- Glue
- Paint pots
- Paint
- Paintbrushes
- Stickers and more stickers
- Stamps
- Date stamp (to use on all portfolio work or tests)
- Old meat trays or yoghurt pots to hold water, glue, and paint
- Paper towel
- Tissues
- Disposable gloves
- Small first aid supply - just bandaids and gloves really
- Air freshener/disinfectant spray - imperative
- Water spray bottle - kids love this on hot days
- Plastic bags
- Elastic bands
- Small snap lock bags

Student Resources You Will Need

(These are all optional but helpful. Don't feel you have to rush out and buy them all now!)

- A few extra of each item on the required stationary list
- Picture story books
- Chapter books
- Craft supplies (stencils, crazy scissors, glue, paper plates, wool, cotton wool etc.)
- Board games
- Card games
- Puzzles
- Dress ups
- A teddy or two
- Toys
- Cushions and/or beanbags
- Scrap paper (you will build up a supply throughout the year)
- Old magazines and newspapers

The Day Before The First Day

You've set your room up and gotten all your classroom and teacher supplies ready. So what next? See if you can find out the answers to these questions.

- Establish where the line up area is for your grade. Will you welcome them by yourself or will the team leader welcome the whole level?
- How are students allowed to visit the toilet in your school?
- Where do your class put their bags?
- Will you name their bag boxes or hooks or let them choose daily?
- Will you let students sit anywhere for the first few days or assign them a table?
- Where do students put their supplies?
- Plan your first few days
- Ensure you have all your resources ready
- Do you have any yard duty on the first day? Work out where your area is and where the yard duty supplies are kept
- What are the lesson and break times?
- Can children bring water bottles into the classroom? Where will they put them?
- Is there an eating time inside prior to outside play?
- Can children eat a healthy snack during lesson time?
- Wander around the school, both inside and out, to become more familiar with it
- Are there areas outside that are restricted for play? Can children climb trees or fences? What happens if a ball goes outside of the school boundaries?
- What is the school discipline policy?
- How will you handle a fight in the schoolyard?
- When and where is whole school assembly?
- Is the school rubbish free? How do you enforce that?
- What happens if you need to send a child to sickbay during class time?
- What happens if you need help during class time?
- Where is the emergency evacuation plan?
- How will you contact other teachers or the office? Is there a phone contact list?
- What if you need to contact a parent? Where are their details?
- How will you mark the roll? Digital or hard copy? Where will you keep the hard copy?

- » Can you connect to the school wifi and Intranet/shared drive?
- » Do you have the right connectors/dongles to work the Interactive Whiteboard or T.V.?
- » Where are the staff toilets and staffroom? Can you use any mug?
- » Do you have any staff room duty? What is involved? Do you owe any tea money?
- » How do you get your students to and from specialists? Where are these located?
- » How do you use the photocopier? Where is it located? Do you need a code or card?
- » Can you print?
- » Who do you ask when you have technical problems?
- » Where can you park your car?
- » Where should you safely store your bag?
- » Is there a lockable filing cabinet or cupboard in your room? Do you have the key?
- » How do notices get sent home?
- » How do you send money to the office?

The First Day/Week

The first day has arrived and no doubt you are feeling nervous. The key to surviving your first few days, weeks and term is preparation and rest. If you have asked many of the questions above then you will be fine. In the first week of a new class your aim should be to learn all the children's names, for them to learn each others', for you to discover a couple of things about each student and to have a good blend of learning and fun. I like to get a bit of communal artwork displayed on a wall and play a variety of getting to know you activities. Listed below are a few ideas that work for me. Your colleagues will have many ideas, as does the Internet.

Activities

Legend: **J** Junior **M** Middle **S** Senior

J **M** **S** CUBE
Use a cube net to create a personal cube. Create your own first so students can learn about you too. Students put something different on each face of the cube about themselves. Suspend from the ceiling when you are finished. For seniors you can use a net with more faces!

M **S** GETTING TO KNOW YOU
(See Get To Know You Game in Templates chapter). Provide a template for each child, and they grab something to lean on and a pen. They must wander the classroom asking the questions listed on the template until they find an affirmative response. Then they write that person's name in the box provided. No double ups of names! You can make your own template up to insert different requests. This game only lasts about ten minutes.

M **S** GUESS WHO
Give each student an index card and ask them to record four facts about themselves. Collect them and then hand out randomly. Students must circulate and ask questions of their classmates to find the owner of the clues. The catch is, they cannot use any words used on the index card.

J **M** **S** JIGSAW
Provide large jigsaw pieces to be coloured and then children write or draw information on them about themselves. They could be put together as a class (if you can stand the chaos) or assemble yourself on a wall for display. This is a possible resource:
http://www.k-3teacherresources.com/jigsaw-puzzle-template.html#.U5f39f32DIY

M **S** JUMBLED NAMES
Have the names of all the students in your class displayed somewhere in the room. Prepare a template with every student's name jumbled. Either as a class or individuals, unjumble them. Extend this further by naming a fact about each person.

M **S** LETTER
Students write a letter of introduction to you. Be specific about what you want to learn. This could perhaps be a homework task. You model a letter of introduction to them.

M **S** LIFE MAP
Provide the template and ask children to name it then either draw or write some major life events in the boxes. Model it first. Children should brainstorm the events prior to beginning, to ensure they get the timeline right.

M **S** MULTIPLE INTELLIGENCES
Find out the many different ways your students are smart by having them complete a multiple intelligences assessment such as this one: http://www.literacynet.org/mi/assessment/findyourstrengths.html For younger students you may like to read out the statements.

J **M** **S** NAME CARDS
Give each child a piece of card and they must write their name clearly and creatively, and decorate the remainder of the space. These can be adhered to tables, backs of chairs, desks, tubs, bag boxes or hooks etc.

[J] [M] [S] PHOTO
Take a photo of each individual in your class and print them out, centred on A3 paper. They must design a frame around the photo and then either draw pictures or write information about themselves.

[J] [M] [S] PHOTO HUNT
This activity works best if you run a 1:1 iPad program or children have access to a class set of iPads. (See Photo Hunt in Templates chapter (26)). Break your class into groups of three to four maximum. They must take photos of the things listed on the template. Once finished they return to the classroom and then need to put the photos they took into an App such as Strip Design to make a story. Share stories on the Interactive Whiteboard or TV using Air Server or a dongle. This activity should take approximately an hour.

[J] [M] [S] READ
Reading is a great calming activity. Many activities can spring from the book you choose. Here are some book suggestions and you can search the Internet for accompanying tasks. The books are mainly focused on the junior level for rules and behaviours but they really can be read to any level, just make the activity age appropriate. Purchase them through Amazon or Fishpond and look at the blurb too. Alternatively, you can borrow them from either your school or local library.

- No David and David Goes to School by David Shannon
- The Little Red Hen by Paul Caldone
- The Little Engine That Could by Watty Piper
- Miss Nelson is Missing by Harry Allard
- Amelia Bedilia's First Day of School by Herman Parish
- Bailey by Harry Bliss
- Miss Malarkey Doesn't Live in Room 10 by Judy Finchler
- Chrysanthemum by Kevin Hinkes
- Teacher From The Black Lagoon by Mike Thaler
- Never Spit On Your Shoes by Denys Cazet
- Alexander and the Terrible, Horrible, No Good, Very Bad Day by David Shannon
- This School Year Will Be The Best by Kay Winters and Renee Adriani
- The Name Jar by Yangsook Choi

[J] [M] [S] SELF PORTRAIT
Draw yourself. You too! Get creative and use unusual materials such as those found in the garden, use newspapers or magazines, pastels etc.

[J] [M] [S] SILHOUETTES
Using a projector, illuminate a side profile of each student onto a piece of A3 paper adhered to a wall. Trace the profile. Students then cut it out and decorate it with information about themselves, either written or drawn. Display.

[J] SING
Junior students love to sing and cannot tell yet whether you have a good voice or not! Sing something you are sure they'll be familiar with and teach them a new song too.

J M S SPIDER WEB
Sit in a circle and you start by holding the end of a ball of wool and throwing the ball to someone, whilst keeping hold of the end piece. As you throw the wool ball you can either state something you would like to do in the class this year, or use it as a name game. The next person holds onto the stretched thread and tosses the ball onto someone else until everyone has had a go and you end up with a 'spider web'. To extend this you could try unravelling by tossing the ball back and repeating what the previous person said.

J M S TOILET PAPER
Pass a roll of toilet paper around a circle and invite children to take as much or as little as they like. When everyone has some, reveal that for every square they took they must share a piece of information about themselves.

J M S TRIBES
If your school is a Tribes Learning Community there are plenty of resources for name games and getting to know you activities. If not, you may be able to access the book of activities either in your school or via a colleague.

J M S T-SHIRT
(See T-Shirt template in Templates chapter (26)). Using the T-Shirt template ask children to write words inside it that mean something about them. You may like to brainstorm ideas of what to include on the whiteboard first. Decorate the T-Shirt also. Display. Thirty minutes plus.

J M S TWO TRUTHS & ONE LIE
Place students in groups of four to five. They must take it in turns to tell everyone in the group two truths and one lie about themselves. The challenge is that the lie must be believable and the rest of the group must determine which is the lie.

M S WORDLE
A Wordle is a tool for generating 'word clouds' from text that you provide. The clouds give greater prominence to words that appear more frequently in the text. You can tweak your clouds with different fonts, layouts and colour schemes. www.wordle.net/ is one example to use. Check children can access and create these on the devices you have at school. Encourage them to create a few so they get the concept and can improve their word cloud. Print and display.

J M S ZIP ZAP
Everyone stands or sits in a circle with one person in the middle, who is 'IT'. The person in the middle points to someone in the circle and says either 'zip' or 'zap'. If zip is said the person in the circle must give the name of the player on their right. If zap is said, name the person on their left. If the wrong name is given then they trade places with 'IT'. If the correct name is give then 'IT' must pick again and after three correct tries switch the person who is 'IT'.

Once you feel thoroughly planned and your resources are all at hand, plan a couple of quick back up activities in case a task takes the children a shorter than expected time to complete and you need a fill in. It's a yucky feeling realising you have some time to fill in and your head is saying 'What am I going to do?" There will always be times that pop up throughout the first few days that need a five minute filler. See my chapter on this for some quick ideas.

First Day/Week Extras

Here is a list of things I like to cover in the first few days to make my classroom well organised and to help the children be as relaxed as possible. Not all of these will be relevant for you, depending on the year level you are teaching.

- Establish your toilet visiting rules (See Chapter 13, Poo Wee Vomit for tips)
- Select monitors - office, library, art smocks, shoe lace tying etc.
- Inform children what you would like them to bring to school - library bag, art smock, novel, box of tissues, school hat etc. Perhaps they could receive a little reward for when they bring the items in, like free time minutes or a sticker/stamp
- Visit important areas of the school if you have a Prep class
- Take an individual photo of each child if you are using them for your roll or an activity
- Introduce or revise school rules
- Make a whole class list for your class expectations
- Talk about your expectations for the classroom
- Select monitors
- Introduce and explain your class reward program
- Getting to know you and name games
- Little bit of numeracy
- Little bit of literacy
- Whole class art/craft project for display
- Some outside or classroom games
- Elect class captains if applicable
- Watch something fun on YouTube
- Establish homework guidelines for the year
- Decorate or label books

> Your aim for week one is to get plenty of sleep and rest, learn everyone's name and get to know each child a little bit. Have a nice balance of work and play in the classroom.

End Of The First Day

- Go home
- Drink wine
- Go to bed early
- Don't stress
- You did a good job
- Tomorrow is a new day
- Believe it or not, one day this job will be easier
- I promise, your head will stop spinning soon (unless you drank the whole bottle of wine)

Classroom Management

Chapter Overview

- » Learning zones/classroom set up
  - Teaching area
  - Learning zones
  - Table seating
  - Floor seating
  - Behaviour management on the floor
  - Movement between tables and floor
- » Gaining children's attention
- » Toilet visits
- » Marking the roll
- » Classroom monitors
- » Food and drink in the classroom
- » Class parties/reward day
- » Tidying up
- » Lining up/movement around the school
- » Team teaching
- » Sharing time
- » Parent helpers
- » Student awards

Learning Zones/Classroom Set Up

Flexible learning zones are ideal in the twenty first century. Your classroom set up is largely dependent upon your school's facilities and the layout of your room. Open learning spaces allow for multiple zones, where children can learn independently, or in small groups. In a traditional classroom with four walls, you can still have multiple learning zones.

Teaching Area

Generally you will have a white/blackboard, some kind of interactive board, or both. This area should be kept free of obstructions. You will need to walk between them frequently and children need to come up to them or stand out the front at times. The chair you teach from (ideally on wheels) should be placed to the side of the board you will use most frequently. If you teach using an interactive whiteboard or T.V. regularly, then you need a small table or bench, running underneath the board, on which to place your laptop or tablet. This allows you to get up to illustrate points or to write something.

As this is your major teaching area it is necessary to store your regularly used resources here. Keep them organised, neat and labelled. Tubs or boxes work well. Ensure you have whiteboard markers, permanent markers and pens all close by too. Teachers always seem to need copious amounts of these.

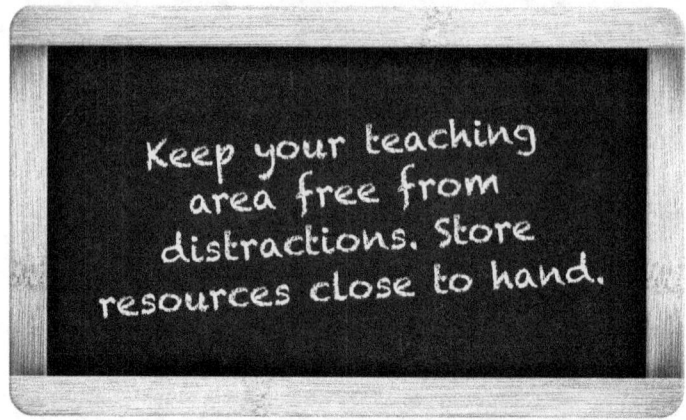

Learning Zones

For years I've had an old futon mattress and scatter cushions in my room. These are always highly coveted, no matter how grotty or tatty they are. So desired in fact, that I've had to create a roster and rules for usage! Time and time again children choose spaces like this to work at. Apart from handwriting, any work can be done sitting on a cushion or comfy chair. Generally children don't abuse this privilege and it helps to make your classroom welcoming and comfortable. Your students should know the rules - producing no work or talking too much means back to tables. Be flexible where children choose to learn; as long as they are concentrating and on task, it doesn't matter where this occurs.

A reading nook near a bookshelf can inspire some independent reading. For juniors, construction zones, home corners, tinkering tables, and arty zones all help to provide a variety of learning experiences. The possibilities are endless...tech areas, puzzles and board games, learning games etc.

After teaching middle and senior students a new numeracy or literacy game, provide an area where you can place the resources into labelled plastic pockets and pin them to a noticeboard. Children can be directed to 'play' one of the games if they finish early.

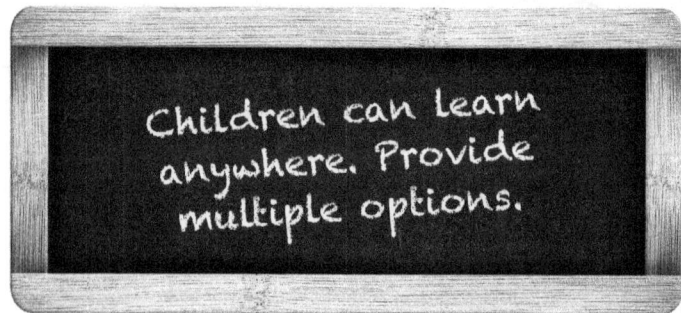

Table Seating

The layout of tables and chairs should be fluid and change regularly, perhaps once a term. Sometimes it takes awhile to get it just right. If you are finding it tricky, ask another teacher for input, or even the students. Try to set the tables into groupings of two-four maximum. Place them so that children aren't pulling chairs back onto the chairs of those behind them. That is a recipe for problems. Keep enough space between the table and chair layout so that you can easily get around them all to attend to everyone.

There are a number of ways to group children for seating. It's personal preference combined with the unique behaviours of some combinations of kids. **Here are a few options:**

- No allocated seating - Kids sit anywhere
- Students choose seating and stay for a predetermined time
- Groups of boy or girl tables
- Mixed sex tables
- Boy/girl alternate seating
- Teacher picks seats - talkers and/or poor behaviours spread evenly. The thinking here is that spreading out the difficult to manage students helps keep behaviour in check. However, sometimes their poor behaviour rubs off on or disturbs those around them, even usually well-behaved students
- Teacher picks seats - talkers and/or poor behaviours all on one table. Choose this only as a last resort after trialling the previous strategy. I have only had to use this once, and by the time I elected to try it, it was clear this group of students weren't going to concentrate or stop disrupting others no matter where I put them. Putting them together meant they only bothered each other and the rest of the class were able to get on with their work uninterrupted. It was an interesting experiment to observe that being constantly distracted ended up bothering the constant distractors!
- Table Torture - Number your tables with either permanent marker or contacted numbers (see Templates chapter), depending on how many students in your class. Laminate a set of matching number cards. Line children up in front of you and flash a card number to them, then they move to that table number. You can repeat this process as often as you like. Let the new groupings settle and see how they work together, possibly moving children if needed
- Mix of arrangements - Pair seating, group tables, individual desks, couches, bean bags, floor etc. Students can sit where they feel they work well, as long as they follow the rules for that area. Move them somewhere else if they are not responsible

> Tables and chairs should be easy to move around. Be creative with student seating arrangements.

The Essential Teacher's Guide

Floor Seating

Children need to be seated on the floor for whole class teaching. Always. This is non negotiable. When you are teaching the whole class it is impossible to teach and have your eyes roaming over the whole classroom to ensure children are on task. At their tables they cannot all see the board or T.V. properly and there are many things for them to fiddle with. Seating children on the floor in a large group has many benefits. Your eyes and attention aren't roaming as far while you teach, it's much easier to pick up on inattentive students or distracting behaviour and the children are closer to the teaching zone and can see and hear better.

Don't be tempted to seat senior students at tables because they are bigger or because they demand it. You are in charge. If you are making this change and they are used to sitting at tables then they will grumble, but they get over it. You can make the floor more enticing by providing floor cushions or letting kids lean against a wall. Try to arrange furniture so that the area they are seated in is cleverly zoned so they cannot spread out too far and provides just enough space for them to all be cross legged on the floor. Children must always sit up when you are teaching.

Seating children on the floor to teach also enables you to sit down. Teachers are on their feet nearly all day so a small respite is welcome. You will still stand to write something or to illustrate a point so ensure children aren't sitting too close. Juniors just love to touch you and run their hands over your feet and lower legs. This personally makes me uncomfortable so I have boundaries around this and I'd probably advise that this is something to discourage. See Boundaries chapter for more detail.

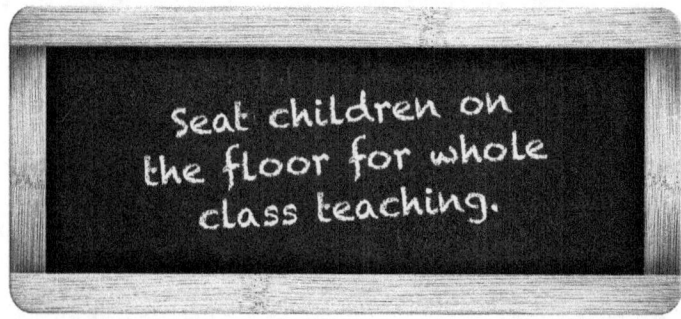

Behaviour Management On The Floor

Keep your whole class teaching to fifteen minutes, maximum, to avoid the wriggles (and boredom). At times I have used masking tape to mark out an area on the floor that children all need to be seated within. Ensure each time you begin teaching that you can see all the children and that they are not hiding behind any furniture. Always move them.

Frequently request that children make appropriate floor seating choices where they won't talk or be distracted. Offer a moment to allow children to decide if they should move. If they choose not to, and you end up needing to move them, they can lose some free time minutes or house points. Don't be afraid to move children. Rarely do they self-monitor or cease whispering to or touching their friend. Split them immediately. Sometimes you will need to direct chronic repeat offenders to 'their' spot, with the most difficult to manage child right at your feet. Very occasionally you may need to be more structured in your floor seating arrangements. Masking taped crosses on the floor with a child's initials on it is a last resort. One year I was team teaching in a double room and we had fifty-four grade five and six children. Amongst that group were six boys who tested our patience every single day to the max! We had to use the masking tape crosses all year. They lost free time minutes for not sitting on them or for ripping them up. It worked quite well.

If a child persists in being rude or distracting others then you need to move them away even further. Try moving them to the back of the classroom, completely away from all other students, or near the door or windows. Keep this to five minutes, maximum. Ask them if they are ready to stay focussed and return to the group. Every now and then a child says no and this is usually good self-monitoring. As soon as possible, ideally when the rest of the class are occupied, make a point of talking to the student you moved away. Ensure you are crouched to their level and maintain eye contact. Ask them to reflect on why you had to move them and also how they can avoid finding themselves in that situation again. Typically, children act out to 'be heard' or to gain attention. They may be feeling a sense of separation from the group and a desire to feel more connected. Calling out or distracting others may be the only way they know how to get this attention. Reiterate how important it is to speak respectfully (in a way that doesn't communicate your dislike or frustration for them) and maintain eye contact as you do this. When children feel heard, frequently their misbehaviour eases. A grade four girl I taught would constantly talk amongst her friends on the floor, distracting both herself and others nearly every session. Moving her didn't help as she talked to whomever she was seated near! After asking her to reflect on why she was keen to talk to others and understand that she was causing others to lose concentration also, she revealed she was uncomfortable telling others not to talk to her and didn't know how to do it. Her parents had taught her it was polite to respond to someone when they spoke to her. We brainstormed a few ways to politely request her friends not chat that she felt comfortable with. Problem solved!

When you separate a child from the rest of the class for discipline reasons, please don't send them to sit outside the classroom or in a corridor. They are unsupervised and often get up to mischief out there with other students passing by. Plus, it's super easy to forget them out there. I have done this! If you feel that a child should be removed from your classroom altogether then have a buddy class you can send them to, along with some quiet work. In all my years of teaching I have never resorted to this as I believe it sends a poor message to the child about your ability to manage them and isn't great for a child's development either. Children are very clever and they will soon cotton on that if they want to get out of class, just play up. Respect is important and students sent out of a classroom more than once will learn very quickly how to push your buttons and they will have minimal respect for you. However, sometimes a child needs to be removed from the classroom for the safety of both yourself and your other students. (See Chapter 7, Behaviour Management).

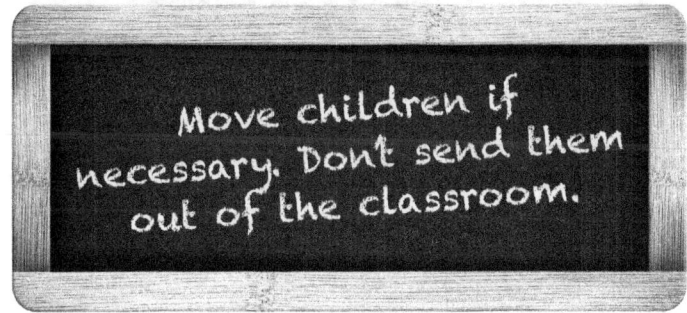

Movement Between Tables and Floor

Too much time can be lost in the movement between floor and tables. A handy system to use is to count down from five to zero. By zero all children need to be seated quietly and on task. If not, then deduct house points or free time minutes. A chiming bell works well too if you don't want to use your voice. You need to be explicit in your expectations and consistent in adhering to them.

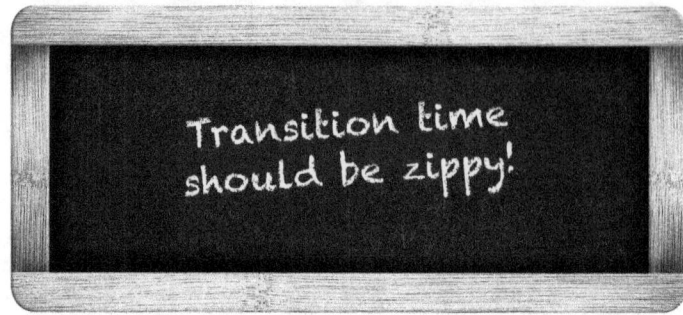

Transition time should be zippy!

Gaining Children's Attention

At times you will need to gain the attention of the whole class. It's personal preference for which method you choose. Just stick to it for the year so your students know what you mean.

Some ideas:

- Clapping hands in a rhythmic pattern and children repeat
- Shhhhing in a pattern and children repeat (best in junior grades)
- Ringing a bell
- Singing a line and children repeat
- Shake a shaker
- Hold your arm up in the air and all children copy and fall silent
- Call out S.L.L. (stop, look, listen)
- Call out S.A.L.A.M.I. (Stop And Look At Me Immediately)

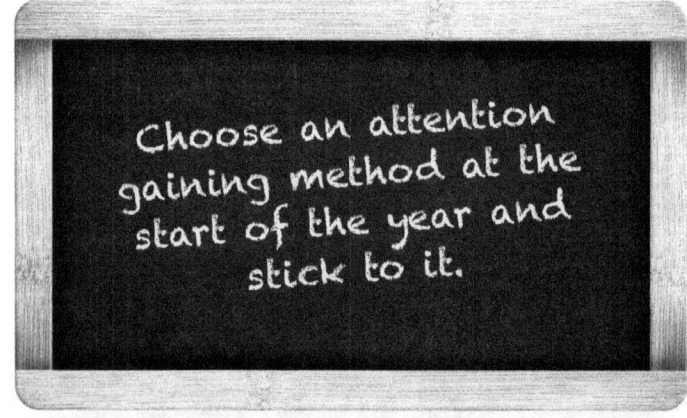

Choose an attention gaining method at the start of the year and stick to it.

Toilet Visits

Anything to get out of class! You will have repeat offenders here. A toilet visit management system is essential and should be introduced on the first day of the new school year. The system I have developed works wonderfully. See Chapter 13 'Poo, Wee, Vomit' and Chapter 26 'Templates', for more information.

Marking the Roll

This is a nice part of the day and an opportunity to individually greet all your students. Children love to be acknowledged and asked how they are going. There are a few fun ways to do this.

> » If you are an extrovert you could sing the roll and children sing back:
> Good morning Darcy - Good morning Nadine
>
> » Children can call the roll themselves by recalling the order they are listed and shouting out their name
>
> » Alliteration nicknames (although if you have a Xavier you may have to stretch the alliteration here!)
>
> » The old fashioned way (but why would you do this when there's so many more fun ways to do it?)
>
> » Interactively - if you use an interactive whiteboard then play around with Easiteach software (or similar software that allows you to type or write). Display each child's name on a class page. Kids enter the room, press their names and their photo comes up. You can use audio and record them saying good morning which plays as they press their name. The teacher then sees who hasn't pressed their name and can quickly note absences. A good rule to have is only press your own name. You can take a screenshot of the page to look at to mark the official roll later on. To extend this idea further, children can drag an emotion that they are feeling and place it near their photo. Use this to track student emotion and wellbeing and to begin some individual conversations

Interactively: Using an online tool such as www.classdojo.com. Children choose monster avatars at the start of the year. Each day you mark the whole class absent so the monster turns red. When children enter the classroom they press their name and then the monster turns green. It's easy to see who is absent by the red monsters. This software is worth exploring for its reward system also. It's free!

Classroom Monitors

Children love helping out and being given a position of responsibility. No matter their ability, they are all capable of fulfilling some type of monitor role. Assign as many as possible and rotate if needed. Clearly display them in your classroom.

The list of possibilities for monitors is endless, however some ideas to get you started are:

- Taking messages and notices to and from the office
- Carrying the art smock/library book tub
- Emptying rubbish or recycling
- Tying shoelaces
- Tidying shelves or areas of the classroom
- Putting up chairs
- Opening windows or turning on fans/air con
- Tallying house points or free time minutes
- Managing sports equipment
- Table monitors for junior classes

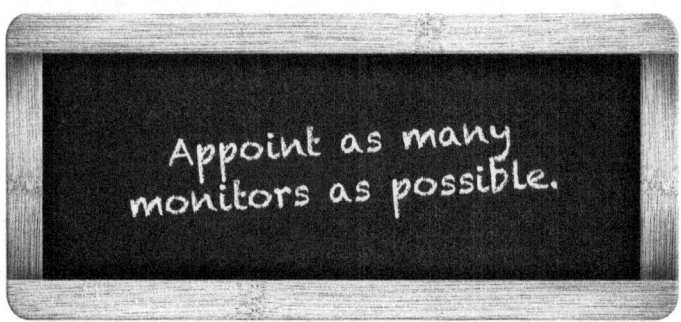

Food and Drink in the Classroom

Schools will have policies on this practice that you will have to adhere to. Make sure you find out from your mentor what the policy is and don't rely on your students telling you. They are good at attempting to convince teachers of something for their benefit.

Drink

Children should only drink water at school. Water consumption throughout the day is important so allow students to refill their drink bottles when they are empty. Send them in pairs if the tap is outside or fill a jug at the start of the day for the kids to refill themselves within the classroom. Encourage children to bring drink bottles to school each day and if a child never brings one it's advisable to contact parents to suggest they provide a bottle.

How you manage the location of drink bottles throughout the day is personal preference. I have found drink bottles during whole class teaching time, when children are on the floor, to be distracting. Save the drinking for independent working time. Generally, junior classrooms should have drink bottles stored on a ledge or in a tub to avoid spills. Middle and senior students are mature enough to manage drink bottles stored on their own tables. Frozen drinks on individual desks are a no no. Throughout the day, as the ice melts, condensation slips down the sides of the bottles and wets the table and work. Store them elsewhere.

Food

If your school allows healthy snack sometime during learning time, carefully monitor what is produced. Only fruit, seeds, nuts and vegetables are suitable (Check your school's nut policy). Junior students should have a specific time when everyone can eat their brain food. Middle and senior students are capable of snacking anytime throughout the day. Generally, after the big lunch break is a good time for a boost of energy, to get through the tiring afternoon session. I allow students to eat their snack during whole class instruction time, but do not allow them to put their skins and peel in the bin. They have to wait until they are sent off to work independently.

Many schools allow some time to eat lunch before children go out to play. This time still needs to have some structure. Wandering in and out of the classroom at differing times to put their lunchbox away should be discouraged as they nearly always meet someone in the hallway for a chat and are unsupervised. Encourage students to remain in their seats to eat as this eliminates silly behaviour. Children think they are 'free' during lunch eating time and start to get boisterous if not monitored. Reading your class serial is perfect during this time.

Occasionally children come to school without lunch or sufficient nutritious food to last them throughout the day. Your school should have procedures in place to respond to this so check with colleagues about what to do. Don't keep a stash of muesli bars or fruit to hand out, as schools need to monitor who is going without for legal reasons. Having a quick glance at what children bring to eat each day is helpful. A family sized block of chocolate or bag of chips is completely unsuitable. Have a quiet word to the student and if the problem continues you need to contact their parents and tactfully suggest some suitable lunch ideas.

Sharing of food between children should be discouraged. This practice is fraught with danger. Not all children are aware of allergies or sensitivities. Some students also use food sharing as a bullying tactic.

Finally, lollies and chocolate are not appropriate rewards. Children eat enough sugar in their regular diet without you contributing. There are many ways to encourage and reward children that don't involve food. Most schools nowadays have a healthy eating policy and I'm pretty sure lollies are not on it.

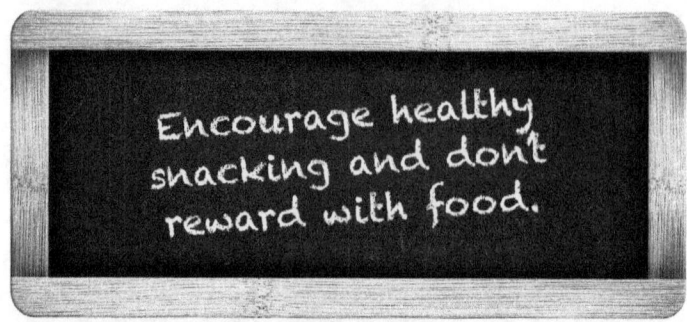

Class Parties/Reward Day

We all love a good party! Class parties are fun and should only occur when there is a genuine purpose and not too frequently. Twice a year is probably sufficient. To end a term, or reward your class in another manner, you could have an afternoon of making cubbies, dressing up, watching an appropriate movie or indulging in a student choice activity. (See Chapter 26, Templates, for class party letter).

The information letter to parents needs to be okayed by leadership and it's preferable if the whole level holds the same activity/party during the same time period. If any kind of dressing up is involved, children love when their teacher participates. Make sure that your requests to parents are not too overwhelming or difficult, nor should they be last minute. They need time to prepare. As a child I loved dress up days and my mother went O.T.T. to kit us out. Nowadays many parents work and are more time poor than in earlier decades. Now I have children of my own I hate dress up days. It doesn't mix well with working full time, so please remember not to be too demanding of parents.

Even though my daughters are in secondary school I still have to source dress ups for myself as I teach primary school. There's always a teacher or two who LOVE dress up days. They are worth their weight in gold. Sniff them out and hit them up for costume ideas. Putting the query out to social media also reaps rewards.

Several years ago I taught a middle school class. At the end of a unit we chose to have a level party. It was one of the most rewarding experiences of my teaching career. The unit was one we'd never taught before so it was written as we went. The topic came under the umbrella of sustainability and we chose to focus on food miles and shopping. Children were asked to source items for our end of unit party that were Australian made and had travelled as few food miles as possible. The efforts and enthusiasm on the part of both the children and parents to provide suitable food were outstanding and exciting.

Another class party that an entire school can participate in is in the last day or two before the school year ends. My current school has held this event for many years successfully. Children are placed in mixed sex groups of four. They are responsible for planning a three course Christmas lunch and decorations. This is planned at least a week in advance and prior to a weekend to allow parents time to source items if needed. Everything from cups, cutlery, tablecloths, food and drink is provided by the group. They must check with their parents to confirm they are comfortable with providing the nominated items. Some classes design menus and placemats as part of their end of year activities. (See Christmas party letter template in Chapter 26).

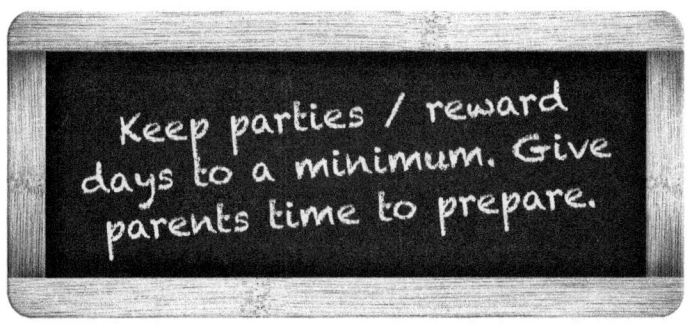

Keep parties / reward days to a minimum. Give parents time to prepare.

Tidying Up

Teachers need to manage their time effectively as we have a very large workload. Putting some classroom tidying up procedures in place is essential. All year levels are capable of pulling their weight and taking pride in a neat workspace. Making it fun where possible is helpful too.

Some tidying up ideas:

» Chairs should always be pushed in, even when returning to the floor for a short time

» Before each break all table tops should be returned to their original condition with pencils and other stationery stored away

» Before each break all paper and other scraps created should be binned or recycled

» Appoint a monitor to be responsible daily for an area of the classroom to tidy, such as bookshelves

» Play Magic Piece each afternoon just before the home time bell. Have your eye on a 'magic' piece but don't actually eyeball it. This could be a tissue, pen or any scrap needing to be picked up off the floor. Send children off to find the magic piece. Keep your eyes roaming over the whole room as they quickly realise if you are looking at one spot then they think they've found it and stop tidying up. Deflect children's questions about if it has been found. When the room is as tidy as you want it, declare the game over and announce who found the piece. Add on some house points or other class reward. This is suitable for all year levels and they never get tired of it. A way to deepen this activity is to choose a person, rather than an item, who have tried hard to pack up well. This encourages good helping and rewards someone deserving.

» Children are not allowed access to cleaning products, apart from water and cloths

» If children spill something then they should be responsible for cleaning it up

» Any unused worksheets should be placed in either recycling or a scrap paper tub each day to avoid a quick build up of paper around the room

» Paint and glue pot lids and brushes should be washed out weekly

» Clarify with leadership what specific jobs the cleaners complete, and when, and what you will be responsible for

The Essential Teacher's Guide

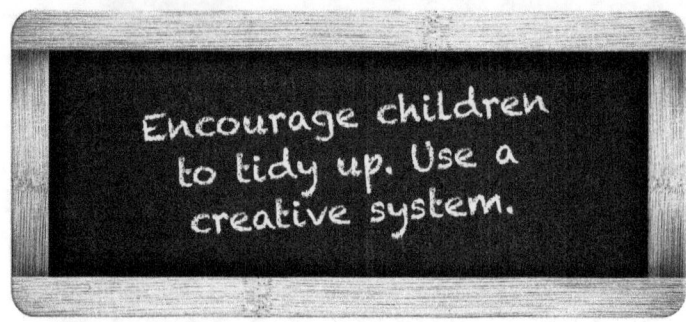

Lining Up/Movement Around The School

Students move around the school quite regularly as they attend specialist classes and other events. It's important that the class is able to stay together and not run or make too much noise. There are a variety of ways to move a whole class, depending on their age groups. Moving the class around the school requires some practise and consistency.

If you have junior students, then learning to line up is imperative, for safety reasons. They need repeated practise and instructions. You will have students who consistently wander off or lag behind, as well as students who will push and pull. The way you form your class lines does not need to be static; you should respond to changes in behaviour throughout the year. In general, lining up in pairs, linking hands, is the ideal. But how does this work when you have some students who refuse to hold the hand of another, or other students who purposefully try to wreck the line?

- Every time you come in from breaks or are moving to another area, always expect that children will form two orderly lines. If they can't then you must wait until they have done so. Moving off before they are in expected positions encourages children to not bother
- In the early part of the year, when you have five minutes spare, have some lining up practise
- Make your expectations clear
- As you move around the school no children should go ahead of you, unless you direct them to
- When walking the line to a new place, repeatedly stop if the line gets too rowdy
- With some grades you may need to have specific partners. If their partner is away then they go to the end of the line
- Direct the children who are always lagging behind to be at the head of the queue
- Some junior grades find it almost impossible to line up outside. Some brightly coloured dots or crosses painted on the ground, at a reasonable distance apart, are good visual reminders for children to line up

Senior and middle classes require less practise and guidance, particularly if the junior classes have worked hard on good lining up behaviour. Middle grades should still move around the school whilst formed into two lines, however the linking of hands becomes unnecessary. By senior level it should become personal teacher preference whether children still line up all the time or not. For several years, the senior team I taught in have allowed children to not line up in the morning and to come straight into the corridors, with the expectation that they are seated and ready to learn by the second bell, which peels right on nine o'clock. This also occurs after recess and lunch breaks. The benefits are that you are able to maximise learning time, children feel a greater sense of responsibility and a reduction in the frequency of children being late to school. Before you attempt this you should have your entire level team on board and definitely make it known to the students that this is a trial, contingent upon how they respect the privilege. Moving around the school as a grade should not always require two lines when in senior school. As long as no child is ahead of you, children are reasonably quiet and no running occurs, then allowing some independence is possible.

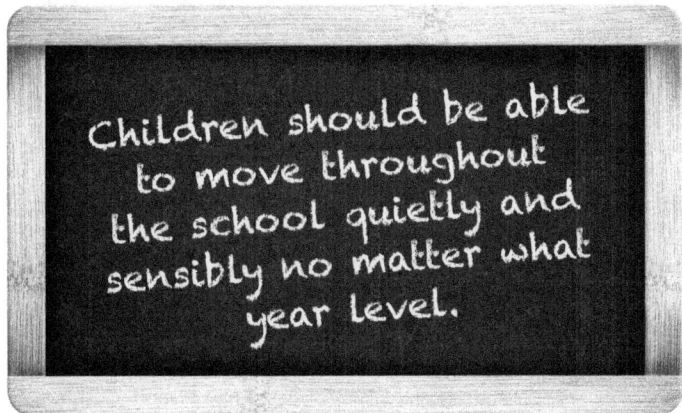

Team Teaching

Team teaching is not job sharing, nor is it you teach this lesson and I'll teach the next. Rather, it is two grades combined together with two teachers teaching at the same time. As a graduate teacher, if you ever get the opportunity to team-teach then you should jump at it. I have team taught with my mentor for two years and on many other occasions. This experience fast tracked my teaching ability and confidence like no other. For the first three weeks or so both teachers are finding their feet with each other, determining what role they will play in the partnership. After this time it usually runs smoothly. As a beginning teacher you will get the wisdom and experience of another teacher to guide you, the workload of teaching a whole class is shared, and the children receive the benefit of two teachers. When teaching small groups, there is an extra pair of eyes and hands to roam the classroom and assist children, whilst you focus on your group. It's great to have another adult in the room with you to share a laugh or to talk about concerns you may have about a particular child.

If there is another teacher in the school that you connect well with, don't be afraid to mention to leadership that you'd like to team-teach with them. Open and shared classrooms are making a comeback so anyone who is willing to embrace this model is appreciated. If this isn't possible on a permanent basis, then link up to teach a few lessons throughout the week. Children really enjoy a larger group to interact with and you will gain some new experiences.

Occasionally you will find yourself team teaching with someone you don't connect well with. This can be really difficult. It's preferable to keep communication lines open between the two of you, discussing the way forward. Perhaps you can each assume responsibility for teaching a particular curriculum area or create a temporary physical barrier in the room in order to split into your own classes.

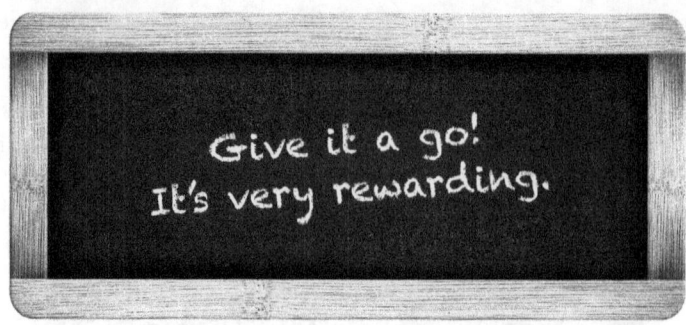

Voice

This is a teacher's major tool of the trade. You need to look after it well! There is no need to yell to be heard as this just encourages children to have a louder base working level. To gain children's attention use your repertoire of tricks, rather than your voice (see section on gaining children's attention).

Teachers need to be able to project their voice so that all children in the group you are teaching can hear you adequately. If you are unable to do this then students quickly lose attention and go off task. Sometimes moving students closer can help, however it really is an essential skill to develop. Using sound systems or microphones in a larger area can assist.

There's no point going to work if you are unwell, especially if it is affecting your throat or voice. Straining can make it worse and do some permanent damage.

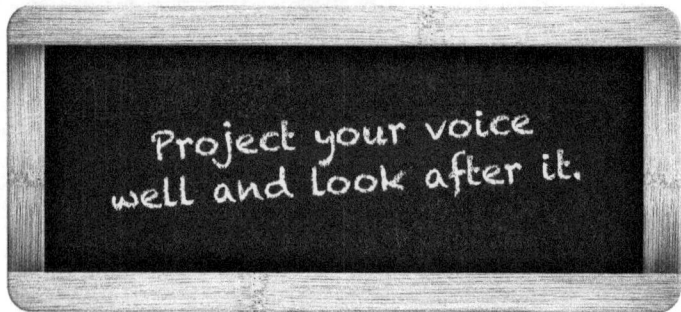

Sharing Time

All children love to share what's happening in their lives outside of school and this should be encouraged as part of speaking and listening. Children also enjoy questioning the sharer! What you don't want is all twenty-five students waffling on and sharing EVERY day. In a crowded curriculum there's no time for this.

You have a few options for making sharing time more effective:

- » Choose one day a week and get through all students. Seat them in a circle or get groups of about four to come to the front before changing groups

- » Randomly request a child ask a question of a sharer to improve their listening and questioning skills

- » Split the grade into four or five groups and assign them a day of the week to share. Spend about fifteen minutes maximum on sharing

- » After you mark the roll on a Monday morning ask students to share about weekend happenings or interesting things. This works well for senior students as they are mostly 'over' the concept of show and tell

- » Split the class into groups of four that remain the same for the whole term. Each week assign a different person to be the 'reporter'. Children get into their groups and take it in turns to share, only within that group. After this the reporter stands in front of the class and reports a few points that each person in their group shared. This works well for grades one to four

- » Encourage children to not bring items of great monetary or sentimental value. You don't want to be responsible for misplacing them! Also, no weapons or toys that encourage violence

Parent Helpers

Parents can be an invaluable assistance both in and out of the classroom. In fact, this is how I ended up becoming a teacher. I was a regular parent helper in my daughter's Foundation class and loved it. I started to match up the skills needed with the skills I possessed and thought it was a good match. Turns out it was a great decision to make!

Check with others in your team before inviting parents into your room, to ensure you are following the school's procedures. Some parents are more helpful than others of course. Parental involvement in the classroom and their child's learning is a key factor in academic achievement. Encourage it wherever possible. Parent helpers work best in junior classes, however it can work at any level. Generally, this section is about junior classrooms and you can adapt for middle and senior as required. Set up a good system from the beginning, where parents are well informed and you will make the most of their assistance.

You may like to team up with the other teachers to hold a 'parent helper session', where you discuss:

- Sorting through home/reading folders in the morning
- Helping with writing - the main job is to listen to the children read back their writing and then scribe. Also inform them to let the students try and write the words themselves, NOT to spell it for them
- Listening to reading
- Sharpening pencils, filling glue pots, cutting out laminating etc., when you are undergoing whole class instruction time
- Activity maths- measurement focussed rotation stations. Provide parents with an instruction card at time of session- they run and monitor small groups to complete tasks
- iTime- (Investigation Time) usually manning a station such as painting, making minibeasts with magiclay, making playdoh, cooking stations etc.
- Gardening sessions
- Library helpers
- P.M.P. and sporting events
- Returning and borrowing library books

It's a good idea to not engage in classroom parent help until Term Two. This allows the students to settle into the routines of school during Term One. All parent helpers need a working with children's (volunteer) check, which can be obtained at the post office for no cost- however they do need to provide a passport sized photo. A copy of this should be filed, in the school office, for their records. See Parent Helpers Letter in Templates chapter (26).

Some further ways parents can help at school:

- Changing readers
- Supervising small groups
- End of term classroom cleaning of equipment such as tables, chairs, glue and paint pots etc.
- Accompanying groups on excursions
- Sharpening pencils
- Laminating or contacting supplies
- Helping to put learning portfolios together
- Assisting where a larger number of adults would be helpful, such as logging on to computers
- Helping during construction or investigation times
- Supervising groups in the garden
- Assisting with extra curricular activities such as choir, gardening, music etc.
- P.M.P. and sporting events always need extra helpers

Train parents to help in many areas of the school.

Student Awards

Most schools have some kind of student award system where students are encouraged for their good deeds either in curriculum areas or social/behavioural areas. Approach your mentor to find out what system your school employs.

Some things to find out:

- Are all students in your class expected to receive an award throughout the year? Sigh. DO NOT MISS ANY STUDENT IF ALL ARE REQUIRED TO RECEIVE ONE. Heaven forbid a child should miss out. This is a bit tedious but parents will be knocking on your door. Or barging in and most likely complaining about you with the rest of the carpark mafia! And then, how genuine is the award they receive next week? Keep a class list template where you record the date and specifics of the award so you can look back for reference
- Is it per year or semester?
- Is it awarded in a public forum?
- Is there a word limit?
- What areas can you give awards for? For example, curriculum, sport, behaviour, friendship etc.
- Can they share with you some sample ideas for award areas to ensure you are on the right track with what you are rewarding? Very important! Recently an angry parent came charging into the staff room one afternoon aghast at what her daughter had been awarded for and in a public forum
- Do you need to inform parents prior to their child receiving the award? And if so, how do you do that? This is a big, big one. I have seen many a parent frothing at the mouth because they had no idea their child was to be awarded and they missed recording it on their iPhone. Whoopdedoo I say, but parents of this century are a little bit precious. If your school contacts parents prior to the presentation, you will really need to have some kind of alert or reminder system in place so you don't forget. That's one less problem you have to deal with then

Some sample award sentences:

- You are consistently putting in an excellent effort during class. Keep up that strong dedication and your future will be very bright. Well done!
- You have made a fabulous start on Junior School Council. You remembered your tasks well and followed up with our class. Well done!
- I am very impressed with the fabulous work ethic and behaviour you are showing in class. You should be very proud. I look forward to a continued improvement. Well done
- You should be very proud of your efforts in class and the way you have transitioned to senior school. You are concentrating and working well
- You always contribute well thought out ideas to our class discussions and have outstanding knowledge of many non-fiction topic areas
- You should be very proud of the dedication and diligence you show towards your school work. An outstanding start to Grade 5. Well done!
- Not only do you always complete your work diligently and to a high standard, but you are a kind, caring and inclusive friend and classmate. You are a valuable asset to our class!
- You have been displaying outstanding patience when working with other students. You should be very proud of your growth in maturity. We are!
- What an outstanding improvement in your decimal knowledge! Super proud of your post-test results. Well done

Resource Organisation

Chapter Overview

- » Importance of resource management
- » What to do daily: Digital and hard copy
- » What to do weekly: Digital and hard copy
- » What to do long term: Digital and hard copy
- » Managing finishing off work: Digital and hard copy
- » Back up!

Importance Of Resource Management

Teachers prepare and source countless amounts of resources in a few weeks, let alone a year or a career! They mount up so quickly it's important you manage them well. I'm all about efficiency in order to utilise my time well as teachers are pretty busy people.

We all have our own way of storing and locating resources. Organisation has always been my strong point, so I have developed a few strategies to manage the copious amounts of 'stuff' teaching generates that we may want to use again. The systems I suggest may not click with you, however it's a good place to start and once you get into the groove of managing your own resources you may find a better system for you. I also think it's important to keep your own workspace and that of the students relatively tidy and organised. When we are reporting on their ability to manage their own resources, it helps if you are teaching them how to do this through demonstrating your own techniques.

Don't file BOTH hard and digital copies – it's a waste of time and space.

What To Do Daily

Digital Copy See Chapter 14, Technology, also

I cannot imagine teaching nowadays without the aid of an interactive whiteboard or television. If you are using this resource, then each morning, well before 9.00 a.m., review all the resources you will require for the day's lessons, in order to determine their availability. When it's planned to use a website for the whole class, type the address into the search bar in a new tab and check to see everything is working. What works at home won't necessarily work at school due to security blocks. Leave it open for when you need to access it later. When it occasionally doesn't work you have time to either fix it or find another comparable resource. It's pretty annoying when your whole lesson is based around an awesome YouTube clip and it doesn't work! Any websites that the children will access also need to be located and checked to see if they are operational.

Before each lesson, locate documents you will be using for whole class instruction in the applicable digital folder on your laptop, open them and then minimise to the dock. (See Weekly Digital section in this chapter). Fluffing around and trying to find them when you are teaching is really awkward. The class become distracted, they start talking, you lose their attention and it's hard to regain. This has happened to me a few times so I have learnt to be prepared!

Recent advances in technology mean that either you or the children may be using a tablet device for learning and teaching. Check to see all documents are in the right location and can be opened by the kids. Do they have the required app? Can you connect to the T.V.? Do you have the connector or Air Server (or equivalent) operational? Are the files in Dropbox (or equivalent)? Tablets don't always support animation so a great web based game you have sourced via your laptop probably won't work on a tablet.

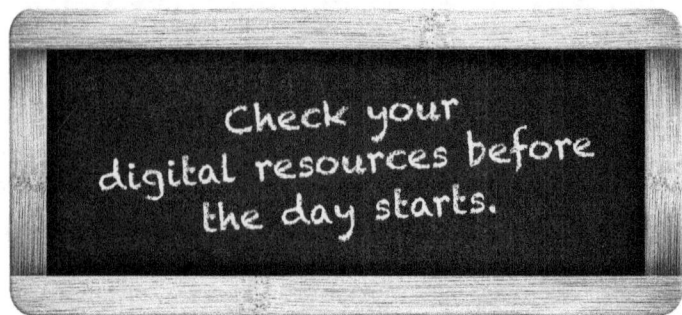

Hard Copy

All resources must be ready AND close at hand when you are teaching. Spending time finding them is wasted teaching and learning time and encourages the class to lose focus and it's harder to keep them on track.

In a box or tub, keep your day's photocopied resources, ready at hand. Locate this right where you teach the whole class. Use plastic pockets or pegs to keep the tasks separate. I prefer plastic pockets which I can either label with a marker or slip in labelled post it notes for me to remember who is doing what. This is especially relevant for differentiated activities where the distinction between tasks may only be minimal.

Any activity that an absent student has missed and needs to catch up on should be kept in the plastic pocket and write their name on the sheet. This is a helpful reminder to you to get them to complete it. Store it in the classroom where you are most likely to visually see it.

We often photocopy more paper than is necessary. A good idea is to have a scrap paper tub in your classroom for children to access, rather than using good paper just for rough copies or planning. Either daily or weekly, sort through your paper resources that are now surplus and transfer them to the scrap paper area. This prevents too much junk accumulating, making an end of term clear out much quicker.

What To Do Weekly

Digital Copy

On your desktop create two folders. Label one 'This Week' and the other 'Next Week'. The folder labelled 'This Week' contains all digital documents you will require for the week's plan. Don't rely on having them stored in a cloud or shared drive as sometimes these go down and you will be caught short when you go to use them in class. Either shortly after you use them or at the end of the week, transfer all used docs to long-term storage (see over page). The 'Next Week' folder has any documents you have prepared or found in advance. Highlight them all and transfer them to the 'This Week' folder. Continue this rotation each week.

Hard Copy

Only file hard copies of anything NOT digital. It's pointless to store paper copies and take up valuable space when it is already stored digitally. On, or near your desk, keep a tray or shallow box in which to put any papers to file more permanently later. Filing every couple of weeks should only take you ten minutes or so. A good time to do this is whilst the children are eating their lunch inside.

Things to store hard copies of are:

- Children's reports *
- Photocopies of good samples of work
- Test results
- Paper copy when digital not available
- Brochures/information booklets
- Professional development certificates

* This refers to any draft copies that were printed. A school may require you to keep hard copies of reports in the school office and to destroy any spare copies.

What to Do Long Term

Digital Copy

Create a folder called 'School' or 'Work'. Store it either on your desktop or dock. Within this folder you will create folders and within those folders you will create more folders! Think about a sensible filing system that you will be able to remember and access quickly.

For example, a folder called 'Writing' may have a folder within it called 'Narrative'. Inside this folder you may have folders named 'Narrative Planners', 'Characters', 'Good Beginnings' and 'Writing Stimulus', all to do with narrative writing. As you build up your teaching experience your writing folder will grow to contain 'Biography', 'Information Report', 'Poetry', 'Persuasive' and 'Advertisements', just to name a few. Most of these writing topics will contain templates or planners too. When you have taught many years your writing folder may be divided even further into 'Junior', 'Middle' and 'Senior'.

Another example is a folder named 'Maths', and then inside that you may have 'Senior'. Inside Senior is 'Decimals'. Decimals contain the files called 'Addition', 'Compare', 'Division', 'Subtraction', 'Multiplication', 'Order' and 'Rounding'. Get the idea?

Don't be tempted to leave all these folders you create on your desktop. They generally don't fall into alphabetical order and it's not an efficient system to access. Every couple of terms go through these files and see if any can merge or if new folders can be created within them. This helps to keep your filing efficient and easy to find. At last count in my School folder I had one hundred and fifty one files! There'd easily be five times that many within that one hundred and fifty one.

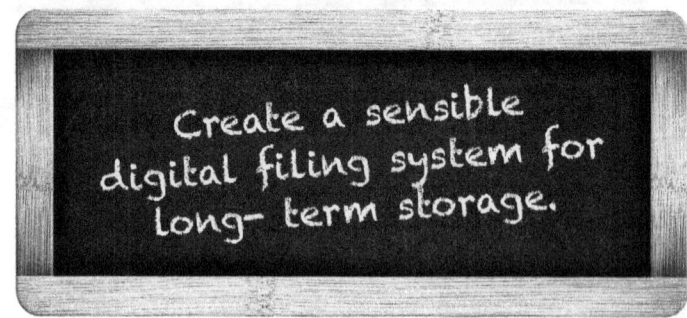

Hard Copy

This is my favourite bit! Display folders and a label maker are your best friends! Seriously, I think it was my best present ever and every box and shelf in my house is labelled. You may laugh, but I can always find anything!

How do you file? You will need to purchase some magazine file holders and display folders. Separate your papers to file into different subject piles, determining which will go into what folder. Then slip them into a display folder, one topic or subject for each book. On the spine either print the file name or use your label maker. Some examples are 'Space', '2014 Tests', 'Social Skills' or 'Government'. Store them upright in the magazine holders, about six per box. If you want you could even file them alphabetically. Done! These can be stored in your classroom in cupboards or on shelving. The magazine holder is pretty crucial. If you skip this, the folders tend to collapse in on each other, making the spines hard to read. Similarly, storing the folders lying down is also harder to access and read your labels. It gets pretty heavy on the bottom of the pile and hard to yank out.

The reason for not using a filing cabinet and suspension files is it's easier to locate and transport display folders. Sometimes you will be planning at home or off site and these display folders are more portable and the risk of papers dropping out is minimal.

Purchasing these items will obviously cost money. Speak to your mentor or area leader about adding these items to your teacher supplies. Unfortunately, we sometimes have to stump up for these items ourselves. Luckily though, display folders and cardboard mag holders are pretty cheap, but make sure you keep all receipts for work purchases for the taxman.

Managing Finishing Off Work

Sometimes students either don't have enough time to complete their work, or they had poor time management. It's important for students to finish off work, especially ahead of any free time activities. There are a few ways to go about storing these ready for the child to access.

Digital Copy

Generally, finishing off tasks that are digital, rely on honesty from the child. There are a few ways around this.

- » All children email you their completed work. You check them off. Anyone who hasn't emailed needs chasing up
- » Use a web-based note-sharing device, such as Evernote, that you can check via your own laptop. Check off completed work. Chase up non-finishers
- » Students place completed work on the school's shared drive, you check and chase up
- » Print out any incomplete work and place it in the finishing off tub (see below)

Hard Copy

An option to store unfinished work is a large box with a named suspension file for each student. You, or they, place any incomplete work for them to go back to when requested. This stops children wasting time searching for their own work in a box that is not divided into files for each child. Alternatively, if children have individual storage areas in tubs or desks, it could be stored in there. The second option is largely an honour system, as the teacher may not see how frequently a child is not completing their work and students can misplace any finishing off. To get around this you could provide a document wallet or display folder for each child to place unfinished work in, to then be stored in their tubs.

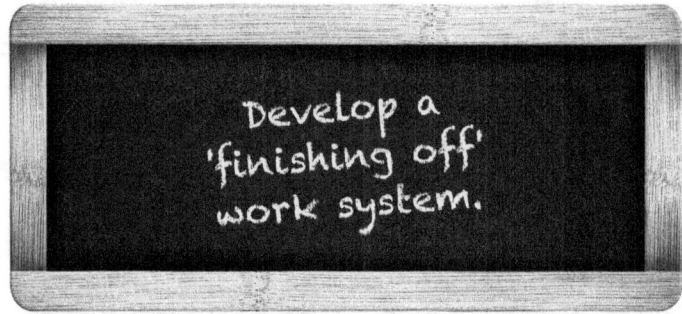

Back Up!

A final word about digital resources. It's very important to regularly back up your files to an external hard drive or cloud option. I can't stress the importance of this. Virtually your entire teaching history, lesson plans and resources are digital nowadays. If your laptop is stolen or the hard drive dies you are in a bit of trouble. Make that a LOT of trouble.

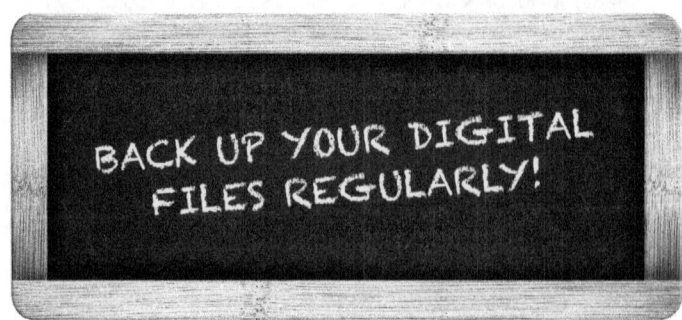

Use this page to document any areas you may want to make changes to within your resource management system.

Behaviour Management

Chapter Overview

- » Make connections and develop strong relationships
- » Make your expectations clear
- » Be consistent
- » Be reasonable and fair
- » Be proactive
- » Intervene quickly
- » Respond only to the behaviour
- » Appropriate discipline – minor behavioural issues
- » Curbing attention seeking
- » Appropriate discipline - major behavioural issues
- » Bullying

CHAPTER 7

One of the major issues that beginning teachers struggle with is behaviour management. You simply cannot teach effectively, nor children learn effectively, if the management of your class' behaviour is not effective. Children respond well to clear and firm boundaries, ones that don't change daily, and that make sense to them. Above all, children need to feel safe and secure. Sometimes the classroom teacher is the only adult in their life who provides that stability. When you discipline a child appropriately and reasonably, it actually brings them closer to you, rather than drives them away. They appreciate the attention, fairness and lack of judgement you bring.

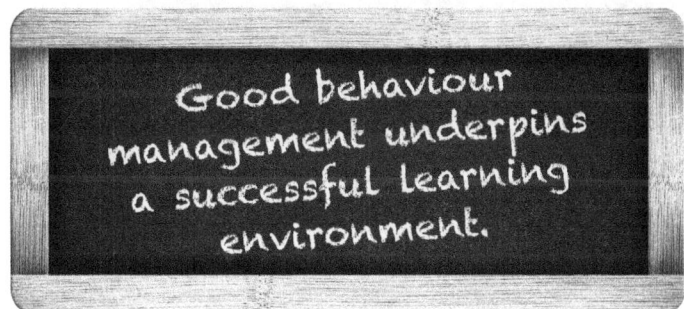

Good behaviour management underpins a successful learning environment.

In my first year Prep class I had many boys that I was finding difficult to manage. I tried strategy after strategy and asked endless advice. Some things worked a little bit. I felt strong pressure from within myself to 'fix' their behaviour before I sent them on to Grade One. This was delusional! My thinking was that my skill set should be able to 'fix' them and, if I couldn't, I wasn't a great teacher. I also worried that their teachers for the following year would think I was a bad teacher. It wasn't until one day, feeling quite despondent about my efforts and their lack of a response, that a very wise teacher spoke some encouraging words to me that helped me immeasurably. She said that social skills are developmental and like any other curriculum area that we teach. Some children won't click until they are in Grade Three, some Grade Six and some never! It is just like numeracy and literacy - some children are just not ready to achieve expected levels but 'switch on' later. Whilst I already knew this, I definitely needed reminding. It was like a switch was flicked that day and I really eased up on my self-imposed pressure to fix these students. I recently taught some of these children again in Grades Five and Six. Some of them are doing really well now with their social skills. Sadly, the 'switch' hasn't flicked on yet behaviourally in others.

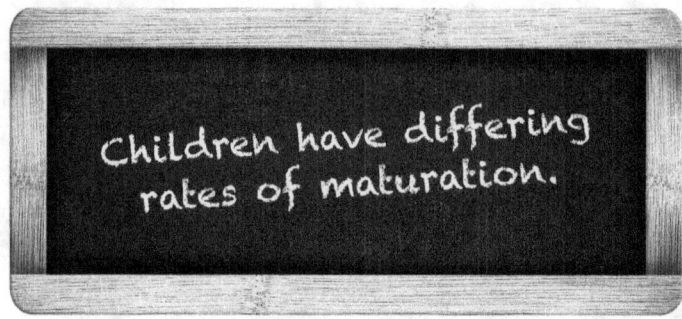

Colleagues with several years experience are your best resource for managing behaviour in the classroom. They have a wealth of knowledge. If you find yourself stumped for what to do, ask your co-workers for some input and ideas. Going to professional development courses and reading appropriate books is also of great assistance. Another invaluable option is peer observation. Either observe the way an experienced teacher manages behavioural issues, or request some observation on your own interactions. Asking for help does not mean you are not doing a good job. There's so much to think about and manage in your first couple of years and you cannot be an expert in them all.

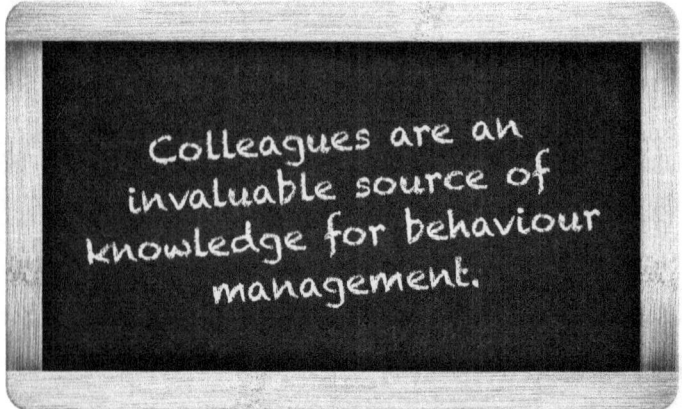

I want to stress that the management techniques outlined in this chapter are mine only. They are not theory based, they are experience based. (Although you will definitely find some of my techniques in behavioural theory). Through trial and error, as well as input from more experienced colleagues at the time, I have developed some actions to respond to poor behaviour, as well as learnt to change my own practices to avoid the behaviour in the first place.

Make Connections and Develop Strong Relationships

The more connected students are with you the more they will strive to be well behaved for you. This is not always the case, but a pretty good rule of thumb. A connection is a link or a bond with someone else. In order to foster this you need to develop strong relationships. So how do you do this?

Think about the impact you want to have, long before the relationship begins. My aim is to foster a sense of security, to be respectful and understanding, include fun and humour, and to inspire.

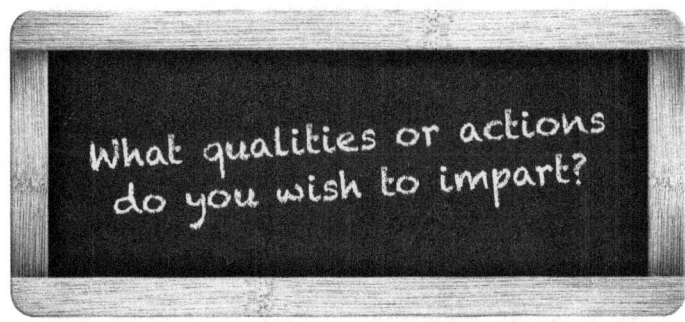

What qualities or actions do you wish to impart?

Once you have decided what your impact will be you need to think about how you will achieve this. I achieve my aims by:

- Making time to actively listen
- Maintaining confidences
- Being patient
- Following up when I say I will
- Sharing parts of my life with the children
- Encouraging children to share parts of their life
- Setting challenging and rewarding tasks
- Rewarding great effort and behaviour
- Being consistent
- Setting clear expectations
- Having fun and a laugh together
- Making allowances where necessary

When you make a good connection with someone then a healthy and strong relationship is possible. Regular reflection on the effectiveness of your connection is essential.

Make Your Expectations Clear

At the start of the year you should outline what your expectations are for behaviour, attitude, effort, presentation and work standard. You will need to go over these regularly, especially if you are working in the junior area. Middle and senior students need clear modelling and repetition of your expectations too. Alongside the school rules, you will have your own personal expectations that you choose to implement. Be patient with children as they learn your way of doing things. Incorporate your expectations into lessons, activities and making posters at the beginning of the year. Do not assume that they will know appropriate expectations, or even fulfil them. Discuss the expectation, model it and have them practise everything you expect from them. Even something as simple as how they walk into the classroom can be modelled and rehearsed. They usually only have to repeat the correct behaviour a couple of times for it to sink in.

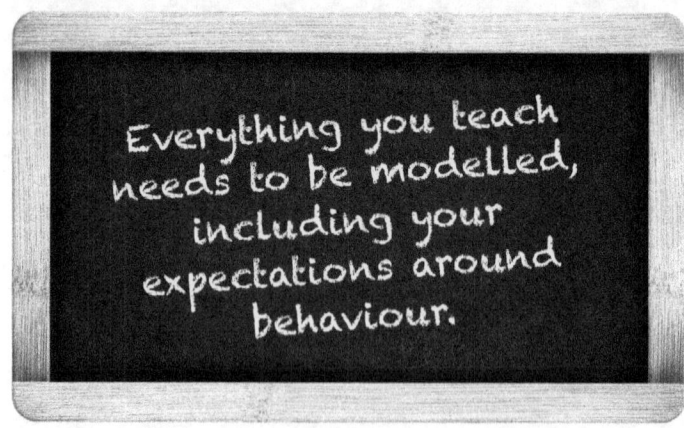

Everything you teach needs to be modelled, including your expectations around behaviour.

In the early days of your career you may not have much idea about what you want your expectations to be. You will begin to develop these as you gain experience. Sometimes, even with many years of experience, you will have a class that requires a new set of expectations and rules. Recognise the importance of flexibility. When you decide upon a new expectation, make it clear to your class what it is and why it is important. We are all inclined to strive to meet expectations if the reason is obvious and we understand it.

If you are first year out, these are some handy expectations to make clear in the first week:

- » Toilet visiting rules
- » Movement around the school
- » Noise level
- » Settling to independent work in the classroom
- » Responsibility for resources and personal equipment
- » Communication between students and how they treat each other

See Chapter 5, Classroom Management, for more details.

Be Consistent

Nothing irks children more than if you appear to have different rules for different kids. Or today you let a child go the toilet with ten minutes until break time and tomorrow you say no. If you decide to change the goal posts, and you are entitled to if something isn't working, then you need to announce it and tell your students why. Then be consistent.

The exception to this is if you have a child with special needs of some sort. You should still have a consistent approach with that particular student, however they may require different expectations to the rest of the class. Many students will pick up on this. Some will take it in their stride and work out for themselves the reason why it appears you are being inconsistent. Others will need an explanation. The way you choose to convey the reason is dependant upon the situation. A tactful whole class chat may work, or a quiet chat with a student or two may be the preferred option.

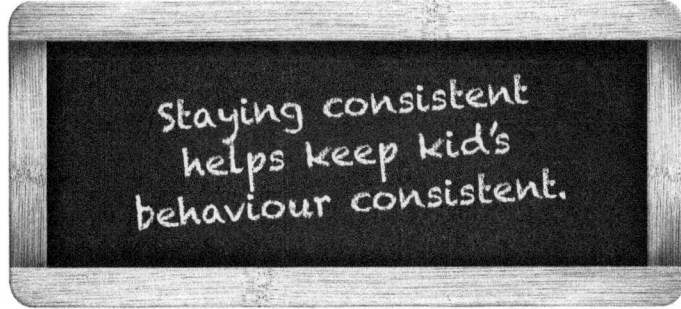

If a child points out you are being inconsistent then you need to own it. A student called me on it once and I realised it was true. It's really, really important to admit when you are wrong and apologise. Children need good modelling about appropriate ways to respond when you are proven wrong. I realised immediately that they were right, told them that, and then apologised. By the look on his face I assumed it wasn't often he'd seen an adult admit they were wrong, let alone apologise. It's powerful. Give it a go.

If you make a threat, such as they need to stay in at recess until work is completed, you need to follow through. This is Classroom Management 101. Children are very clever and will pick up quickly when you are not consistent. If you threaten them with staying in at recess, but don't actually do it, the students will know your threats are hollow. You will find your classroom control is really challenging. Your discipline techniques need to be easy to follow through on and consistent.

Be Reasonable and Fair

Your expectations of children should be age appropriate and reasonable. Too often I see teachers expecting children to behave years beyond their developmental ability, especially if the child is tall. Sounds silly, but it's true.

Examine your motives behind any discipline. Are you quick to discipline students who have a particular behaviour that you really dislike? Does it tap into your own issues? This is a common problem. Often teachers will discuss in the staffroom a student that they just can't connect with and who pushes their buttons. Yet other teachers who have taught the same child really liked them and connected well. The student is most likely displaying behaviours that trigger a reaction in you, based on your past experiences. When this is the case, it's possible you are treating this child differently to the rest of your class, in the way you respond to them. This creates a snowball effect, whereby you continue to clash and probably don't handle their behaviour positively. Do you have a student who triggers you to 'overreact'? There always seems to be one per class for me! Self-reflection is really important here. Ask yourself, if this behaviour occurred in another student that you connected well with, how would you respond?

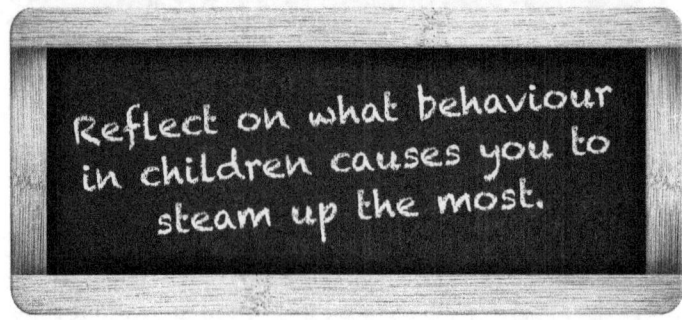

When children experience the feeling of being treated in an unreasonable or unfair manner, it is NOT going to improve their behaviour. Put yourself in the child's shoes in order to empathise. Why do they need to behave that way? Realistically, if someone was disciplining you the way you are disciplining them, do you think you are likely to be motivated to improve? A vicious cycle will occur with you escalating your intervention through frustration and stress and the student increasingly frustrated and stressed resulting in an escalation of their behaviour.

Reacting in a fair and reasonable manner to ALL the students you interact with will foster trust and self motivate students to want to behave well. Being overly punitive in your responses or inconsistent in the way you discipline individuals translates to erratic behaviour in children, just the thing you are trying to avoid.

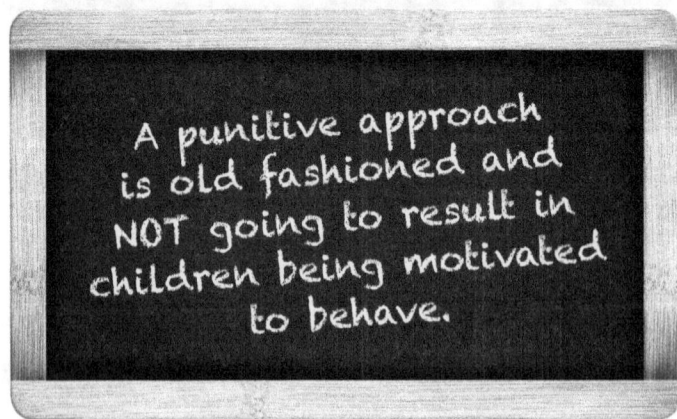

Be Proactive

Being proactive, with regards to behaviour management, helps to avoid misbehaviour in the first place. Not always, but often! Proactive means to be forward thinking by developing plans and strategies for your classroom management and reward programs. Children feel safest when boundaries are clear and they understand the rules.

Be proactive by:

- Stating clearly your classroom rules and behaviour expectations at the beginning of the year
- Role play the rules and expectations if necessary, for all year levels
- Repeat the rules and expectations often
- Make posters or incorporate the rules into activities and lessons
- Getting to know your students so you are well equipped to notice minor behavioural changes
- Talking to children individually when you notice some changes
- Speaking to parents as soon as you are concerned
- Using incidents that occur with other students in the school as a way to discuss and reinforce to your own class appropriate behaviour. (Don't use names or identifying information)
- Intentionally developing good relationships with students
- Modelling consistency, fairness and reliable behaviour.

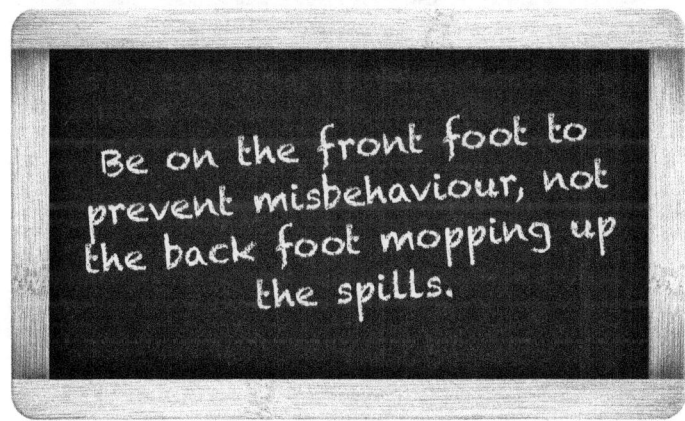

Be on the front foot to prevent misbehaviour, not the back foot mopping up the spills.

Teachers have a massive workload. If I choose to help, how much time is this going to cost me? If I choose to take this extra time, will it be worth it? Sometimes we observe interactions amongst children that need intervention, and quickly weigh up in our mind if we should intervene or not. If no child complains about it then it's doubly easy to choose to not intervene. However, choosing to discuss the situation with the students involved is a good way to avoid bigger problems down the track. Some children are not good at speaking up for themselves, so by initiating a discussion, you may well be helping these students too.

Intervene Quickly

The power in behaviour management lies in quick intervention. The earlier you can talk to students the better the outcome. When you leave an issue for a few hours or sometimes a couple of days, it's harder for the students to connect to how they felt and recall their exact behaviours, especially for children on the spectrum or with behaviour issues. However, make sure both the students and you have had time to 'calm down' first.

Frequently students return from recess or lunch play with a tale of injustices. Some are completely trivial and don't require much more from you than to listen and acknowledge their emotional hurt. Other issues require discussion and reflection. When you are teaching, it's hard to put that aside to deal with student problems, because the rest of your class will start to act up. A strategy is to acknowledge to the complainer that what they have to say is important and that you will follow it up shortly. Teach your whole class lesson, or get the students working independently on a task. Once they are settled, then speak to the students involved and help them to resolve the problem. It's important to remember to do this if you have promised students you will. It may make life more difficult for you if the child informs their parents about an issue that you knew about but have not followed up on. Issues can also be followed up in the next break if it's not convenient during class time.

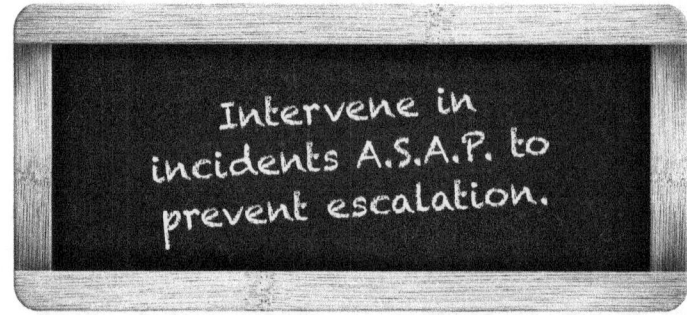

Children should also not have multiple chances regarding the same behaviour. For example, during whole class instruction a student is talking to his neighbours. Warn ONCE only. "Xxx, you need to stop talking please or I will move you." As soon as he starts talking again, move him as you said you would. Giving multiple chances is not an effective behaviour management technique. Your aim is to curb the undesired behaviour as quickly as possible and to display to the class that you are in control.

Respond Only to the Behaviour

Separating the behaviour from the child is imperative. The language you use is very important when chatting with children. They need to know that you don't dislike them, but that you dislike the behaviour. Let's examine some unhelpful comments and determine some better dialogue.

'You are annoying me' (Or insert frustrating, aggravating and making me angry). Straight up, you are giving your power to the child. They clearly know now that their behaviour is affecting you. 'Woohoo!,' they are thinking, 'I've managed to annoy the teacher. I'm going to keep doing this!' Sure they may be annoying you, but it's your job to not show it or impart it to children. A comment like 'You are annoying me' comes from an emotional position and your aim should be to separate your own emotions from interactions with students. Sentences that start with 'you are' are accusatory. Imagine you are a child again and a teacher is telling you that you are annoying or frustrating. Immediately you will either shut down emotionally or lash back in some way. There is no way you will have an effective interaction if these are the types of phrases you use.

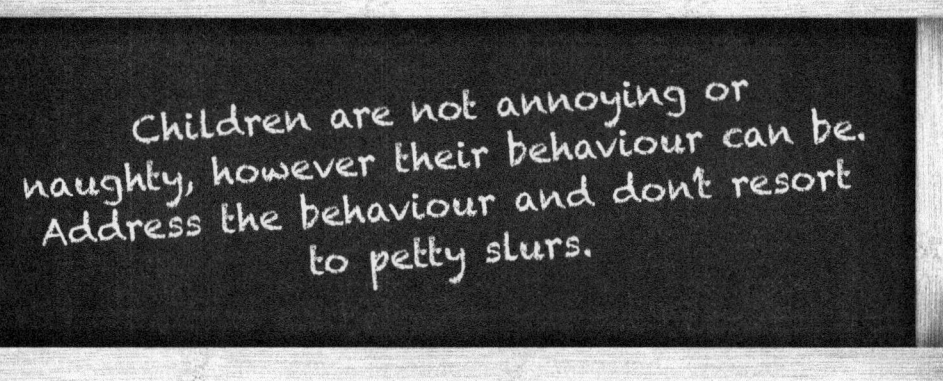

Children are not annoying or naughty, however their behaviour can be. Address the behaviour and don't resort to petty slurs.

A better response - so a child is annoying, frustrating or aggravating you. Recognise that and own that you are having an emotional response to their behaviour. Now separate your emotion from the behaviour. What is the behaviour? Constant calling out? Frequent disregard for the classroom rules? Once you have identified the behaviour you are better placed to respond to it in a helpful manner and to request the child do some self-reflection. Below is a sample conversation.

I have noticed that you are calling out a lot this morning.
(Identifying the behaviour only).

Have you noticed that too?
(Asking child to identify and own the behaviour).

Last week we talked about how calling out during class time can be disruptive to both teachers and your classmates.
(Referencing that this is a repeated behaviour that's already been discussed and is disruptive).

Can you tell me why calling out isn't a helpful behaviour in the classroom?
(Asking child to recognise why their behaviour is unhelpful. If they cannot do this then the teacher needs to list a couple of reasons).

How could you get my attention in a way that isn't disruptive?
(Asking child to think of more appropriate behaviour helps them to take ownership).

Those are great ideas. So you suggest putting up your hand or coming over to me and waiting patiently until I am free to talk to you. Fantastic. You are showing me that you are very clever. I know you can do this.
(Encouraging and then feeding back to the child their ideas in order to reinforce them).

Let's practise it now.
(Role play to reinforce how to behave appropriately. Possibly works better with junior students).

'You are naughty' (Or insert stupid, a pest or an idiot). There is absolutely no helpful purpose to these types of statements. Like the example above, it is accusatory, and a child will either feel angry at you or shut down and not participate well in a conversation. When you read the examples of stupid, a pest or an idiot, did you think they were a bit far fetched? In an ideal school you wouldn't hear these sorts of assertions, but unfortunately I have heard teachers using them. The statement 'That's naughty' or 'You are naughty' raises its head most often. I'm guilty of using it too. So what's wrong with telling a child they are naughty? For starters, you are labelling the child. If they hear it often enough they will begin to believe that they are naughty or identify themselves as a naughty child. The statement 'You are naughty' does not directly tell the child what they have done wrong. Choosing to not be specific about undesired behaviours will not help a child identify what it is they need to work on.

A better response - Identify the undesirable behaviour and make your conversation with the child solely about this, without attaching any emotional accusations to it.

* I just saw and heard you encouraging someone to smash their iPad down onto the desk and now the screen is completely broken.
(Telling the child specifically what you observed, keeping to the facts, no emotional accusations).

Encouraging someone to wreck their own property is not the right thing to do. Can you tell me why?
(Specifically stating what action was wrong. Asking child to recognise why their behaviour is unhelpful. If they cannot do this then the teacher needs to list a couple of reasons).

That is correct. It means that they are likely to get into trouble too and it is a mean thing to do.
(Reinforcing that they can identify why their behaviour is wrong and restating their thoughts to keep them clear to all).

Can you tell me what possible consequences will occur now that the iPad is broken?
(Asking the child to identify ramifications of their actions).

You have told me three possible consequences. They will be without an iPad to work on, it will cost a lot of money to replace and their parents will be angry.
(Feeding back to the child their ideas in order to reinforce them and to check you are both clear what was said).

I can think of some more consequences. Can you?
(Identifying that there are other consequences and asking the child for some more reflection. If they cannot do this then the teacher needs to list more reasons).

Exactly. Your parents might ask you to pay for a new iPad.
(Feeding back to the child their ideas in order to reinforce them).

How can you stop yourself from encouraging someone to do the wrong thing again?

(Requesting self-reflection to take ownership of the poor judgement. If they cannot do this then the teacher needs to suggest some ideas).

I suggest that you make sure you don't sit next to that student again and to remind yourself that encouraging others to do the wrong thing is an unkind and unhelpful behaviour.
(Stating clearly an action plan).

* I have simplified the interaction in order to give you the gist of a conversation such as this.

'I've told you a thousand times not to do that, why are you still doing it?' - It's so very tempting to ask children WHY they are doing something. And there's certainly a place for it. However, the majority of the time, particularly with younger students, they are not yet able to explain their actions. Pushing children to name reasons for the behaviour is counterproductive. It's also tempting to show your frustration by pointing out you have told the child the same thing over and over. There's really no point to doing this. When a student continues to repeat the same behaviour, despite past requests to change it, then connections have not yet been made between their trigger and reaction. Perhaps they are not mature enough yet, or you have not managed to convey in an appropriate way why they shouldn't be doing something. Even when a person can identify 'why', it doesn't excuse their behaviour.

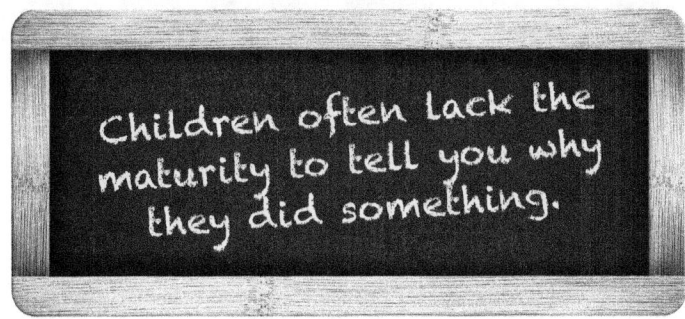

A better response - You are an adult and have a lot more life experience and maturity than a child. This helps you to critically assess why a child has made poor choices. If you are able to determine a reason for their behaviour it is not always necessary to point it out. Because their parents are getting divorced or because grandpa died are reasons for you to just apply more tolerance or understanding to the situation. Sometimes it's enough to just ask if they are feeling sad. If a child chooses to not share reasons, this should be respected and not pushed.

When you are fairly certain the reason a child is misbehaving is not too complex then it's feasible to talk them through it.

- » I have noticed that when you feel a little lonely then you....
- » I have noticed that when Xxx stirs you up or teases you then you....
- » I have noticed that when you play with Xxx then you....
- » I have noticed that when you return from P.E. you...

It's important not to force your opinion onto children. If you make a suggestion as to the reason for their behaviour, you need to ask them if that is possible. You could potentially be wrong so if they disagree, ask them if they have an alternative reason. See the Appropriate Discipline section on the next page for behaviour management strategies.

These sample conversations are guidelines only. Feel free to personalise them for yourself, just make sure that the purpose of your interactions when disciplining maintains the integrity of my suggestions.

Appropriate Discipline – Minor Behavioural Issues

Despite our best efforts, it may be necessary at times to respond to some poor behaviour choices. Opt for minimal intervention for early offences and escalate or change your discipline responses if the behaviour continues. A punitive approach as a first step will not be successful in curbing the undesired behaviour. However, there are times when a very serious offence occurs, such as cruel and intentional harming of another child, where more serious discipline needs to occur. If this is the case, then leadership and parents need to be involved.

Whenever you are disciplining a child for any reason, it's important to make that a private conversation. Talking to children about their behaviour in front of others has the potential for humiliation and they are unlikely to be totally focussed on your conversation due to worry about what their peers are thinking. You are aiming to correct the behaviour, not to humiliate.

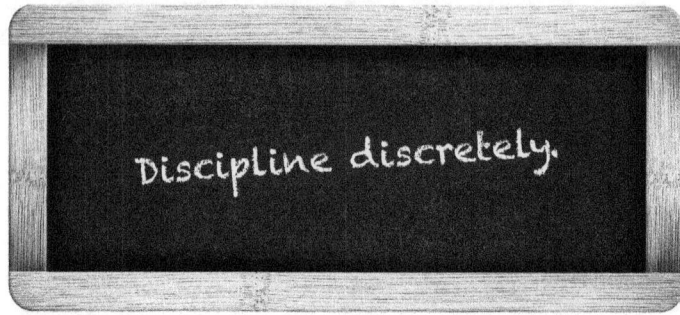

Document all discipline you do - what you said, what they said, what action you took. This is helpful for back up with aggressive or accusatory parents, and as a record of frequency of behaviours. How you choose to document the discipline is up to you, although a digital copy is preferable for long-term record keeping (and don't forget to back up regularly!).

Discipline should only be for the children with behavioural issues. Deducting points or rewards from the whole class, when it's only a few children acting up, is punitive for the well-behaved majority. Do this regularly and you will quickly find your easy to manage children have little incentive to focus and work well.

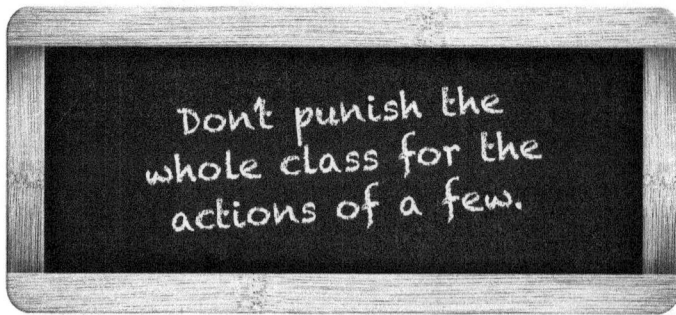

Matching misbehaviour to the correct consequence is essential. It is more powerful when the child understands how their behaviour impacts both themselves and others.

Minor Behavioural Issues:

- » Calling out frequently during whole class instruction
- » Talking during class time
- » Off task behaviour
- » Unable to keep hands and/or feet to self
- » Offensive language
- » Throwing rocks, sticks and bark during outside play
- » Not returning from recess promptly

For minor behavioural issues the first step is always to talk to the student, guide them through some self-reflection and ownership of the issue and to come up with an achievable plan to lessen the undesired behaviour. This process may need to be repeated several times as it is unrealistic to expect children to improve immediately, especially as behaviour meets an unstated need. Generally, most behaviour that doesn't meet societal expectations of 'normal' can be considered attention seeking. The reasons why we seek attention are many and varied. As a teacher, it is not necessary to determine that reason, that's the job of trained professionals and parents! Teachers just need to be aware that most minor behavioural issues are attention seeking.

Curbing Attention Seeking

Attention seeking behaviour can be frustrating for teachers, particularly when students don't seem to mind if they are receiving positive OR negative attention. It's easy for kids and teachers to get stuck in a negative cycle. A student misbehaves, the teacher reprimands for the behaviour and the student finds the negative teacher attention reinforcing. The child continues to act up and the teacher finds more and more ways to reprimand. You can break out of this cycle though by practising 'random positive attention' with students. They receive some positive attention when they are not misbehaving and eventually make the internal link that they can still receive attention in a more beneficial way.

Ways to practice Random Positive Attention:

- » Make eye contact and smile
- » Ask student a question during whole class instruction (that you are fairly sure they know the answer to)
- » Give specific feedback on good behaviour when they are doing the desired thing
- » Give the student a few quiet words of encouragement
- » Give the student a role in the classroom such as to hand out/collect papers or take something to the office
- » Share a joke
- » Write them an encouraging email or note
- » Call their parents to share some good news
- » Give them a pat on their shoulder

Sometimes, despite your best efforts, children seem quite unmotivated or incapable of adjusting their behaviour. Examine your expectations. Is it worth not worrying about it? Should you let it go? If so, how could you alter your mindset so that it bothers you a whole lot less?

Is it disrupting other students too much, or could potentially worsen, so still needs to be addressed? Intervention at this stage will be highly dependent on the issue. Below are suggested interventions, not a comprehensive total solution.

Calling out frequently during whole class instruction:

- » Whole class regular reminders about not calling out and why
- » Examine if there's a reason behind it that you could address. For example, a student who is very active might talk to others when they have to listen for a long time. Perhaps a 'fiddle toy' would be helpful, so that part of their body is moving while they are listening. Shorten your instruction time too
- » Give to the student some small laminated cards with hands printed on them, possibly three maximum per session, that they need to use if they have something to say
- » Move student to right at your feet when instructing the class
- » Reward program for when they raise their hand (See chapter on Classroom Management for more details)

Talking during class time:

- » Examine if there's a reason behind it that you could address. (See notes, above, on students calling out)
- » Speak to the student, ask for self-reflection regarding why they are talking
- » Ask for suggestions from the student about how to curtail their talking
- » Move who the student sits next to, position table so it faces a wall (less visual cues)
- » Reward program for not talking
- » Move to sit near your feet during whole class instruction
- » Give children a chance to choose a spot on the floor where they won't be tempted
- » As a last resort - masking tape crosses on the floor for certain bottoms to sit on!

Off task behaviour:

- » Examine if there's a reason behind it that you could address. (See notes, above, on students calling out)
- » Determine if this occurs whilst seated next to particular children
- » Move seats for independent work
- » Seat them at your feet during whole class instruction
- » Catch and praise when on task
- » Set realistic guidelines of what needs to be done in each session
- » Remove any distractions such as toys or pencil cases
- » Situate their table so it faces a wall (but doesn't isolate them)
- » Check they know what they need to do
- » Write a checklist if they frequently forget

Unable to keep hands and/or feet to self:

- » Incorporate as a whole class rule
- » Determine if this happens with specific children
- » Talk about the consequences (hurt child, lose friends etc.)
- » Remove triggers where possible
- » Introduce behaviour plan for repeat offenders (with parent and leadership input)
- » Reward program for keeping hands and/or feet to self
- » Remind to use words not bodies to communicate
- » Provide fiddle toys to satisfy their need for touch

Offensive language:

- » Talk about importance of not using offensive language as a whole class
- » Talk to the individual to remind
- » Determine what triggers bad language
- » Ask them to pause when triggered to take a breath
- » Speak to parents if language continues to ask for support (but beware, home may well be the place they learnt the words in the first place)
- » Reward program for not swearing

Throwing rocks, sticks and bark during outside play:

- » Reminders before sending out to play
- » Walking with the teacher on duty
- » Playing in an area without rocks, sticks or bark
- » Spending part of outside playtime inside in a safer environment
- » Speaking to parents

Not returning from recess promptly:

- » Reminders before sending out to play
- » Suggesting toilet visits happen before the bell to come inside goes
- » Playing closer to the classroom
- » Walking with the teacher on duty

Sending out of the classroom:
It's very tempting to want to remove a child from your classroom, temporarily, when you are angry or feel unable to control their behaviour. However, the message you are sending to the child is unhelpful and unhealthy. It says, "I'm fed up and can no longer cope with you." It also serves to exclude a child, the opposite of what you should be striving for in your behaviour management strategies. This really should be as a last resort if the behaviour is unsafe towards either themselves or anyone else. One useful strategy may be to send a child to the office or to another classroom with a message. It provides you with a brief respite and offers the child an opportunity to break the 'cycle'. Just don't make it a regular occurrence.

Appropriate Discipline – Major Behavioural Issues

- » Bullying
- » Biting, pinching, spitting
- » Furniture throwing
- » Abusive towards staff
- » Leaving school grounds
- » Stealing
- » Ruining others' property

Generally, major behavioural issues indicate serious disturbance or stress in a child. They could arise due to a change in circumstances or be fairly constantly present for a number of reasons. Intellectual, psychological or emotional disabilities, or trauma, can be the basis for many of these behaviours. It's always worth speaking to previous teachers of the child and reading their file for background information.

Many of the problems listed above will require meetings and intervention with leadership and parents. A first incident could be handled within your own classroom or team, but further incidents need mediation and assistance from the wider school community and family. Behaviour plans may need to be written along with referral to specialists such as social workers and educational psychologists. You will require support and mentoring. Don't try to handle these issues alone.

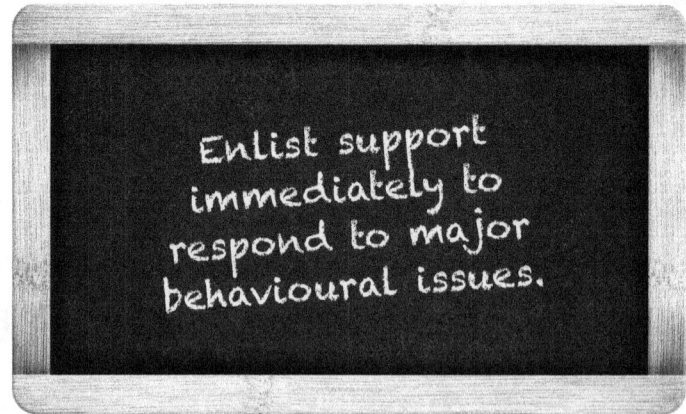

Enlist support immediately to respond to major behavioural issues.

The only major behaviour problem I will briefly address is bullying, as you will very likely experience this issue in every classroom and level that you teach. The other issues listed are less common and hopefully in your first few years of teaching you don't encounter them. If you do, seek advice and assistance immediately from leadership as they are complex problems to handle and must be addressed.

Bullying

Bullying has been a very hot topic for many years. Bullying is described as **repeated** verbal, physical, social or psychological behaviour intentionally directed towards another individual or group that is harmful or involves the misuse of power. Children and parents readily label what has happened to them as bullying but further delving often reveals it was just one occasion. This is not to minimise what has happened to them, but a once off incident is not bullying.

All schools will have a bullying policy and information about what it is and how to handle it should be incorporated into your classroom lessons. Please have a zero tolerance for bullying in your classroom and school. One year I had a grade five boy intentionally bullying pretty much anyone he wanted to. He had immigrated to Australia about twelve months before from a Western country. When all efforts to curb his bullying had failed I thought perhaps it was a cultural difference and that bullying behaviour was tolerated in his home country. "No, I got in trouble for it over there too. I just like to do it." Suffice to say the intervention escalated rapidly and more severely after this. Luckily we saw some gradual improvement.

There are copious amounts of excellent resources on the web to access to help you understand the issue and learn how to manage it. Bullying No Way is an Australian government site http://bullyingnoway.gov.au/index.html to access. Each state government has resource sites also. Cyber bullying is a major problem in the twenty first century also. See Chapter 14 on Technology for more advice.

Final Word

Behaviour management is a massive part of your day as a teacher, so the amount of information here reflects this. It's not recommended to undertake multiple changes in your classroom after reading this chapter. You will have more success if you work on one area at a time, master that technique and then add another.

Planning

Chapter Overview

- What to plan
- When to plan
- How to plan
- Planning for colleagues
- Planning with colleagues
- Filing
- Planning templates

Whilst completing your course you will have spent countless hours planning individual lessons, lesson sequences and units. Generally, students emerge from university feeling most confident about how to plan curriculum and where to access resources. Learning how to do this is an ongoing process, constantly being refined, and heavily dependent upon the level you are teaching.

When you are first starting out teaching, it can seem like you have to plan an overwhelming amount of lessons and have no 'bank' of previously taught lessons or stack of resources to call upon. This is tough! Hopefully you are in a generous team who will share their experience with you. In all the years I have been teaching I have found it is pretty rare to use an exact lesson or resource that I have used previously. In my home state there is a two year scope and sequence for integrated topics, plus I have never taught the same year level two years in a row! When I have had the opportunity to teach the same concept to the same year level again I have always adjusted or improved it anyway. I'm very easily bored and like to stretch myself too.

It can feel scary or overwhelming when you begin planning because you may be unsure of what, when and how to plan effectively. If it is worrying you too much, seek assistance immediately. Don't let it drag on, as this will only build your anxiety. Your mentor is a good place to start.

What To Plan

Will you be planning the whole curriculum content by yourself? Will you be responsible for a particular content area? Will you be planning with anyone else? Your team should have a meeting prior to each term to discuss what will be taught and who is responsible for planning each curriculum area. Once you are clear on what will be your responsibility for the year or term, determine if there's anyone in the team who has planned that area previously and ask them to share their resources or lesson sequences. If not, and no guidance is forthcoming, look at your state's curriculum documents as a starting point.

You may have a tendency to over plan in the early days. Even experienced teachers who switch levels may do this too. Within the same level some grades take longer to complete tasks than others, or some teachers are slower to impart information. You will get to know the right amount to plan as your experience increases.

A helpful tip is to plan a little too much so that you are in the position of having to drop something, rather than scrambling to find a fill in task. Begin collecting some emergency fill in lessons or five-minute fillers so you don't find yourself in that heart pumping situation of panicking, "What do I do? What do I do?" Chapter 21 on Five Minute Fillers is a good place to start. During my first year of teaching, in Prep, there seemed to be endless times I was grasping for a fill in activity. Those Preps sure complete work fast!

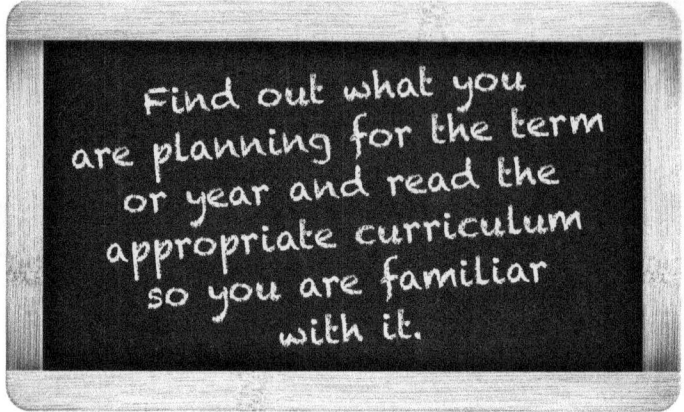

When To Plan

Will you be planning with another team member? Will you all plan together? If so, do you then refine the plan and find resources independently? These are a few questions to answer before you will be able to begin planning.

There's no right or wrong way to time your planning, it's heavily dependent on the team and it's specific protocols. The timing of your team planning will change from year to year, depending on when your team are able to meet. Personally, I prefer to plan late in the week for the following week. This allows you to reflect on how the lessons for the current week are progressing and know the areas that children need more repetition or experience in.

When your team arrangement is such that you plan a particular content area and then share that with the rest of the team, it is imperative that you don't let them down. Manage your time effectively so that you have lessons and resources prepared for them by the appointed time. That's good teamwork and professionalism!

Planning time should be focussed and uninterrupted. It's difficult to find that space during school hours. The allocated planning time at school is often taken up with administrative and management tasks, although it is possible to search for physical resources in the school such as books or equipment. Planning out of school hours, or when there are no children or parents around, is more effective. (See Chapter 3 on Enjoying Teaching for more tips).

Lesson plans need to be very clear and sequential. One year a teacher in my team would write lessons week after week that were unteachable. The team leader and myself sat with her often to assist her and model good planning methods and writing, to no avail. Each week I'd read through her lesson plans that she was expecting me to teach, take the topic only, then do a complete rewrite. It was really awkward but I refuse to teach my students rubbish or to be put under stress due to inappropriate lesson plans. If you are receiving guidance from colleagues on how to write lessons, please take their advice!

> *Plan at a time that allows you to be uninterrupted and productive. Plan early enough to share with your colleagues.*

How To Plan

What is the lesson's learning intention? How will you know, or how will the students know, if the lesson is successful? Begin all lesson planning with the learning intention clear. When this is not the case it is difficult to plan effectively and the learning outcomes will be murkier. Once you know the learning intention, determine the content of the lesson before finally deciding on the activity. Don't be tempted to find a good activity and work backwards.

Ask colleagues for their suggestions regarding the best resources to use to underpin your planning, both online references and sites as well as books. There's plenty of great lesson plans for all subjects on the Internet, however use these for ideas and stimulus only. Rarely will a lesson be exactly what you need, you will need to tailor it specifically for your own student's unique learning needs.

Ensure lessons are scaffolded, sequential and differentiated. (See Chapter 9, Differentiation. for more detail). When you begin your own independent planning as you launch your career, keep checking with your mentor to make sure you are on the right track. If you are struggling, speak up and ask them for some extra assistance. When a lesson is not planned properly you can feel like you are drowning as you attempt to teach it. This is especially so when the learning intention is not clear.

Some more questions to consider are:

- » How long will your lessons be?
- » Have you provided for a short whole class lesson (emphasis on the short)?
- » Is this followed by an activity where the students practise or consolidate the concept you have just taught?
- » Is there time at the end for reflection or sharing?

At the end of each day, or when there is some time throughout the day, reflect on what you have taught. Regular self-reflection is really important in teaching, to enable improvement and development of your skills.

- Was the learning intention apparent to both you and the students?
- If not, how could you improve that?
- Was the activity appropriate?
- Did you differentiate?
- Did the whole class lesson drag on too long?
- Were the children sitting too long?
- Did you have all the resources to hand?
- Do students need more lessons on the concept?
- Do you need to sit with your mentor to fine-tune the planning process?

Planning With Colleagues

Depending on how big your team is, you may have the opportunity to plan with another colleague. This is great when you are a newly graduated teacher, or just starting at a different school as it gives you some experience with the school and team's expectations. Be guided by when and how they wish to plan, but make sure you speak up so you get some planning experience.

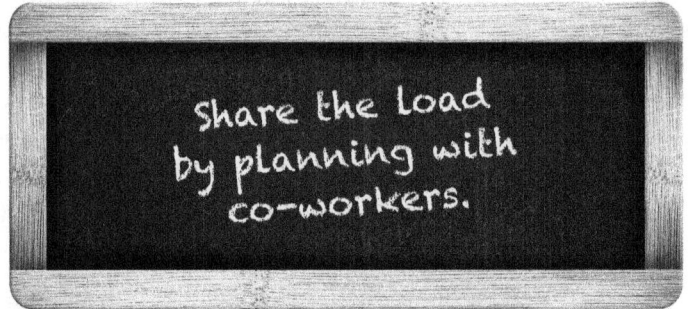

Planning For Colleagues

When you are assigned a curriculum area to plan for the term, perhaps Numeracy, you will need to ensure you are making your lesson plans clear enough for others to understand. Imagine you have been given the lesson to teach. Let's look at two examples to compare. Could you teach them both?

Sample 1

SUBTRACTION
Demo Multidigit.

Group 1: Multidigit

Group 2 & 3: Teacher group

Group 4: Sheet

Sample 2

Learning Intention:
Be able to understand how to subtract whole numbers

Success Criteria:
You will be able to use rounding, estimating and subtracting 2, 3 and 4 digit numbers in a game.

Subtraction. Context: Game – Multidigit.

Whole Class:
Multidigit demo.etng

Aim to get the highest possible number after subtracting. Roll dice one at a time, fill in top row first in order of choice, then bottom row. Do subtraction. What was the highest possible result? Lowest possible?

Easiteach whole class demonstration, then do as whole group with individual sheets

Group 1:
Play Multidigit.

Groups 2 & 3:
Teacher group – subtraction across zero with emphasis on USEFUL EASY rounding and estimating.

Group 4:
Sheet: M.A.B. Subtraction. Student records formal algorithm.

Sample 2 has enough detail for you to be able to teach the lesson, particularly if you didn't plan it. The more helpful information you can put in, the better. Your aim when writing lesson plans that will be shared, is to include enough detail so that your colleagues have no questions about what is to be taught.

Sample 1 is easily open to misinterpretation. There's no learning intention, success criteria or reference to any documents and resources needed. No mention was made regarding rounding or estimating whilst subtracting, so this important focus would most likely be missed. The teacher group focus was not stated and group 4 has a sheet. What sheet?

If you received a lesson plan such as Sample 1, you would find it difficult to teach effectively and with appropriate focus and depth. Chasing up the teacher to ask for clarification takes time and is annoying.

There is a lot of detail in Sample 2. If you were writing a lesson plan just for yourself then so much information is probably overkill. However, in your first few years, detail is necessary so you don't go off track or lose your focus. You still need to write your purpose or learning intention before you plan any lesson.

Once you have planned the lessons for the week, how will you be sharing them with your colleagues? It's advisable to have a weekly meeting where you all 'hand over' your curriculum area lessons and resources. Hopefully they can all be shared and stored digitally, a much more efficient system than handing out sheets.

If you are required to save your plans and resources to a central point, it's appreciated if you have uploaded them all prior to your team's planning meeting or before the week finishes. Ask your team for help with uploading or saving appropriately.

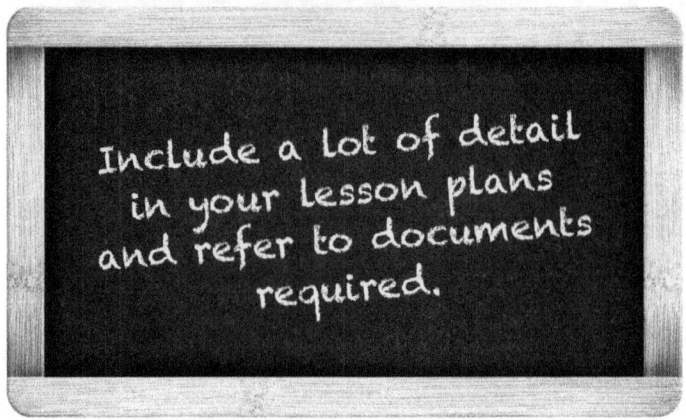

Filing

Once the years start to go by, we possibly repeat what we have taught in the past. Finding what you planned last time is an excellent starting point for planning in your current year. Filing, using a good system, is essential.

Chapter 6 on Resource Organisation has detailed methods listed for storing and filing your lesson plans and resources. A brief overview (can refer to either digital or hard copy filing):

- » Create a folder for each topic. For example, subtraction, government
- » Store all resources within the relevant folder
- » Create a folder for each term
- » File the term overview
- » File each week's FULL lesson plan
- » Save files with easy to locate names. For example, Term 3 Week 1 2015

When you have listed specific document names in your lesson plans it is far easier to locate these when you want to reuse them.

Planning Templates

There are countless templates available on the Internet and through colleagues. Every teacher I know uses a different one. It's a matter of trialling some to see those which suit you best. When you set your own template up, make sure you include when children are at specialists or any other special events for the week.

For example:

9.00 House Captain Elections.	**11.30** Maths 5 Flip chart. Work on project with partner. Individual/small group help with drawing regular polygons when needed.	**2.30** Finishing off – writing, unit. Free Choice Time
10.00 SENIOR SPORT		
	12.30 Spelling Groups - Low Grp – sounds	

It's your choice how much or how detailed you make your weekly template. I like to have as much detail as possible so if I go off on a tangent part way through teaching (never happens of course!) then the plan reminds me how to get back on track.

I also print a couple of weekly plans and locate them at my desk and at my teaching spot so I can grab them if necessary. I like the security of having a printed plan, just in case my computer carks it, which has happened once or twice.

You also need to have your weekly or daily plan clearly visible on your desk. This is in case you are unexpectedly absent and the relief teacher has easy access to your plan.

See Chapter 6 on Resource Organisation for more details about planning templates and management. Refer to the Templates chapter (26) for samples to use.

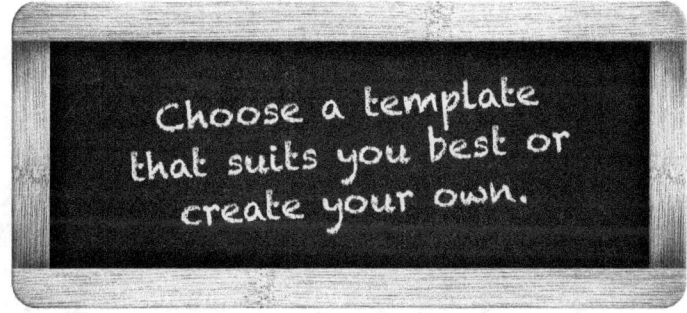

Differentiation

Chapter Overview

- » Why differentiate
- » How to differentiate
  - Pretesting
  - Grouping
  - Planning
- » Learning styles

When I went to primary school it was a one size fits all approach. Too bad if you needed extension or extra support!

I was horrified to read an Australian education textbook, published in 2004, advocating that the differentiated classroom was a bit difficult to manage and too much work for the teacher! The concept of differentiation has gained justified momentum in more recent years, to the point where it should now be considered an essential part of your teaching toolkit.

Briefly, differentiation is a useful framework for effective teaching that provides students with different options for learning the same, or a similar, concept. You will have covered this concept in depth at university and perhaps even completed an assignment or two on it. Therefore, I will only briefly comment on this topic, detailing some personal experience that may also be beneficial to you.

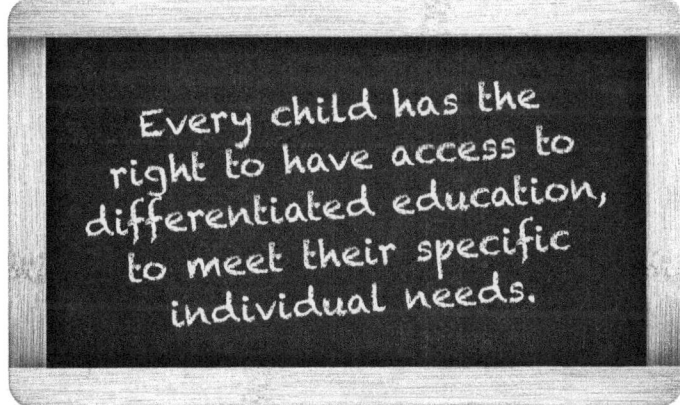

Every child has the right to have access to differentiated education, to meet their specific individual needs.

Why Differentiate

Personally, I have found evidence of the validity of a differentiated classroom throughout my teaching career. I believe that students who are provided with appropriate learning activities that meet their individual needs are more likely to remain on task, enjoy learning, rise to a challenge and exhibit improved on task behaviour. The benefits are more far-reaching than this and you will discover more for yourself as you establish your own culture of differentiation.

Opposition to differentiation still occurs. It is likely you will encounter some teachers who are set in their ways and a bit lazy. 'Planning the same task for every student was how we did it twenty years ago, it seemed okay to me, why should I change?' Tread carefully with these teachers, they can make your working day extremely difficult. If you have voiced your belief in differentiation and encountered a roadblock, it may be beneficial to approach another teacher who you believe may support your ideas. Perhaps they can advise you on how to approach these roadblock teachers. Alternatively, they may be able to support you as you go it alone if necessary. If you are team teaching or in an open shared area, then this may not be possible. Your only option here may be to put in a request with your principal to be placed with like-minded teachers the following year. Does the assistant principal or principal advocate for and support a differentiated classroom? Arrange a meeting time with them to find out. It's important to be guided by leadership, as they are your employers.

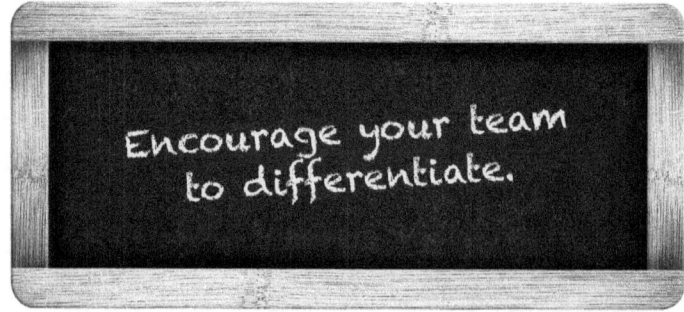

Presented with the evidence you discovered at university regarding differentiation, and your experience either as a pre-service teacher or new graduate, how could you NOT differentiate? You should always aim for best practice in your teaching career and be dedicated to reading current research and curriculum documents. It is highly likely you will be required to teach students with disabilities or specific learning needs. I have not had a classroom without them! It makes sense to differentiate their program. Within each class there will be students below, at level and above expected level, sometimes significantly so. It's discriminatory to not tailor learning tasks for all children. If you choose not to differentiate then you are choosing to not offer each child the best education possible. I wouldn't want that on my conscience!

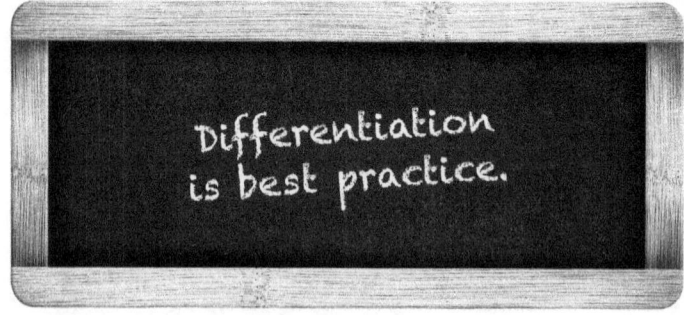

It's a joy to hear a small group of students exclaim with pleasure over a challenging task you have given them. It's rewarding to sit with children requiring some consolidation of a concept and to see their face light up when they 'get' it. Imagine each group of children with the opposite task. Not much joy or reward there; in fact giving students an inappropriate task for their ability, understanding or learning style can be damaging to self-esteem and their long-term view of learning.

How To Differentiate

Feeling a little overwhelmed? Sounds like a lot of extra work, doesn't it? I can hear you saying, 'I already have approximately twenty-five hours to plan for each week with good quality, imaginative, creative and relevant lessons. I have three to four meetings to attend and jobs that arise from those. I have to meet with a few parents, have several yard duties and extra responsibilities to attend to. I can't do any more, my head is already spinning and overloaded!'

Teaching DOES involve many facets and is very time consuming. I get that. If you are currently not doing any differentiation you can begin by taking baby steps. Choose a lesson a day (or a subject area) and slowly increase until this becomes an ingrained behaviour and ask sympathetic colleagues for suggestions. Request some professional development on the topic or share planning with co-workers for a while.

Pre-testing

Before any new topic is started you need to establish your baseline. What do your students already know, want to know or have no idea about? This can be in the form of standardised tests, tests you or colleagues have developed, thinkboards, K.W.L.s, mind maps, interviews or concept maps. This is not a definitive list. Assess your student's results and then group them accordingly.

Grouping

Choose whether you need two, three or four groups. Social studies may only require two groups and mathematics perhaps four. Importantly, these groups aren't static. As you teach the concept you may realise some children need to move groups. Each time you pretest for a new topic area your student groupings will alter. Never assume because a child is in the lower ability groups for numeracy that this will be the case for all mathematical areas. I have had students excel at fractions but no other numeracy topic. Groupings are fluid.

Should you tell students what group they are in? This is personal preference. I publish groups on the classroom wall but am very careful how I do that. The groups are never numbered or given names that indicate ability. Colours, movie or book characters, superheroes, animals or insects are some ideas.

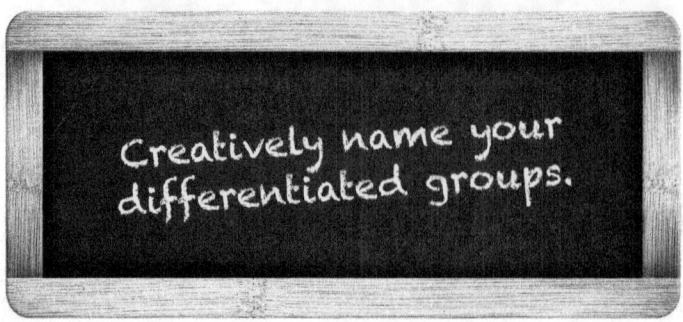

Planning

Occasionally, several years down the track, a family will sue either individual teachers or the school for not providing a tailored program to help their child. Keeping a digital record of groupings and the pre and post testing for each concept you are teaching is good practice and an excellent way to cover your back. Additionally, the record is easily accessible when you are planning, if this is done away from school.

For stand alone lessons

Essentially, determine your learning intention and then a whole class focus for approximately ten minutes (pitched at the middle), and then source activities that support that learning intention. For example, if you have three groups, choose an appropriate activity for the children at level and then determine how you can make it slightly easier and slightly harder. This is applicable for every curriculum area. You may also need to allow for cultural or language differences. Below is a sample lesson using a differentiated approach. The learning intention and success criteria were for a sequence of lessons and not all were covered in this individual lesson.

Learning Intention:
To add and subtract fractions with different denominators.

Success Criteria:
You will be able to find the lowest common multiple of different denominators.
You will be able to make equivalent fractions with the lowest common denominator.
You will be able to explain to someone how to add and subtract fractions with different denominators.

Whole class:
http://nlvm.usu.edu/en/nav/category_g_2_t_1.html (Fractions-adding)
Model game BEAN BAG THROW using beanbag throwing

Individual:
Yellow group: Add fractions, subtract fractions sheet (Dropbox)
Green group: Teacher group - focussing on adding fractions with different denominators
Blue group: Bean Bag throw (accessing instructions and scoresheet in Dropbox)
Red group: Mathletics on own iPads

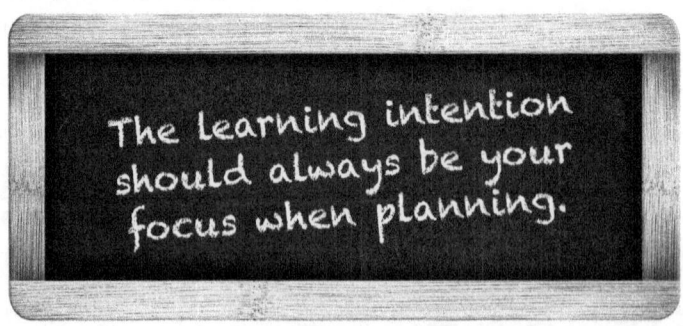

For projects or whole topic areas

Many topics don't necessarily need different activities for different abilities; sometimes all that is required is to inform a student what you would expect them to complete. For example, provide open-ended activities, give a variety of ways for the task to be completed or presented, prepare rubrics, choose three activities from the list of five to complete or reflective journal responses. This is not a comprehensive list, just a starting point.

For students with severe disabilities

From time to time you will have a child in your class with a severe or profound disability of some sort that prohibits them from accessing the curriculum, even when differentiated. In this case you will have to write a completely different program for them. Do not ignore the fact they cannot access lessons without modification.

For two years I taught a beautiful girl in grades five and six. She had a severe language disorder and Dyslexia, trouble consolidating mathematical concepts and poor short-term memory. Sadly, she had no funding. Each Sunday I would go through my lesson plans for the week through the lenses of this student. I would then prepare more appropriate activities for her, based on what the rest of the class were learning. When it came to report writing I wrote two different versions. Her parents read the legal copy that I was required to write and they did not show her this, as it was too disheartening for her. What she did read was a special report I prepared that focussed on her skills, abilities and growth areas. This was not a burden in any way. It was a pleasure to see her excited to read a school report and appreciate where she had grown.

There are a vast variety of disabilities that you will need to differentiate for, including behavioural, social and emotional, psychological, physical and intellectual. Language or cultural differences may also require some differentiation.

For E.A.L. students

English as an Additional Language (E.A.L.) students are the trickiest to differentiate for in my experience. Whilst these children may be quite intelligent, the first twelve months of learning English can be overwhelming. Assimilating with a new culture is very difficult and sometimes these students arrive traumatised or with very little previous formal schooling.

All activities need to be modified and the simplest of instructions given. Even when you do this it is not uncommon for the child to misinterpret the activity and complete it incorrectly. Teachers need to be encouraging and supportive, demonstrating where possible the desired activity outcome. Keep responses, requiring writing, to a minimum, along with reading large slabs of text. A good strategy, along with differentiating the task, is to buddy them up with a kind student who can model expectations.

For students with disabilities or who are E.A.L., it's helpful to seek advice from more experienced teachers regarding differentiation. Not all teachers at your school will have a kind heart towards students that require extra planning for. See if you can find help from those that do.

Learning Styles

All human beings have a preferred mode of learning style. Much has been written on this topic in recent years and at university you would've planned lessons that cater for differences. When differentiating, you should also take this into account. Provide the opportunity for students to respond to a task in a variety of different ways. Differ the way you present lessons. Get outside to teach and learn occasionally. A colleague working in senior school was responsible for planning spelling lessons for the lower ability students. Each week she presented the lesson and activities via a different learning style, such as singing spelling words and making the words with their bodies. A little bit of creativity and effort with differentiation really helped engage these learners with a topic that was normally hard work for them.

Seek out professional development.

Final Word

If you think you need more education regarding differentiation, then this is a topic that you should be able to find professional development in. Ask your school's leaders if there is money in the budget for you to attend some. There is also plenty of information on the Internet to search for and read about. Alternatively, ask more experienced colleagues for some guidance.

Use this page to document the steps you need to take to improve differentiation.

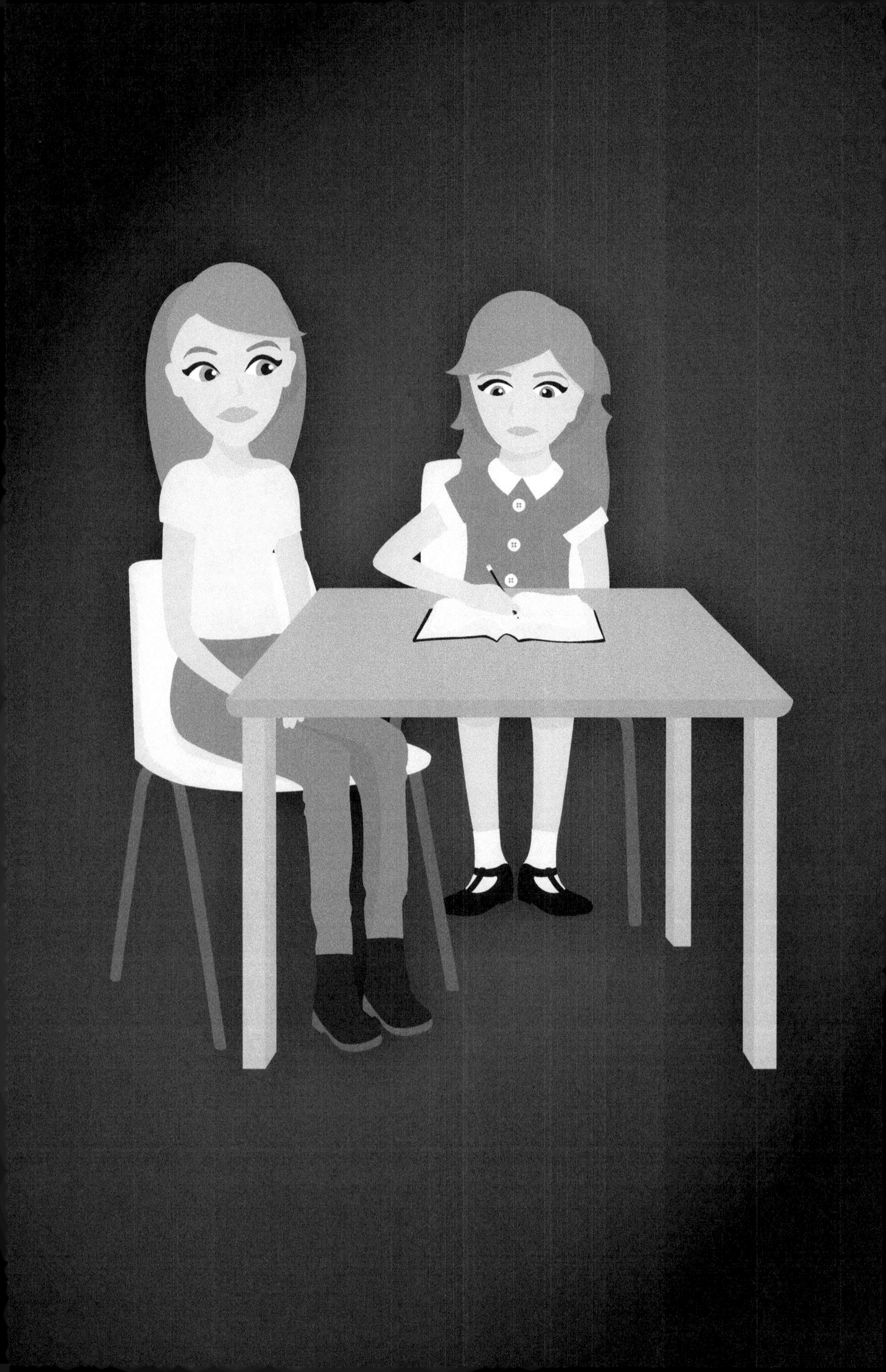

Aides

Chapter Overview

- The teacher and aide's role
- Planning
- Learning plans
- Support
- Instruction time
- Resources
- Parent meetings
- Reporting

The Teacher and Aide's Role

An integration aide works alongside the teacher to plan and implement a learning support program for students with disabilities. This is a great opportunity for a partnership between teacher and aide that can be mutually beneficial. You will come across some awesome aides and, unfortunately, some dismal ones. I've experienced both and have developed some helpful ideas and tips to make the most of whichever type of aide you have in your classroom. Prior to becoming a teacher I completed a Bachelor degree in Disability Studies and then years later an Integration Aide course. I worked as an aide for a few years and have some perspective on the experiences of both aide and teacher!

Whilst you are not the aide's boss, you are there to give direction, as the teacher is ultimately responsible for the integrated child's learning experiences. A supportive and friendly relationship is paramount and it's important you spend time chatting with your aide about both of your expectations and strive to keep interactions professional and respectful at all times. My experience has been that the clearer direction and support you give to the aide, the better the outcomes for the three-way partnership - aide, teacher and child. These small things communicate to the child that you are equal and both play a part in the child's learning.

Aim for a supportive and friendly partnership.

Instruction Time

You must insist the aide is present in the classroom for the instructional phase of the lesson. It's very annoying having just taught the whole class and provided an explanation of the task, only to have the aide wander in just after, and then require another explanation. You don't have time then to explain again, you need to be focussed on the children. If your aide is consistently late then you need to have a little chat with them. Find out why they are late and stress the importance of being present for the whole class instruction time. Sometimes it just takes someone to call them out on their lateness for them to improve. If this doesn't work then it's a good idea to have a quiet word with leadership, just to clarify what time they are supposed to be in your room and to let them know your aide isn't there on time! I would always opt for talking to the aide first in order to keep your working relationship as smooth and professional as possible.

Where the aide sits in the classroom is up to you. Some children are fairly independent and prefer the aide to not sit with them during whole class instruction, yet others will require the aide alongside them at all times. It's important a spot is chosen in the classroom that doesn't appear to physically exclude the child from their peers. Provide the aide with an adult sized chair. Too often they are expected to make do with a child's chair and by Friday they have a sore back.

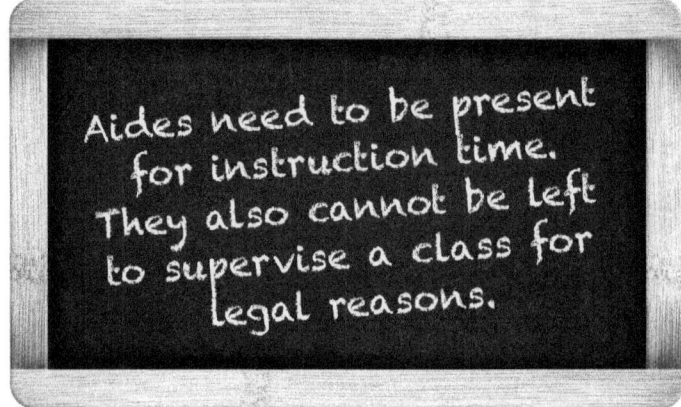

Planning

When I have a child or children in my class that require an aide, every Sunday I email through to the aide my plan for the week. This helps them to get their head around topics, locations and events coming up and a great aide may even have time to plan some activities to support the whole class plan. If you can't manage a week in advance, a few days is helpful also. For some integrated students, this is all that is required as they may be able to work on the same tasks as their peers and the aide's duty is to keep them focussed, on task and behaving well.

It is the teacher's responsibility to provide appropriate learning activities and for some integrated students your plan will need to be differentiated, sometimes markedly so. My strategy is to look in detail at each lesson planned and determine what the student can and can't do. I then source appropriate activities that mirror the content taught to the remainder of the class. Using a similar template to the weekly plan for the whole class, I then amend the task in the plan for the aide to use. Indicating whether the student should remain in the classroom or find a quiet space with the aide is also helpful.

Both the classroom teacher and integration aide will get to know the student quite well. Specialist teachers may only have one session per week with them so would benefit from your input. Sharing your management or instructional strategies for the child with other teachers helps with a smooth transition from class to class. Sometimes the student has aide time during specialist lessons and this is a great help to those teachers.

Resources

Keep a display folder in a designated place in your classroom for the aide to access easily. In this folder you should place each week the whole class plan, amended plan for the aide and all photocopied resources needed for that week for the student. I label the pages by the days of the week and slip the resources into the appropriate day. The reason for using hard copies is that in the event of your aide being absent, there's an easily accessible folder for a replacement to find everything they will need. That utilises your time well also, as you don't have to spend too much time explaining to a new person. The folder should also contain a brief run down of the child's learning requirements, behavioural issues or personal care needed. Additionally, appropriate extra worksheets should be added to the rear of the folder. Information on individual students is confidential so it's important that this folder is kept out of reach of students.

An outstanding aide may be willing to find or prepare their own resources to support your program and the child they are working with. These aides are worth their weight in gold; don't take them for granted! Inevitably, as they work so closely with the integrated student, they will get to know them better than the teacher. Listen to what they have to say and take on board their tips and suggestions for planning and managing the student.

Learning Plans

(See Chapter (11) on Disabilities for more information)

It is likely you will have to develop a learning plan or goals of some sort for integrated students. Ask for a template that the school uses and to also look at completed plans of other students. If a student has had an aide in previous years then their file should contain prior plans. Sometimes an aide has worked with the same child for several years and they may have copies of plans also.

When you have thought about some ideas for possible goals, it's a good idea to sit down with the aide to formulate them together. In reality, it is the aide who will be spending the most time with the student and working regularly on the goals, so it makes sense to have them involved.

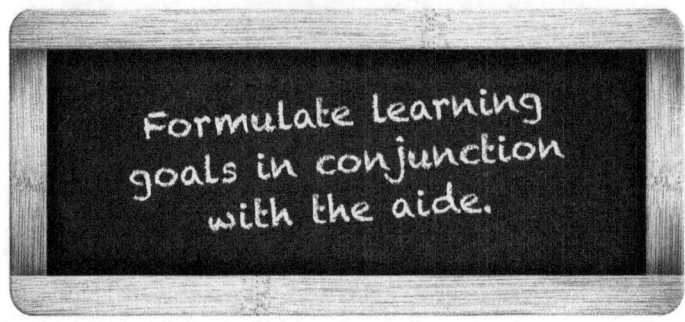

Parent Meetings

(See Chapter 11 on Disabilities for more information)

S.S.G.s, P.S.G.s etc., etc. Whatever the acronym (and they do change yearly it seems!), you will be required to meet on a semi regular basis with a representative from leadership, the family and the integration aide. The purpose is to set goals or to inform the parent of their child's progress around specific goals that you have set together.

Prior to any meeting with a parent of a child with funding it's imperative that you meet with your aide. Work together to set attainable goals, reflect on the goals they have already been working towards and make adjustments. It's important that you show a united front to parents and impart that you plan together for the best possible outcomes for their child. Sometimes families can be difficult to work with so this is where it's really important to plan with your aide before a meeting with parents.

As you get to know the parents you can potentially predict their reactions and responses. Going into a meeting equipped with ways you will respond to any difficulties is really helpful. Don't just rock up to a meeting unprepared, as you will feel on the back foot (and in front of leadership too)!

During the meeting if you are asked a question that you feel the aide will be able to answer better, remember to defer to their expertise.

Support

Hopefully you have laid the foundations early in the year for a great working relationship with your aide. Sometimes an individual child can be very challenging to work with. Supporting each other is very beneficial to you both. Two heads are often better than one in coming up with a new approach or strategy when you are tearing your hair out!

Everybody is capable of pushing your buttons in some way and, often, difficult students with disabilities do a lot of pushing! I've worked with a traumatised student with severe behavioural issues. It was challenging for all people involved with his care and education. Many times the aide and teachers discussed strategies for managing and improving his outcomes, whilst maintaining our own (and other students') safety. I could not imagine coping by myself in the classroom and school grounds without the support of his aide.

Speaking to a child's previous teacher and aide is a really fantastic strategy for improving your understanding about how they learn, behave and interact. If you know what pushes their buttons or what motivates them then you are off to a great start. You would speak with previous teachers for the mainstream class and it is equally important to do this for a child with an assistant. After you have taught them for a few weeks you have gotten to know the student reasonably well. Now is a good time to check back in again with a previous aide or teacher for extra tips and fine-tuning.

Some years you will find yourself with an aide that is not on the same wavelength as you and the partnership between you is not ideal. If you have tried many of the strategies already outlined in this chapter and they are not working, then here are some further options to try in order to maintain the best possible educational outcomes for the child.

- » Speak to a more experienced teacher or your mentor to request ideas for improving your partnership
- » Make a list of what is not working and your thoughts on why. Don't play the blame game here. You need to reflect and own your contribution
- » Understand you cannot change the way someone else behaves and thinks. You can only change your own behaviour, thoughts and responses
- » Speak to leadership about your concerns regarding the aide and the steps you have taken to improve the situation. Requesting your mentor sit in on this meeting will give more weight to your concerns
- » Ask leadership for their suggestions to make the partnership more workable
- » Ask leadership if there's any option for shuffling aides within the school, although it's pretty doubtful this will occur
- » At all times maintain your professionalism - don't resort to whinging to others. This is not constructive and quite possibly damaging
- » Seek to have at the forefront of your mind at all times the best possible outcomes for the integrated child

Another area requiring support relates to the specialists that visit the integrated child. Often, the student may be visited by O.T.s, speech therapists, psychologists, social workers or physiotherapists. The aide is expected to be the go between and this can be problematic. Frequently the teacher does not know when these visits are occurring, however it's suggested you ask your aide to update you. To make the most of these fleeting visits the teacher and aide need to set a short time aside to chat about anything to be discussed prior to the meeting taking place.

The Essential Teacher's Guide

Encourage your aide to take charge of work books, notes, feedback regarding specialist visits and following up on work sheets, exercises, activities that specialists leave to be done between visits. It's very important for the aide to show initiative and do the tasks set, or the therapist visits are wasted time and expense from limited disability budgets.

Reporting

(see Chapter 22, Reporting Writing, for more information)

You will be required to report in some format on an integrated child, whether that is in the same format as mainstream children or in a unique template your school prepares. As the aide works very closely with the child it is useful to get their input. There are three ways to do this.

1 Write your report and then ask them to read it and give feedback or input

2 Write the report together

3 Ask them for some input prior to writing.

I tend to use the first way but it wouldn't really matter which format you used as long as it worked for you both.

Use this page to document how you could improve your relationship and systems with your aide.

Disabilities

CHAPTER 11

Chapter Overview

- Disability Types:
  - Physical
  - Intellectual
  - Sensory
  - Spectrum disorders
  - Emotional/Behavioural
  - Learning
- Integration
- Inclusion
- Start of the year
- Integration aides
- Areas of adjustment
- Stick to your expertise
- How to share concerns with parents
- Parent reactions
- After diagnosis
- Learning plans
- Reports
- Parent meetings
- Communication books

Every mainstream class you teach will typically have between one to three children with a significant disability/disorder of some sort, and five to ten others with a lesser degree of some sort of disability. Some will have been diagnosed and some are yet to be. Sometimes they become apparent in the junior years and sometimes not until the senior primary years. Whatever the situation, you must always treat the child with respect and seek to understand the conditions under which they learn best.

Educating a child with a significant disability is a team effort, so don't worry, you won't be required to do this on your own. Seek assistance from the child's parents, colleagues, integration aides, leadership and any agencies involved in applicable service provision. Most of the time it is enjoyable and rewarding, but for those extra challenging times, make sure you call on others in the child's team.

Disability Types

Throughout your teacher training you will have learnt about the types of disabilities you will encounter in the classroom. Perhaps you even taught some children with disabilities on placements. No two disabilities are alike, just as mainstream children are also unique. It's very common to present with multiple disabilities so it's impossible to have a 'one size fits all' approach. Listed below are some disability types. It is not a comprehensive checklist, so if a child in your classroom does not fit neatly into any of these categories, you will have to do some research.

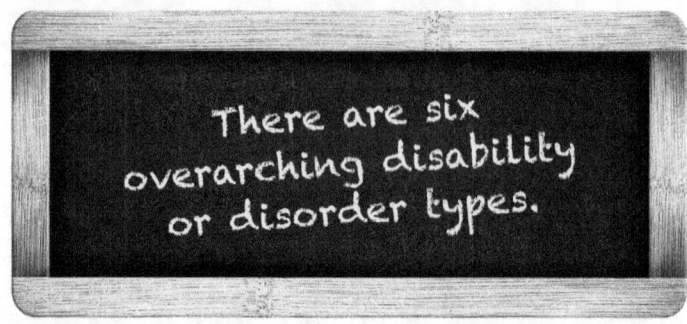

Physical disabilities are a partial or total loss of a person's physical functioning. Examples include cerebral palsy, amputation, birth defect or spina bifida. Children may require walking aids, wheelchairs, splints, helmets or braces. Medical issues can be included in this category, such as diabetes, anaphylaxis or severe asthma.

Intellectual disability is characterised by significant impairment in intellectual functioning and adaptive skills. It can be mild, moderate, severe or profound. In the mainstream classroom you are most likely to encounter mild or moderate. A mild intellectual disability can tend to be undiagnosed, depending on the child's age and background.

Sensory disabilities fall into the category of physical disabilities to some extent. These include visual or auditory loss.

Spectrum disorders are most commonly known as Autism, Asperger's Syndrome and Pervasive Developmental Disorder. In my experience, every classroom will have at least one student on the spectrum, either diagnosed or undiagnosed. It is a lifelong developmental disorder, characterised by difficulties in social interaction, communication, restricted and repetitive interests and behaviours, and sensory sensitivities.

Emotional/Behavioural disorders refer to a condition in which a child's emotional or behavioural responses to a situation are very different to the accepted age appropriate responses of their peers, and of cultural norms. It may adversely effect their self care, learning, personal adjustment and relationships.

Learning disabilities are numerous and, again, each classroom will have at least a child or two who struggle in this area. Children are of average or above-average intelligence yet have difficulty acquiring skills that impact their performance in all areas their entire life. Examples include Dyslexia, Language disorders, Attention Deficit disorders, and Auditory Processing difficulties.

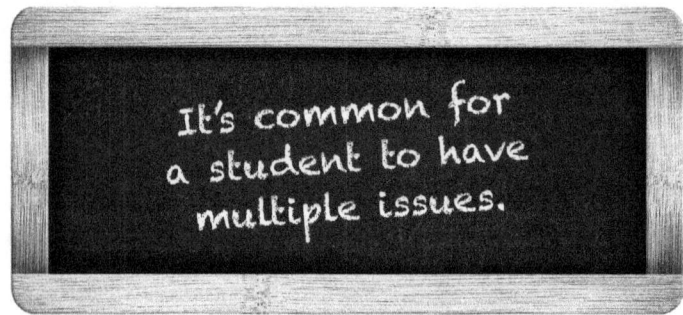

Integration

All children have the right to equal access to the curriculum, activities and resources. Teaching a child with a disability will require more thought and planning, to enable them fair opportunity and to maintain their dignity. You should treat a disabled child in the same manner as you would a child with no disability - with respect and fairness, whilst providing a safe and nurturing atmosphere where inclusiveness is promoted.

Inclusion

Simply integrating a child with a disability is not enough. Inclusion is a human right for all and includes availability of opportunity, acceptance of disability and an absence of bias, prejudice or inequality. You, and your school, need to be proactive in identifying barriers and obstacles learners face to a quality education, as well as removing these barriers. Some of this is big picture and out of your control. What you can control however, is your own classroom.

Some ways to be inclusive:

- Accept diversity as normal and a rich experience for all your students
- Respond to the diverse needs of all your children
- Accommodate different learning styles and rates of learning
- Collaborate with other professionals on a regular basis
- Create a structured classroom
- Display classroom rules and develop them together
- Post the daily schedule
- Plan for transition times
- Help students be organised through checklists etc.
- Differentiate
- Use flexible groupings
- Model inclusive behaviours and expectations
- Have zero tolerance for bullying
- Listen attentively and actively
- Provide consistency
- Build strong relationships
- Explicitly teach inclusivity
- Provide open-ended tasks or differing entry and exit points

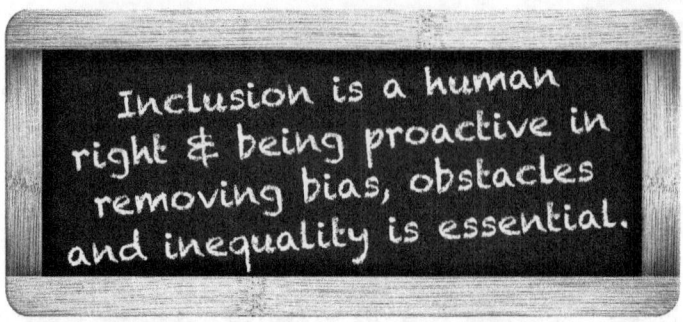

Start Of The Year

You will usually have access to student files before the year commences. Read them all carefully, but pay particular attention to those with a diagnosed disability. It helps to take some notes for yourself so that when you begin teaching them you have a head start regarding managing and planning.

Find out if any of your students have funding for an integration aide and who this will be. (Chapter 10 gives great detail on how to work with them and their role). Try to meet with them in the first week (or before if possible) to have a chat. Has this aide worked with the student before? If so, they are a great resource for you. Ask them how they are integrated, how to manage behavioural issues and where they need the most assistance. If neither of you have worked with the student before, seek out past teachers and aides for input.

You also need to know how many hours the aide will be in your classroom and when that will be. As the first term progresses it will become obvious to you where the funded student requires the most input. Sometimes it's numeracy, maybe literacy, perhaps socially, or all three! If possible, schedule your lessons around when the aide is in your room and the student needs most assistance. This isn't always practical, but a good rule of thumb to apply.

Is the student unfunded? If so, arrange to talk to previous teachers on the best way to manage their learning and behaviour. Sometimes students can be very difficult and have a major impact on your classroom, so knowing in advance how to balance their dynamics is really beneficial. It will still be a learning curve for you, however some forward planning and knowledge is helpful.

Funded students will have an official learning plan and many unfunded students with disabilities have one also. Seek these out and read them carefully. Later in this chapter is more information on how to write learning plans.

In the first couple of weeks, arrange a meeting time with the student's parents to introduce yourself and to ask questions. They know their child better than anyone so this is your best resource.

Some questions to ask are:

- » What does your child enjoy?
- » What are they good at?
- » What is the best way to motivate them?
- » In your own words, how would you describe their disability?

- » How does their disability impact upon their learning?
- » What aspects of school does your child find most challenging?
- » Do they have a communication book?

- » If there are medical issues, how should I manage them?
- » Under what circumstances would you need to be contacted about your child?
- » Who are their friends?
- » What are your greatest concerns?

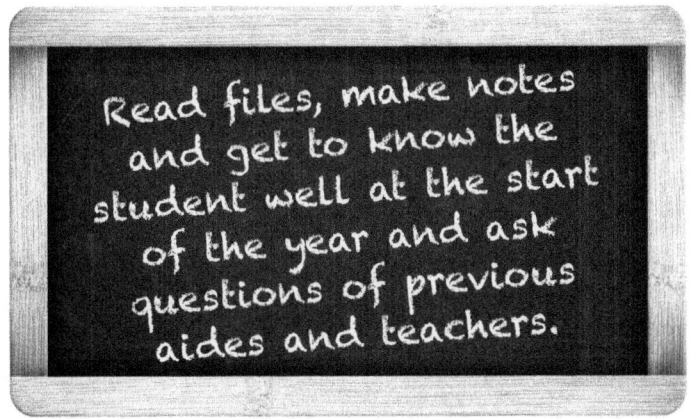

Integration Aides

Aides are an excellent support and resource for both you and the students in your class. Treat them with respect and professionalism and you will get the best out of them. I've nearly always had an aide in my class and the best ones are awesome. Sometimes they will be kind enough to take another student or two under their wing who may be unfunded. I cannot overstate how helpful this is to you AND the students.

Having an integration aide in the room does not mean you leave curriculum up to them. You are responsible for each student's learning in your classroom and need to plan accordingly. Make it known you are happy for input and ideas from the aide, especially as most likely they will know the student better than yourself.

When it comes to writing Individual Learning Plans and reports, request suggestions and feedback from your aide. Either write together, or, after you have written, get them to offer some comments and editing.

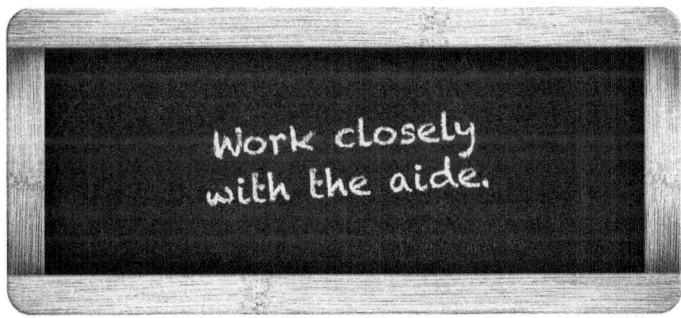

Areas Of Adjustment

No matter the disability or disorder type, you will need to make adjustments for these children to best meet their needs for successful learning and integration. It is going to take you some time each week to plan and adjust, and this is just part of teaching nowadays. No use complaining or avoiding it. If you avoid making any changes, it will come back to bite you on the butt.

You are not expected to be an expert in any disability or disorder type, however doing some research about the particular needs of children in your class is necessary. The adjustment suggestions below are brief and broad. You will need to do your own research to supplement this beginning list. Taking the time to learn about the disorder/disability will be worth it. Putting strategies into place to support the student not only makes their learning life easier, it will also markedly help you, as you will have less issues to deal with. Getting to really know the child will assist you to fine tune and modify tasks and equipment. Your main aim always is inclusion and access to appropriate resources, facilities and curriculum. An integration aide may assume some of the responsibility for inclusive access.

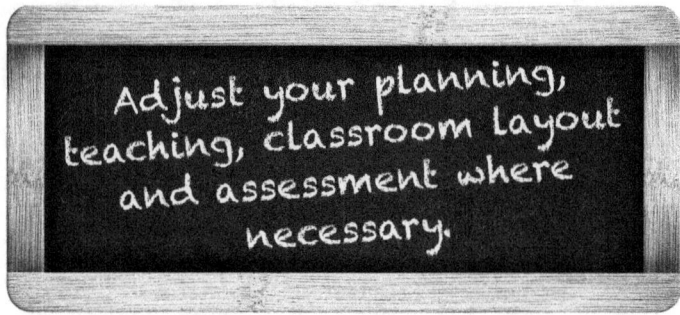

Physical disabilities

In the classroom, adjustments may need to be made for inclusive access, such as higher desks, specialised equipment or specific resources. This is not totally your responsibility; the school, parents, aides and agencies involved share this load. Your responsibility is to ensure the equipment is utilised and kept in good working order.

- » Ask the student what they would like. Don't assume anything
- » Is the classroom layout accessible for a wheelchair or walking frame?
- » Do you need to do any training to manage illnesses, conditions or equipment?
- » Do parents require a daily update for specific reasons?
- » What action do you take in case of emergency?

- » What modifications do you need to make to tasks? For example, can work be typed and not handwritten? Can you scribe for them? Can they remain in a wheelchair whilst the rest of the class are on the floor? Have you provided a range of task response options that suit multiple students?
- » Do you need to speak to the rest of the class about the student's limitations, needs or behaviour?

- » Are you promoting an inclusive, safe and tolerant atmosphere in your classroom?
- » Who do you speak to if equipment is required or requires adjustment/ mending?
- » Do you need to write a learning plan for them?
- » How can an aide best assist?
- » Will you need to help the student with toileting?

Intellectual disabilities

- Investigate lower levels of the curriculum for each topic you teach
- Group children when appropriate for tasks, to help support them
- Simplify materials and texts
- Provide a step by step task summary
- Use small group instruction as often as possible
- Directly teach routines and behaviour expectations
- Model and use concrete examples
- Plan an appropriate task for every lesson
- Ensure your expectations are accurate
- Do you need to speak to the rest of the class about the student's limitations, needs or behaviour?
- Are you promoting an inclusive, safe and tolerant atmosphere in your classroom?
- Do you need to write a learning plan for them?
- How can an aide best assist?
- Provide open ended tasks or differing entry and exit points
- Provide a quiet workspace, free from distractions (not always possible I know!)
- Lots of repetition

Sensory disabilities

- Do you need to speak to the rest of the class about the student's limitations, needs or behaviour?
- Are you promoting an inclusive, safe and tolerant atmosphere in your classroom?
- Do you need to write a learning plan for them?
- Provide a step by step task summary
- How can an aide best assist?
- What modifications do you need to make to tasks? For example, provide written instructions for all tasks? Enlarge worksheets?
- Seat them close by during whole class instruction & ensure they are attentive when you are teaching
- Keep the classroom free from trip hazards
- Promote a quiet working environment
- Adjust expectations for some tasks
- Provide open ended tasks or differing entry and exit points
- Group children when appropriate for tasks, to help support them

Spectrum disorders

- Visuals, visuals and more visuals! These are excellent for transitions, timetables and personal visual emotional gauges
- Timers on iPads
- Use their fixations as a reward and motivator
- Discourage fixations when necessary
- Work on fine motor skills regularly
- Encourage touch typing skills using specialist programs
- Use technology as much as possible
- Use social stories
- Explicitly teach social norms and emotion recognition
- List the day's lessons on the board
- Do you need to write a learning plan for them?
- Provide a step by step task summary
- What modifications do you need to make to tasks? For example, "Finish up to step three then take a two minute break," "After ten minutes work you may have one minute on the iPad."
- Are you promoting an inclusive, safe and tolerant atmosphere in your classroom?
- Avoid using sarcasm, euphemisms and idioms unless you are specifically teaching them
- Provide warning for routine changes as much as possible
- Set up a chill out zone or safe hiding spot. Include this in the Learning Plan
- Are break times stressful for the student? If so, you may need to modify their play or set up lunchtime interest groups
- Do you need to make yourself aware of possible 'escape' zones in the school grounds?

> Further reading is highly recommended for Spectrum disorders. Richard Eisenmajer, Sue Larkey and Tony Atwood are outstanding experts in this field.

Emotional/behavioural disorders

- » Do you need to speak to the rest of the class about the student's limitations, needs or behaviour?
- » Are you promoting an inclusive, safe and tolerant atmosphere in your classroom?
- » Do you need to write a learning plan for them?
- » Set up activities and seating arrangements to promote social interactions and connections
- » Avoid triggers for outbursts where possible
- » Have clear expectations and guidelines for behaviour and be consistent with these
- » Provide a behaviour contract if necessary that the student helps to write
- » Keep goals achievable
- » Set up a chill out zone or safe hiding spot
- » Provide warning for routine changes as much as possible
- » What action do you take in case of emergency? You may need to have a written plan - this is also helpful for other staff and C.R.T.s
- » Communicate with parents to provide a consistent approach
- » Teach self-talk to relieve stress and anxiety
- » Allow time in the classroom to use relaxation techniques or meditation
- » Access student wellbeing support if you have it in your school

Learning difficulties

- » Are you promoting an inclusive, safe and tolerant atmosphere in your classroom?
- » Do you need to write a learning plan for them?
- » Ensure they use their personal resources such as plastic coloured sheets that go over the top of work or glasses
- » Provide text in an appropriate font and size
- » Provide text on buff coloured paper
- » Use headphones to listen to audio recordings rather than read
- » Provide a scribe
- » Regularly use graphic organisers
- » Use a spelling dictionary or online dictionary
- » List instructions
- » Allow more time for task completion
- » Assist with organisational skills
- » Break up work tasks into smaller chunks

Stick To Your Expertise

There will be occasions when you begin to form an opinion that a child in your class requires some type of diagnosis or intervention. Let me make myself quite clear here.

YOU ARE NOT A DISABILITY EXPERT. IT IS NOT YOUR JOB TO DIAGNOSE. DON'T. DO. IT. EVER!

Why not? Well, for starters, are you a paediatrician or educational psychologist? I'm betting not. And even if this was your career prior to beginning teaching, this is not your position now. How presumptuous it would be of you to diagnose a disorder with no qualifications to do so. Now, your unofficial diagnosis might be spot on, but it's not your position to inform parents of this.

Secondly, a diagnosis of any type of disability or disorder is potentially quite devastating to parents. You want to steer well clear of causing any angst or anger for them, whilst maintaining a supportive role.

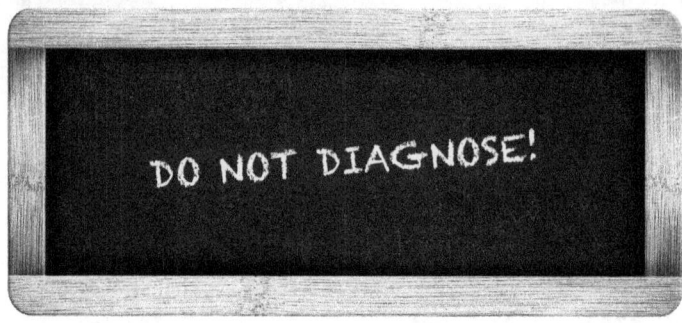

How To Share Concerns With Parents

If you suspect a child requires a diagnosis, there are a number of steps to follow, prior to talking to their parents.

- » Read their file. Has any previous testing been done? Do they already have a diagnosis and you weren't aware of it?
- » Read their previous reports. Did former teachers assess them as struggling in the same areas you think they are struggling in?
- » Write down all the symptoms and behaviours you have observed. When and how do they manifest?
- » Speak to former teachers. What was their opinion? What did they notice? Did they attempt to speak to the parents? If so, what was their reaction? This is crucial as it informs the manner in which you approach the parents
- » Speak to your team leader and other more experienced teachers in your team. This is to confirm your opinion and to seek ideas on handling parent communication
- » Gather any evidence such as videos, writing samples, examples of behavioural problems and assessments
- » Do some research. What broad area of disability/disorder do you think they may have? This is simply to determine what avenues you can suggest that parents follow up with

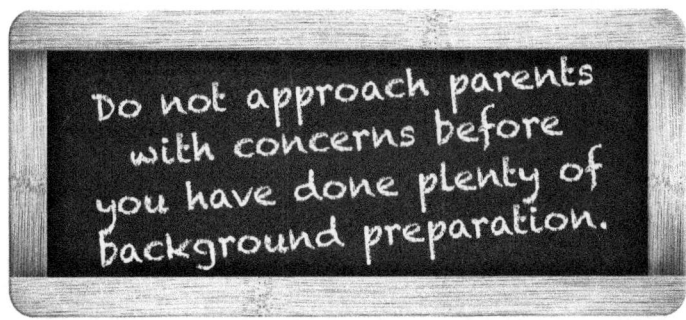

Now that you have completed your preparation, it is time to contact parents to share your concerns. Give them a phone call, requesting they come in for a chat about their child's learning/behaviour and some concerns you have. Don't leave a message on their phone, this is best done in a more personal manner. Just keep calling back until you reach them. They may suggest the meeting is done over the phone, or press you for more details prior to the arranged meeting. It's a good idea to resist this pressure and maintain that you'd prefer to chat in person. Unless it's completely unavoidable, a meeting time before school is not preferable, as you want to allow yourself plenty of time.

If you are particularly nervous about the approaching meeting, ask your team leader or another senior staff member if they will sit in with you. It may also be appropriate to have a Special Needs Co-ordinator (if your school has one) sit in on these meetings. Begin by thanking the parents for coming in and outline the problem. For example, "Through my observations and assessments I have formed the opinion that Xxx is finding literacy particularly difficult. My testing shows that she is several years behind expected levels. She copes well with all other curriculum areas, however, when she is required to write or read for set tasks she can often find herself a little muddled. For example, today I asked her to read aloud to me this piece of text. In most sentences she would switch either words or letter blends around. This meant her reading was stilted as she was trying to make meaning from jumbled words and sentences. When I read the text to her she was able to tell me exactly what it was conveying, including subtle inferences. Have you noticed any difficulties with her reading and writing at home?"

After a discussion about what the parents have observed, it's time to suggest some further investigation from professionals. "I'd like to refer you for further investigation with trained professionals. I'm not qualified to assess or diagnose what might be going on for Xxx and I believe further assessment would be really helpful. Educational psychologists will be able to give us some specific strategies to help her learning." At this point, if parents are amenable, you can plan the pathway with the parent, depending upon the school's input and their own finances.

Always stress that you want to investigate further to be able to make learning easier and less stressful for the child, not because we want to label them.

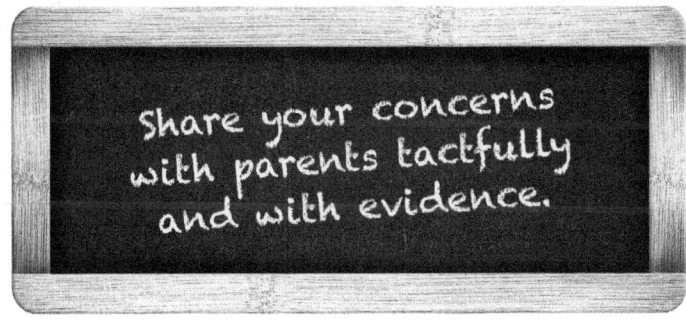

Parent Reactions

When you suggest to a parent that their child may need a diagnosis of some sort you will get a variety of responses. The chapter on Partnering Positively with Parents will be of assistance, particularly if you have already done your homework and determined the type of parent you are dealing with. The key here is to tread softly, to be prepared with evidence and to keep following up with them.

1. Denial. This is reasonably common. "I was like that in school and I turned out alright." Or, "I don't agree with you, I don't think there's anything wrong with my child." When faced with this reaction, restate your educated opinion and implore them to think about it. Perhaps suggest another meeting in a couple of weeks, after they've had a chance to process and regroup. A father reacted with denial when I suggested his daughter may have some learning difficulties, possibly Dyslexia, which then morphed into sadness. His only other child, a son, was autistic and he just wanted a 'normal' child. Both parents followed up and she was diagnosed with Dyslexia, amongst a few other learning difficulties.

2. Apathy. Not usually too apparent in your meeting, apathy may emerge in the coming weeks when they do nothing about making appointments or getting referrals. Again, this is quite a common response. They often promise to do something, perhaps with the full intention of doing so, but end up doing nothing. You can keep checking in but there's only so far you can push it. If the child has a severe issue impacting the classroom, then you need to keep insisting, this time with leadership involved. You will occasionally see the same child progress through their entire primary schooling with each year's teacher suggesting testing, and nothing occurring. Meanwhile their child's problem is becoming more and more apparent or difficult to manage. Apathy may also appear as a masked situation of the parent being completely overwhelmed.

3. Anger. This is a pretty rare response. Anger emerges either when they had no idea and your suggestion has come out of the blue, or when they see a child as an extension of themselves. They think you are criticising or questioning their child, therefore you are doing the same to them. Attempt to talk them down, "I can see that you are really upset. I'm sorry that you feel that way. Would you like some time to think about what I've said and we meet again in a week's time?" You have recognised they're upset and you have also empathised. By suggesting another meeting time you are giving them time to regroup and taking the pressure off an immediate decision needing to be made. Try to book in a meeting before they leave.

4. Sadness. In some circumstances a parent will be quite saddened, possibly even tearing up. This is normal, especially if they've suspected their child has an issue already or is diagnosed with other disabilities. One year I began to suspect a student I taught for two years may have had learning difficulties on top of his diagnosed Asperger's Syndrome. When I raised it with mum you could see her visibly shrink and feel overcome. She felt she was on a treadmill of appointment after appointment already and was dismayed by the thought of yet more.

5. Acceptance. These parents are glad and appreciative that you know their child well enough to suggest a concern you have with their learning and are willing to seek further testing. They may still feel sadness, but the predominant emotion projected to you is that of acceptance.

Always stress that there are strategies that will greatly benefit the child that are readily available and achievable. Don't promise you can fix it - you can't - but that there are lots of things you can do that will help significantly.

When a family elects to investigate further, it is most likely they will give you a form of some sort to give a detailed overview to the tester about how the child responds and learns. Fill these in honestly. It is tempting to gloss over some distressing points, but if you are not transparent then an accurate diagnosis is less likely.

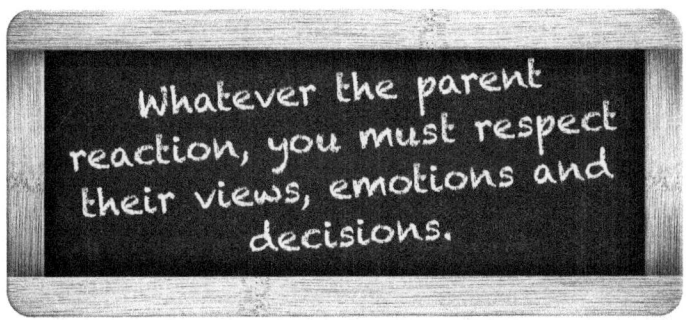

Whatever the parent reaction, you must respect their views, emotions and decisions.

After Diagnosis

Once a parent or school goes down the path of testing and assessing, it can be months before a report is prepared by an educational psychologist or paediatrician. Due to privacy laws, this report goes to the parent only, but usually it is suggested they provide a copy for you.

Upon receipt of a report, read it through carefully a couple of times and make some notes regarding what has been suggested that can be done at school to assist the child. Think about how you can make these changes in your classroom. Not all adjustments or suggestions will be possible; the report details all ideal changes. Determine what changes you can make. Then it's time to have a meeting with the parents to talk about what the report proposed and how you will respond to those ideas.

Share the report with the staff member whose role it is to apply for funding. They will begin the process of applying for support and this will require you to fill in some more forms. When you complete these forms you really need to have your 'worst case scenario' glasses on. The worse you make it appear, the higher the chances of funding coming through. However, do not lie. Think of the worst days they have and fill the form in based on that.

A copy of the report needs to go into the child's file at school. At the beginning of a school year you must read through any reports in files and make notes. During mid year parent teacher interviews I once was taken aback to hear from a parent that their child had A.D.H.D. I'd read the file but somehow missed it and his classroom behaviour hadn't thrown up any red flags for me. It doesn't look good if a parent has provided information to the school but you haven't seen it!

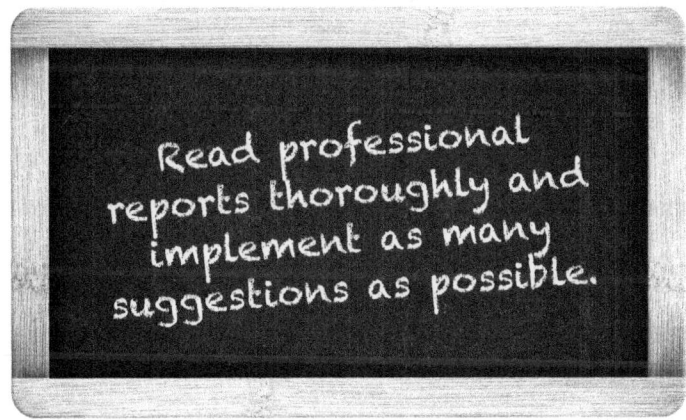

Read professional reports thoroughly and implement as many suggestions as possible.

Learning Plans

The acronym for these gets changed pretty regularly and could possibly be Individual Learning Plans (I.L.P.) or Individual Education Plans (I.E.P.). I will refer to these as Learning Plans (L.P.s) for the remainder of this chapter.

It's highly likely that all children with funding will require an L.P. A school may also direct teachers to write L.P.s for undiagnosed students who may be twelve months, or more, behind in major curriculum areas. When you begin planning for, and writing, a plan, the school will provide you with a template and the structure that they use. Ask questions of your team leader or assistant principal if you are stuck. If the child has an integration aide, include them in the writing process.

Many of the children you need to write plans for will already have an existing plan and it's important to use this as a basis for writing a new one. Children mature and learn at differing rates so the previous L.P. may be quite irrelevant, or another teacher may have felt an area was more important to focus on than you do. Generally, L.P.s are updated around once a term.

When you begin to write the goals, keep it to three maximum (unless you are directed otherwise). I tend to write a literacy goal, a numeracy goal and a behavioural/social goal. This is not a hard and fast rule though. Your student may be great at numeracy and only require extra support in literacy. Or academically be at or above level and only require behavioural goals. Goals should be attainable and small. Some schools require many more goals and for them to be reviewed each term. Below is a learning goal I used for a child diagnosed with Asperger's Syndrome. He exhibited poor fine motor skills and slow processing. He loved technology however!

FOR EXAMPLE:

Goal: To develop touch typing skills. As Xxx has poor fine motor skills and difficulty in note taking, he will need to become increasingly reliant on typing.

Learning Outcomes: To automatically know which fingers sit where on the keyboard for touch-typing.

Entry Skills: No knowledge.

The goal for the first plan was very small and easily attainable; to know where the fingers rest for touch-typing. I knew he had no knowledge as I found a touch-typing tuition program online and had him sit it with his aide. He was plodding away, any finger on any key and managed five words per minute to start with. Once Xxx could rest his fingers on the right keys, the next goal would perhaps be to type ten words a minute with 80% accuracy using a touch-typing program. If he meets that goal quicker than expected, I'd revise it mid term.

Goals must be attainable. If you are going term to term with no improvement then there is a problem. Either the goals are wrong or the skills are not being taught correctly. Ouch! Goals are also not static - you can change them if a more pressing concern emerges.

Goals must also be appropriate. What are the most important skills the student needs to achieve? Formal addition or subtraction algorithms are useless if place value has not been consolidated. Social skill goals might be necessary but you need to explicitly teach to the goal for success to occur.

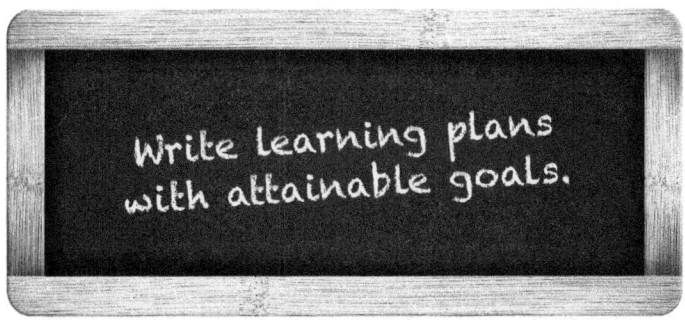

Reports

In your report you should refer to the fact that the child has a specialised learning plan and works closely with the aide. The purpose of this is for legal reasons - a future investigation into whether the school has attempted to meet the needs of the integrated child is always a possibility. This is the sentence I use, "An Individual Learning Plan (I.L.P.) was developed to target his specific learning needs." You would need to adjust the sentence to reflect the official acronym you are required to use. You could also be more explicit, "An Individual Learning Plan (I.L.P.) was developed to target his specific numeracy needs."

Where a child requires assistance or works in a teacher group, you need to state this too. For example, "Writing continues to be a difficult process for Xxx. He requires support to come up with ideas, plan thoroughly and to edit and proofread." Or, "Xxx works regularly in a small teacher group to improve his mathematical skills."

Parent Meetings

Parents of children with disabilities have many concerns and worries. They will appreciate your thoroughness and willingness to get to know and understand their child. Parent meetings are an opportunity to reflect to the parent the breakthroughs, gains and positives their child has achieved. You MUST do this. Parents with disabled students too often hear negatives and are crying out to hear some great things, no matter how small a gain.

After sharing some good stuff, talk about the goals you have set and why you have chosen those ones. It's important to justify why you have selected these goals in particular. Ask for parent feedback - have they noticed similar behaviour or issues at home? List some ways for parents to work on the goals at home, if they are receptive and keen. You may have limited success with this, but it is important to involve parents in this process.

If you are suggesting extra testing or intervention at any stage it's important you know the purpose and to have researched what options are available. Understandably, it can be really difficult for parents to accept yet more specialists, testing and intervention.

Meetings with parents are generally held once a term with the whole support team. You do not have to meet too often with parents. Some want their hands held too much or to interfere, so be firm and only set meetings when you feel there is a genuine need. As long as you aren't avoiding your responsibilities to the child's learning, this is perfectly acceptable.

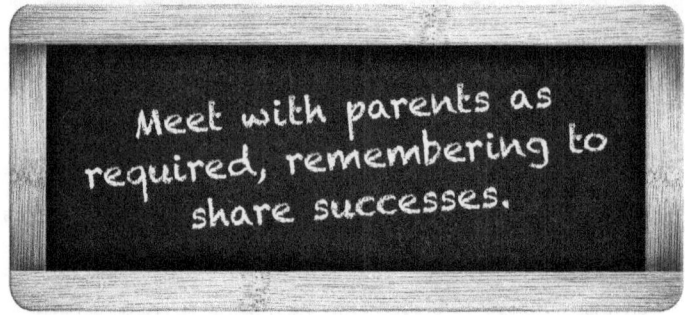

Communication Books

Sigh. I hate these for a few reasons. If you are working closely on some important behavioural goals or there are medical reasons, then perhaps a book is appropriate. In my experience though, parents who want a communication book are wishing to be overly controlling and expect detailed notes daily. This is impossible and unreasonable. If there's nothing of interest to report, there's nothing to communicate.

I have seen parents use this as a way to vilify, criticise and complain about anything and everything. It's easy to get caught up in their dysfunction. Anything you write down is there forever and can be used by an unscrupulous parent in a negative way.

If the child is funded then it should be the aide's responsibility to complete the communication book. An unfunded child means the responsibility falls to you. It's virtually impossible to find time, whilst you are supervising twenty-five kids, to write a detailed note.

Where possible discourage the use of communication books. You may need to wean a parent off them (!) or enlist the support of leadership.

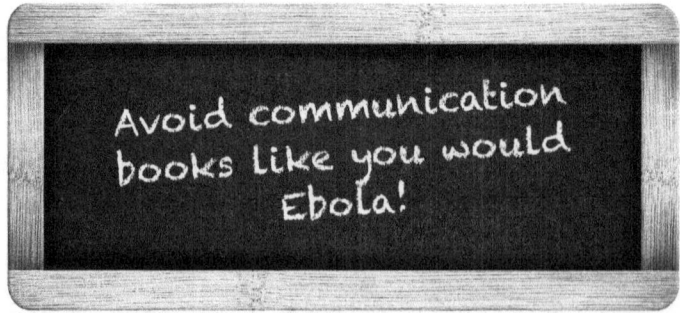

Use this page to document ways you could improve outcomes for students with additional needs.

Student Hygiene

CHAPTER 12

Chapter Overview

- » Nose picking
- » Body odour
- » Farting
- » Lice
- » Illnesses
- » Periods
- » Unwashed bodies/clothes

Student hygiene is a contentious issue that can have quite a big impact on your classroom. Most classes would have a student that, at times, can have hygiene issues. It needs to be addressed and handled sensitively. I have been really surprised over the years how tolerant other students are of their classmates with hygiene issues. At times you will need to send a child to the office for assessment or treatment, so check with your team or mentor for the correct procedure, as each school will have its own format for how you send children to the office or sick bay during teaching hours.

Nose Picking

Let's be honest here - we all do a little bit of this. It's not the occasional pick that is a problem. It's the chronic finger up the nose, wiping it somewhere distasteful, or worse - eating it. Ughhhh. Juniors are particularly prone to nose picking. By middle and senior, children have a good idea that nose picking isn't socially acceptable so generally try and hide it a bit more. They hide it from their peers who are most likely to tease them, but they don't hide it from their teacher. There are a few ways to handle it.

- » A whole class chat or two at the start of the year to outline your expectations
- » Children may not know that germs can be spread through this activity so teach them
- » Provide tissues (if none are provided by your school, encourage students to bring in a box each for communal use. Give a suitable reward for those who bring one in)
- » Model to juniors blowing their nose, disposing of tissue and washing hands

The Essential Teacher's Guide

> » Find a YouTube video to share with juniors that models appropriate behaviour on this topic. A social story: http://www.youtube.com/watch?v=UV_tY6JHTMA or a fun song to help remind them http://www.youtube.com/watch?v=rStT_re35pg
>
> » For seniors I get tougher. Fingers creep into noses most often during whole class instruction. I have an expectation chat and detail consequences. If I notice a finger going in I will say their name and just have a subtle shake of my head. Often the behaviour ceases. If not, I ask them to go to the bathroom and wash their hands. Sometimes a child may be sent more than once per session. I'm careful to not say 'Stop picking your nose', to avoid shaming. Children understand why they are being sent to wash their hands

Body Odour

Generally this becomes a problem when puberty is approaching, and of course it's worse in summer than winter. I think we've all opened a senior classroom door or walked into the senior corridor and been slammed with B.O. Or slammed with Lynx! Many years ago I worked in an office environment and every three months a window cleaner would be employed. His B.O. was so bad that air freshener, open windows and exhaust fans couldn't diminish it. It made our eyes water and sometimes it was so disgusting we'd gag. It took about four hours for the offices to be free of his smell. Luckily I've never had a student with B.O. that bad and fingers crossed you don't either.

Remind students regularly that as we all work and sit close together on a daily basis we need to be mindful of our body odour. Ask students to make suggestions on how to manage it. It's more powerful coming from them. You will also need to point out that overuse of deodorant can cause the same problem to our noses as B.O. does. My eldest daughter thinks teachers should start a chant or make a poster with these words, "Use some deo for your B.O.!"

Often the whole class chat that you had misses the key students who really need to wear deodorant. Take them aside for a discreet private chat. Tell them you have noticed that they have body odour at times. Ask them if they can tell you ways to best manage B.O. (daily showering, clothes washed regularly, applying deodorant each morning and after exercise). Find out if they wear deodorant. If they do, remind them to apply it each morning and shower daily to help. If they don't, ask if it's possible for their parents to purchase some for them and to apply it each morning. Gently impress upon them that the people who sit near them would probably appreciate if they were better able to manage their B.O. Use the term body odour when having individual chats with students as the acronym B.O. has a more negative connotation.

Word of warning: despite your best efforts, some people either ignore you or are unable to manage their B.O. Your options are to keep trying, talk to parents, or to let it go. I'd let it go after a couple of chats.

We live in a very multicultural society, which translates to a multicultural classroom. Some cultures have stronger odours than others and some do not use deodorant for various reasons. This is a sensitive issue to address. You could attempt to educate the class in the hope the message is received by the relevant students. There's a very slim chance of this working. You may have more success by speaking to the individual child, with the best chance of an improvement probably with senior students. If it really is intolerable and you've tried whole class chat and individual chat, seek counsel from leadership about whether it's appropriate to speak to the parents.

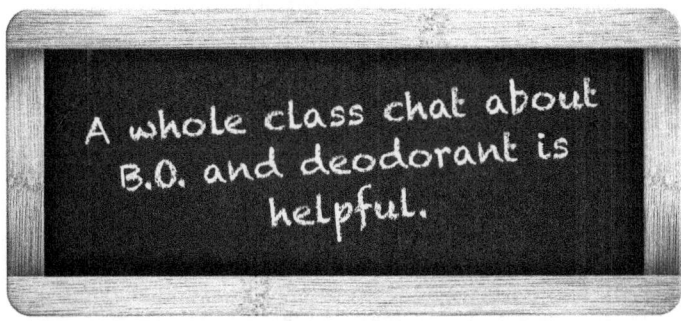

Farting

I have always referred to flatulence in my classroom as farting. That's what the students call it and it doesn't bother me. There's definitely no confusion over what I'm talking about, as I don't use euphemisms like bottom burps or passing wind.

The main aim with this issue is to manage behaviour surrounding it. Request children say 'excuse me' when they fart and don't tolerate purposeful farting for laughs. A private chat with these offenders is a very easy way to deal with the problem. The suggestion that you might have to ring mum because you are worried they have a tummy bug due to all the flatulence should cure the silliness immediately!

Don't tolerate shaming of people with flatulence issues by fellow classmates. A regular farter, when you have established the reason is not due to showing off, may need reminding to go to the toilet. Mostly they will deny this, but you should insist, even going so far as to suggest that you are aware they are farting and it's often a sign they need to go to the toilet. This is a private conversation!

In my class one year I had a student with severe and silent flatulence that was ongoing for a few months. It took awhile to determine who it was - the students helped me by reacting with horror around the child, even naming them at times. My approach involved a few strategies. I started with a whole class discussion, informing children that farting was often a sign that we needed to use the toilet and to feel free to leave the classroom to do so. Didn't work. The smell was so bad that we had to open windows and spray air freshener. I then rang the child's mother to tactfully raise it and ask if she'd noticed it at home. In fact, they'd been changing his diet to try and solve this problem themselves, so they were fully aware of it. Mum requested I let her know if there was no change in the next few weeks. Luckily, there was significant improvement for us all in that little classroom.

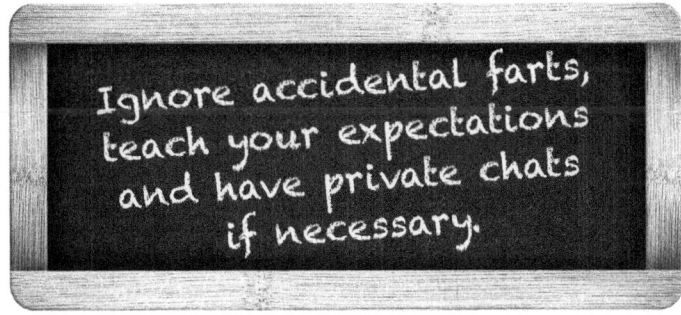

Lice

This scourge doesn't discriminate against social class and is notoriously hard to get rid of. It's always late on a Sunday night when I hear "Mum, my head's been itchy for a few days!" GRRRRRRR.

This hygiene issue will need to be guided by your school's policy. If you haven't had children yourself and require more information about transmission and treatment, check out your state government's health website. The education department in each state will also have online information for you to view. In all my years of teaching, despite living with two daughters who had head lice periodically, I have never had it myself. Unless your head is pressed against a child's head, it's highly unlikely you will contract lice yourself, as lice do not jump.

If you suspect a child in your class has head lice, by viewing live critters crawling or eggs, contact the school office for direction. Please don't physically part the child's hair to examine for live bugs. Parents get a little testy nowadays with teachers doing anything they perceive is not their job and also quite defensive about anything that might potentially question their parenting skills. Suspecting head lice can only occur via observation, not by touching.

Illness

Everyone gets sick at some time or another. Exclusion from school when a child is sick is important. A miserable child cannot concentrate and is possibly unintentionally spreading germs to others, including you. You are within your rights to contact the office if a child arrives at school and you feel they should really be in bed. Constant coughing and sneezing, glazed eyes, temperatures, suspicious rashes or spots, gunky eyes and nausea/headaches are all symptoms that you could feel justified in sending the child to the office. If you mention that you think the child should go home, then the office is most likely to follow through on this. Sometimes illnesses develop throughout the day. Again, send to the office when you think their symptoms are impairing their concentration and ability to work well.

For more serious and contagious illnesses each school will have a policy to follow as dictated by the education department in that state. It pays to familiarise yourself with the policy if you become aware that a child in your class has an illness that requires exclusion for a short period. If they arrive back at school too early, contact the office for direction. It may be possible for office staff to call parents for clarification.

Sadly, too often children are sent to school unwell, as their parents need to work. You, and the children in your class, have the right to a healthy classroom environment. Enlist the help of leadership if you are concerned this is happening and you would like support in dealing with parents.

For vomit and poo related issues, see Chapter 13 on Poo Wee Vomit, for tips. My main suggestion, without going into detail in this chapter, is to get the child to sickbay as soon as possible. Avoid vomit in the classroom!

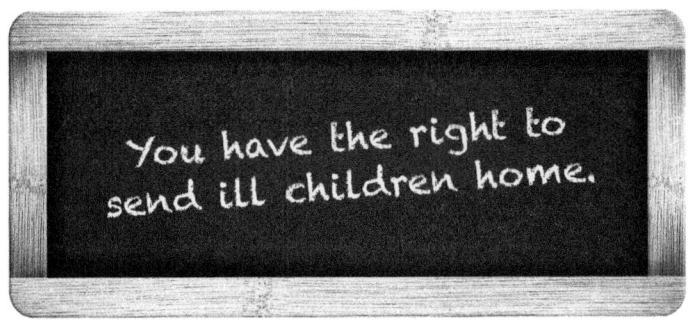

Periods

Hopefully your school will have an excellent sexuality education unit some time during the senior years. Most schools provide some sort of sex ed., either within the classroom or outsourced out of hours. Nowadays it would be pretty rare for a girl to get her period and not know what it was. Getting a period for the first time is a huge shock, even if you know what it is, but especially in primary school.

Age at beginning menstruation has been trending downwards in recent decades. Every primary school will have girls who have their period. As a teacher, apart from general education as required by the curriculum, the only assistance you will ever have to provide will be if you are approached by a child for help. Sick bays have supplies of pads if necessary. Ideally, all teachers will feel comfortable and be approachable, both male and female, if a student requires assistance. If you are supremely uncomfortable or feel it is inappropriate for some reason to help, please take the student immediately to a compassionate teacher.

Unwashed Bodies/Clothes

This is the most difficult hygiene problem to deal with for a variety of reasons. Children coming to school each day who smell ghastly due to unwashed bodies and clothes usually don't come from functional families. Approaching the problem requires much forethought and delicacy. As stated earlier, you have the right to work in a healthy environment. Children have the right to live and learn in a clean and healthy environment. Parents have the right to raise their children in whatever manner and environment that they wish, as long as they are not breaking the law through neglect or abuse. So whose rights trump another? It's an impossible question to answer.

Here are some ways to address the problem:

- DO NOT speak to the child by yourself. This requires some discussion with a number of staff members
- Check their file - is there any relevant information or notes from an earlier meeting to discuss hygiene?
- If applicable, speak to the child's previous teachers to ask for history. Was this issue addressed in previous years? Is this a new change or an ongoing issue?
- Is the Department of Human Services (or equivalent) involved with the family?
- Once you have enough background, meet with relevant staff at school to decide on an approach. Perhaps the child is quite connected with or trusts a particular staff member and they could be involved.
- Do they have a social worker you can discuss this with?
- This is not the child's problem. It is the caregiver's problem and as such, ultimately should be raised with them

- » If an odour is from soiling or urination the school can call the caregivers and ask them to collect the child, shower them and redress in clean clothes before returning them to school
- » If the odour is causing problems with other students in the classroom it's important to address this by having a whole class chat, whilst the student is absent. Impress upon them that it's not the child's fault, perhaps they are not taught the same things at home as them, it's not the child's responsibility to wash clothes or to remember to have a shower. Request tolerance and understanding and indicate that teasing or bullying will not be tolerated

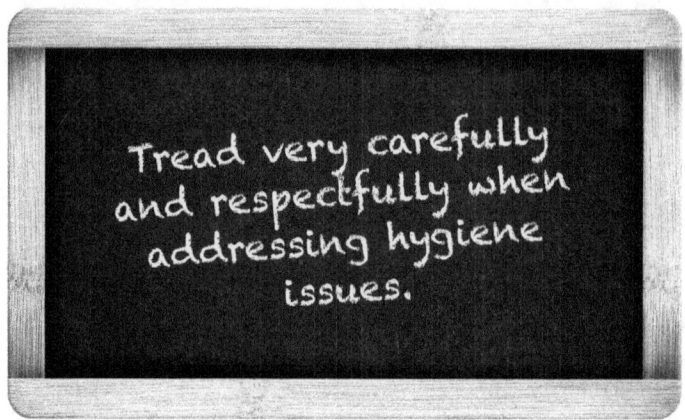

For adults without hygiene problems, it seems like common sense that children with this issue require and/or desire assistance. Sometimes this is definitely the case, however frequently the problem is so intertwined with layers of complications (and judgements) that assistance is not welcomed. I have been involved with several families with severe hygiene issues and despite many support workers and leadership being involved, they proved incapable or unwilling to show improvement. In those situations, managing the odour as best as you can, whilst demonstrating respectful behaviour towards them, is the only option.

Write down your own funny student hygiene stories here and send them to me!

Poo Wee Vomit

Chapter Overview

- » Vomit
- » Wee
- » Poo
- » Excursions and vomit
- » Toilet visits

Unfortunately, in my first year of teaching I became well acquainted with this trio of emissions. In every situation it's essential to remember that the child may well be embarrassed and to handle with compassion and discretion. You can have a laugh later in the staffroom because without doubt, each of these occurrences will throw up (pun intended) a funny reaction from one of the kids in your classroom.

If you are alone in your room, you cannot leave your class unsupervised to clean up the area or the child. You will have to improvise. Not to worry though, improvising is what teachers do best and is at the core of our business. Call the office for help or send a child to the office or the nearest classroom for help. Sometimes, if it's not super urgent you can set the class to the task and then turn your attention to helping the child.

Vomit

A clever teacher will learn to read the signs early that a child feels ill. I like to avoid dealing with vomit at all costs! What are the signs? Getting to know your children is the key. When you know them well enough you will more easily be able to spot unusual behaviours. The chatty child going unusually silent, an inability to focus on an activity, staring off into space, looking a bit pale or sweaty or telling you they feel sick! If a child asks to go the toilet because they feel unwell (and you know they aren't work dodging), let them go. A great question to ask is "Do you think you will be able to go outside to play at lunchtime?" If so, they aren't really all that unwell.

It helps to have a supply of disposable gloves, air freshener (this will have to be kept in a locked cupboard, thanks very much O.H. & S.), tissues, moist wipes and paper towel. A sink in your classroom is a bonus! The school will have a vomit kit somewhere for carpet spills and a more experienced teacher can tell you where. Sometimes the A.P. will do the deed for you, if you are lucky.

I have managed to catch vomit in the classroom rubbish bin, a lunchbox, a hat and a jumper. All better than the carpet, the child or others! A colleague related to me this vomit story. "I remember my very first day teaching – doing C.R.T., I got a late call at 9.00 a.m. to come in and teach Grade 1. I was so nervous and I knew I'd have to hit the ground running when I got there. So I went in and took over from the A.P. and he told me they were doing journal writing. All good, a nice easy start. Gorgeous kids all writing quietly. Then they started to bring their work to show me (all at once of course) and one little boy pushed into the line to see me and I was just about to let him know he shouldn't push in and needed to wait for his turn when he says, I feel S I C K and projectile vomited all over my leg. I can't remember what happened next but it didn't turn me off teaching. I came back for more!" Another teacher had this to offer. "I had a class of five year olds and they were eating lunch, seated at their tables. A child vomited into his lunchbox and the three remaining students at the table just watched and continued to eat from their own lunch boxes. My stomach was churning and I was shocked the other kids just kept eating!" I have lunged across a classroom on a few occasions, grabbing whatever receptacle was handy on the way, and thrust it under a child's mouth.

> You will need for your classroom:
> 1) disposable gloves   2) paper towel
> 3) tissues   4) air freshener
> 5) moist wipes

Excursions and Vomit

It's never fun when a child vomits on the bus. One memorable camping trip we had three! Always, always, always have a box to tick on the permission form for parents to tell you if their child gets travelsick, and then sit them at the front. Older kids know the drill and happily sit there but younger kids often forget. I always do a walk through on any bus trip longer than ten minutes to do a last minute call out for anyone who needs to sit at the front. I've never had a child seated at the front vomit. Sadly, the bus vomiters mostly never tell you in time, if at all, and it's often up to their seatmate to warn you. I have learnt from experience to always take vomit bags with me and to get them out of the first aid kit in readiness. Several times I have been caught short. Dealing with the aftermath is never pretty, especially with limited resources and a long trip still to go. Once I even mopped up vomit from a child and the bus floor with spare sports tops as we were on our way to a basketball competition. My teenage daughter was returning from an interstate band competition by bus when a boy quietly vomited on the floor and didn't tell anyone, nor did anyone notice. They stopped off for a while, still no one had realised, and the bus was left to bake in the sun. That ended up being a twelve-hour bus trip from hell.

A gorgeous teacher friend gave me a tip for avoiding vomit on bus trips that she swears by. "We always get the 'bus sick' kids to sit on a small stack of newspaper. It may be an old wives tale, but it seems to work!" I guess the added bonus is there is something to mop up any spills with...

> Look for the early warning vomit signs.
> Take vomit bags on excursions.
> Find out who gets travelsick and seat them at the front.

Wee

Sometimes little boys in junior classes make you laugh out loud with their toilet antics. Never assume children have been taught toilet etiquette at home, particularly regarding communal toilets. Boys think it's a great activity to have a 'wee' sword fight whilst standing at the urinal! I have known boys to wee in the playground, purposefully wait until recess to wee at a tree and use weeing on another boy as a way to bully.

Toilet Visits

Junior

When children start school for the first time they are not used to waiting too long to visit the toilet. It takes up a lot of time to visit as a whole class for the first few weeks, until they get the hang of where the toilet is and the school's toilet rules, but it is very important to lay this foundation. I'd much rather do that, than deal with the consequences! When you feel confident that 90% of them have got the hang of it then you can start sending children in same sex pairs. Over the years I have had to conduct mini lessons (either individual or whole class) on: not holding your penis or vagina when you need to go to the toilet, not leaving it too late to go, not going too often, flushing the toilet, weeing in the toilet and not out in the schoolyard, not weeing on the bathroom floor, not weeing on your friends and washing your hands. That's not something they teach you at university! I have two daughters, so talking to boys about using the toilet was far outside my experience and comfort zone.

WARNING: Never tie little boy's shoelaces up. After what I have written above, I'm sure you can guess what is often on them. In week one of a new school year I always find out who can tie shoelaces already and appoint them our class shoelace monitor. They feel proud of the responsibility bestowed upon them and your problem is solved!

Accidents will, unfortunately, still happen for a variety of reasons and is to be expected. The school will usually have some spare undies, shorts and socks for you to use. If you are uncomfortable doing any changing or cleaning up you have a few options. Either send them to sickbay for the school nurse to attend to or ask another teacher. Children are also able to clean themselves up. That's my preferred option. Give them all the resources they will need to do it themselves and a plastic bag to chuck their wet clothes into.

Some children, due to medical issues or a disadvantaged background, may need special understanding. It's extremely important to never shame children for accidents or for coming to school smelly. Before arranging a meeting with parents or caregivers, speak to colleagues, in particular the child's previous teacher/s, to determine the best way to speak to the family and to find out any circumstances you should be aware of. Families can be very sensitive around this issue so tread very cautiously. This is applicable for all age groups.

During class time I have always tried to minimise children visiting the toilet, but understand that sometimes it is unavoidable (for us too!). To help junior children to understand this concept I will conduct a whole class lesson a few days into a new school year, and together make a poster for display. This will have to be revised frequently at first, modelled and adjusted depending upon which age group you are working with. Younger children won't remember a lot of these guidelines.

Generally the rules I have found most helpful are:

- » Only one visit per session
- » Take a sensible partner (one you know the teacher will approve of)
- » Ask the teacher before you go
- » Always go at recess and lunch time

- » Wash your hands
- » Don't muck around while you are there
- » Not in the first thirty minutes after class starts
- » Not in the last ten minutes before class ends

Middle & Senior

By this stage children should have good control over their bladder and accidents will be very rare. Personally, at this age I would never physically assist a child, to clean themselves up, or to change their clothes, unless they have a diagnosed disability and this is part of their management plan.

The toilet visit rules formulated for juniors are still applicable for older students. Less time needs to be spent on teaching these rules and it should be done in the first couple of days of a new class starting. I stick the laminated poster onto the classroom door so there's no excuse for not seeing the rules. The individual school will guide you whether students still need to walk in pairs to the toilet. When in senior school I prefer children to go by themselves. I also hate being asked every few minutes "Can I go to the toilet?" A senior colleague shared with me the peg system and I have used it successfully for years now. At the start of the year, write each child's name in texta on an individual clothes peg and chuck them all into a container. When students go to the toilet during class time they just find their peg and clip it onto the side of the box, removing it when they return. This allows me to not be bothered by frequent requests and I also know who is at the toilet. If you use wooden pegs it's fun to get the kids to decorate and personalise them.

The rules and the pegs work well, but I still needed more. Work dodging becomes a problem at these ages and more commonly boys are the culprits here. A year or so into my teaching career I came up with a plan to avoid this and have found it works a treat.

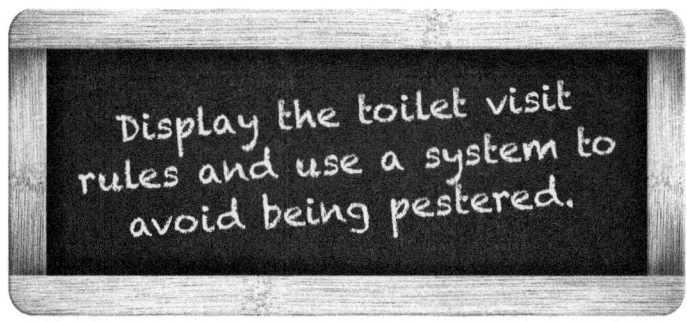

Toilet Visit Template

This system works on reward, not punishment, which is far more effective. I made a template with every child's name down the left-hand side and the days of the week across the top. (See Chapter 26, Templates). I tend to add multiple weeks to the one template to save paper. When students put up their peg to go to the toilet they also mark the box on the template that corresponds to their name and the day. This is an honour system, however, in general, I have found my students to be pretty honest. At the end of the week I give a quick shout out for anyone to add a mark if they have forgotten to do so during the week. The premise is that for each day a child doesn't go to the toilet during class time they receive a reward. It's up to you what sort of reward you use. It should be small but effective. On Friday afternoons many schools have some sort of free time period. I add two minutes free time for each day a student doesn't leave the classroom for the bathroom, potentially allowing them ten extra minutes for the whole week. When I first developed this system I was shocked how effective it was and it has remained so for all the years it has been in use. Some alternatives to free time minutes could be time on tablets or computers, house points, lucky dip, seat choice, other whole class choice etc.

It's important to check what your school's policy is on toilet visits during learning time. Some schools may not allow it.

Poo

Tip number one: When you call a parent to tell them their child has pooed their pants and for them to bring up a change of clothes, make sure you call the right parent. Yes, this really happened to me. We'd come in from lunch and I could smell an accident. I zeroed in on the suspect, did some surreptitious sniffing and then asked him privately if he'd had an accident. He nodded. That was my first mistake. I should've been more specific and said, "Have you done poo in your pants?" but I was trying to be sensitive. An accident in his mind was bumping into someone or falling over. My next mistake was to ask him questions but not really allow him to answer. "Did it happen at lunchtime? Did you just forget to go and it was too late? Did you feel unwell? " Etc., etc. He just nodded again. His dad came up and took him to the toilet to change him, whereupon he discovered he was clean. Oops. Very embarrassed teacher!

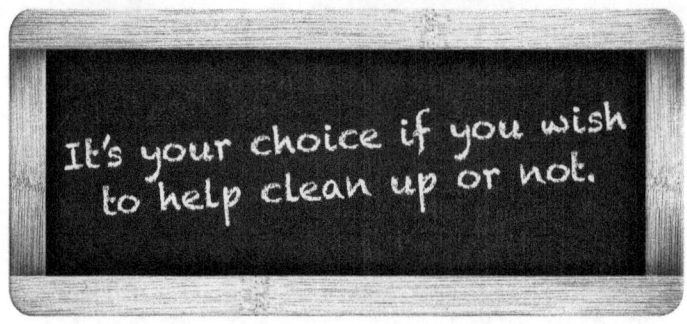

Tip number two: You can disguise poo on the carpet as pebbles. True! I was reading a picture storybook to my junior class and then explaining the task. As they stood to approach me and receive the handout I noticed brown poo balls on the carpet in front of me. I jumped up and quickly guided the line of kids to another part of the room, to avoid them standing on it and squashing it into the carpet. They had been spotted though and I had kids telling me there were pebbles on the floor. I ran with that idea and the kids were none the wiser. How poo pebbles dropped out of a child's underpants AND shorts I will never know!

Tip number three: A giant can of air freshener is your best friend. Children will put up with, or not even seem to notice, a lot of smells but poo in pants is not one of them.

Tip number four: Pooing pants on purpose requires a heavy-duty intervention. I have had a Grade 6 boy do this and refuse to clean himself up. And then wear the same jocks and not shower for the next three days. In thirty-five degree heat! Nasty. There were extenuating circumstances around that family, however you also have the right to a healthy work environment. Speak up and complain hard to management. I remained pleasant and professional to the boy, however the rest of the class were distressed also. It's a really fine line to walk - compassion for the situation and the child and standing up for your own rights. Let's hope it's not a problem you come across!

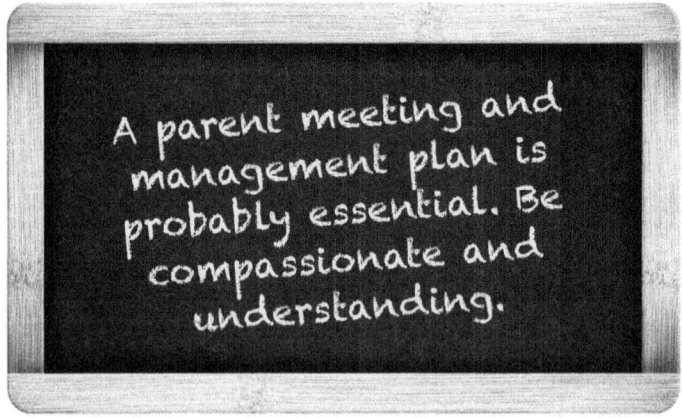

In all seriousness though, a child soiling their pants at school is usually a sign of a bigger picture issue. When it is a regular or semi regular occurrence, the same guidelines apply for talking to parents and colleagues as they do for wet pants. It's up to the individual teacher whether you wish to help clean up or not. This is where I draw the line. I would either provide the student with all the necessary resources and guidance to clean up, or call their parent. If there is no established medical cause for soiling, then some reflection on the emotional causes with a social worker or psychologist should be suggested. Get leadership approval or support first.

Contact professionals for advice if needed.

Devise your own toilet visit management system here.

Technology

Chapter Overview

- Importance of technology
- Embedding technology into lessons and a sample lesson plan
- S.A.M.R. model
- Application - essentials
- Application suggestions for junior, middle and senior
- Website suggestions
- Web 2.0 technology
  - wikis
  - blogs
  - social networking
- Virtual worlds
- Email
- Cyber safety
- Device management
- Username/Password management

Importance of Technology

There are pros and cons for using technology with children in our classrooms. I'm a big advocate for it, having seen first-hand the benefits. There are ways to plan to avoid the negatives, however they can never be completely eliminated. Students are individuals and sometimes they do silly things, despite our best planning and teaching. Just as kids have always looked up rude words in the dictionary, they will look up questionable topics on the Internet! I've had students discover some nude pics a couple of times when the school's security blocks were temporarily down. Luckily the children's parents were very understanding.

Let's face it, as adults we use some form of personal technology for multiple hours a day. There are plenty of articles around where the author has gone without their devices for a week and then written about the difficulties it caused for them. Not the addiction issues, but because we now conduct a large part of our daily life by navigating, connecting and working via some sort of device.

Technology is not going away; embrace it! Technology should be embedded in your lesson plans and no longer stand-alone. Many primary aged children of today will have careers using technology that we cannot even conceive of. It's important to acknowledge that children will usually know more about technology and be more comfortable using it than their parent's generation. Admitting that means you are cool with asking kids for help. There's always someone in your class who is an expert. These students love to share their knowledge and help you and others.

Embedding Technology Into Lessons and a Sample Lesson Plan

The more frequently you practise writing technology into your lesson plans, the easier it becomes. Soon it will be second nature! At university I am sure you have prepared lessons and units using technology. Below is a sample sequence of lessons I wrote for Grade 5 and 6 students.

Lesson 1

Purpose: Examine samples and features of procedural text (P.T.). Write a simple P.T.

Independent: Make a paper plane each with no instructions. Leave on desk.

Whole Class: Ask – "What is the purpose of P.T.?" Record responses on Interactive Whiteboard using Easiteach.

Independent: Using Dropbox on own iPad, view pdf of scanned procedural text examples. Record in English book features in common.

Whole Class: Share features. View Powerpoint on P.T.. Slide 1. Discuss. Where would we find P.T.? Slide 2 Discuss What does a P.T. contain?

Independent: Attempt to write a P.T. on how to make a paper aeroplane.

Lesson 2

Purpose: Review knowledge of P.T. and add information on language features.

Whole Class: View slides 3 & 4 of P.T. Powerpoint on Interactive Whiteboard. Discuss. Watch http://www.youtube.com/watch?v=I0a0p8ygfQM (video of how to make a paper aeroplane).

Independent: Rewrite procedural text from day before, improving on language features and sequencing.

Lesson 3 and 4

Purpose: Convert a procedural text using an iPad app creating tool into a visual text.

Whole Class: Explain task.

Independent: In pairs or solo, make an animation or film of the paper aeroplane procedural text. Can use Popplet, Prezi, iMovie or Explain Everything. It can be done orally, using text, adding diagrams, using animation, or drawings. Share with teacher via Dropbox or export and send via email.

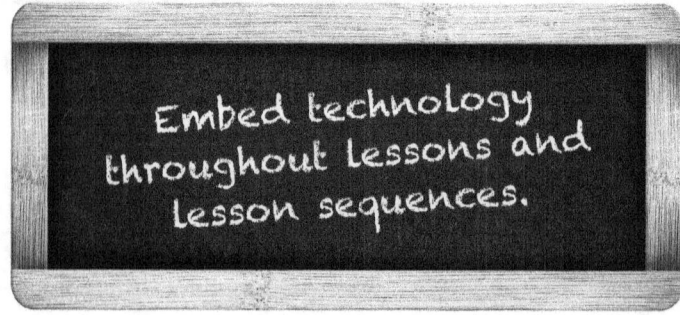

This chapter will only skim the surface of the 'What' and the 'How' to use technology in the classroom. It covers the major ways technology is usable as a solid educational tool.

S.A.M.R. Model

The S.A.M.R. model, developed by Dr Ruben Puentedura, offers best practice for using technology and a fantastic break down of the different levels on the continuum.

Legend: **S** Substitution **A** Augmentation **M** Modification **R** Redefinition

There is a place in the classroom for all of the levels on this model, however it is recommended that your usage is aimed at the M and R level to extend and encourage higher order thinking.

S Substitution: technology acts as a direct tool substitute with no functional change. For example, typing up a story in Google Docs instead of handwriting it.

A Augmentation: technology acts as a direct tool substitute with functional improvement. For example, children use Google Docs to improve their writing through the tools in word processing - spell check, grammar check and thesaurus. It's also easy to embed images into the writing.

M Modification: technology allows for significant task redesign. For example, collaborative writing with a student in another classroom using Google Drive. They can conduct peer editing and feedback during, or out of, class time. Students can invite the teacher to have access to their writing for feedback too.

R Redefinition: technology allows for the creation of new tasks, previously inconceivable. For example, students collaborate with another class, either locally or globally, via web conferencing. Students use a range of multimedia to collect, communicate and distribute their findings and conclusions on a selected research topic.

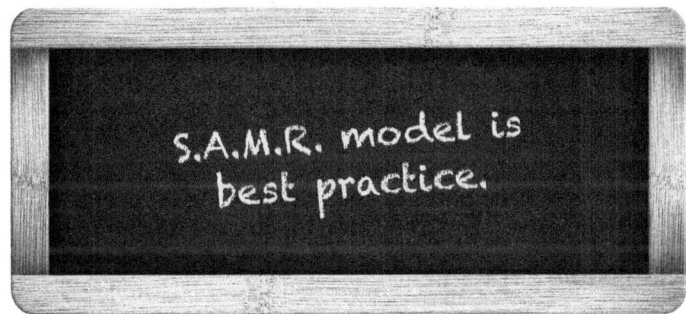

Applications

Websites and applications (apps) are a fantastic addition to your educational toolbox. After reading the app list that follows, you may be feeling a bit overwhelmed with all the new things to learn. Haven't you got enough to do already? A rule of thumb is NEVER teach a student how to use an app. Provide a session for them to play, explore and share their findings with you and their peers. Ask them how they think the app can be used for their learning. Apps are great for all levels of learning and abilities. Prior to iPads I found working with technology in junior grades to be frustrating. I remember whole lessons devoted JUST to logging in! That's tear your hair out pain! Apps are so much easier to use. Why type in an address, with a very high chance of students getting a letter wrong, when they can open an app just by tapping?

Application Essentials

The apps listed below have an initial/s next to them, indicating how they are rated in relation to the S.A.M.R. model. If you are having trouble finding the app when searching the App Store, search for it in Google. This will provide you a direct link back to the store. The list contains both free and paid apps, however I have chosen not to indicate this as it can change with upgrades. If they are on the list then I think they are worthwhile downloading, paid or not.

Legend: **S** Substitution **A** Augmentation **M** Modification **R** Redefinition

You can't run an iPad program without these (or equivalent) apps. All grade levels will require these.

» **Air Server.**
(not an app, but teacher needs to download).
An airplay receiver for Mac or PC. Allows you to mirror what is on a child's iPad without the use of fiddly iPad dongles.
http://www.airserver.com

» **Air Parrot 2**
by **Airsquirrels**.com. Similar to Air Server

» **S A M R**
Dropbox by Dropbox File hosting service.
Put your resources in Dropbox and access them from anywhere

» **S A M R**
Evernote by Evernote.
Designed for note taking and archiving. Notes can be sorted, tagged, annotated, edited, given comments, searched and exported as part of a notebook

» **S A M R**
Explain Everything by MorrisCooke.
GET THIS APP!! Cannot rave enough about it for the classroom. Annotate, animate, narrate, import, and export almost anything to and from almost anywhere

» **S A M R**
Good Reader by Good.iWare Ltd.
Allows children to open and read pdfs, annotate, import, export and collaborate. Store the files in Dropbox

» **S A M R**
Google Drive by Google, Inc.
Storage system that allows file sharing and collaborative editing.

» **S A M R**
Popplet by Notion.
Includes Docs, Sheets and Slides. Capture ideas, sort them visually, and collaborate with others in real-time. Mind mapping

» **S A M R**
Qrafter.
2D barcode scanner that provides access to an image, a website or information instantly

Application Suggestions

Junior

» **S**
1st High Frequency Words by Josh Robbins.
Listen, read and write

» **S**
ABC iView by Australian Broadcasting Corporation.
Watch catch up TV such as children's programs and documentaries

» **S A**
ABC Magnets by Christoper DeOrio.
Manipulate letters or digits, audio and export

» **S**
ABC Phonics Word Family by Abitalk Incorporated.
Word phonics spelling, beginning sound, word family phonics, short vowel sound, and images with a lot of animations and interactions for each word

» **S**
Chicktionary by Blockdot Inc.
Unscramble letters to make as many words as possible

» **S A**
Dominos Addition by Aleesha Kondys.
Builds on basic subitising by using the dot pattern on dominoes for addition equations

» **S A M**
Doodle Buddy for iPad by Pinger, Inc.
Paint, write text, draw and export

» **S A**
Four in a Row Free by Optime Software LLC.
Similar to Connect Four. Game only

» **S A**
Friends of Ten by Aleesha Kondys.
Understanding, recognising, subitising and counting numbers to ten

» **S A M**
Google Earth by Google, Inc.
Real time mapping tool in 3D

» **S A M**
Google Search by Google, Inc.
Fast search engine

» **S A M**
Kids Tell Time by ZurApps Research Inc.
Digital and analogue clocks - matching, telling and setting the time

» **S A**
Math Evolve by Zephyr Games.
Practise maths facts, mental maths and number sense. Story or practise mode in arcade game style

» **S A M**
Mathletics Student by 3P Learning.
Currently the online version is better than the app. Mathematics challenges, practise, tutorials and games. Worldwide challenges available

» **S**
Montessori Place Value by Montessori Tech.
Learn and practice the decimal place value system by manipulation of numbers

» **S A M**
Mystery Number by Aleesha Kondys.
Activities involving, more or less, missing number, mystery number and number lines

» **S A M R**
My Story by HiDef Websolutions.
Create and share ebooks, publish on iBooks

» **S A**
Natural Dice by Nathan Hansen Games.
Select many sided dice and eliminate noisy rolling in the classroom

» **S A M**
PM eCollection by Cengage Learning Australia.
Guided reading for iPads

» **S A M**
Puppet Pals 2 by Polished Play.
Create a show or story using animation and audio

» **S A**
Quick Voice Recorder by nFininity Inc.
Easy to use. Excellent for children with disabilities and for both literacy and numeracy

» **S** A M R
School Writing (Australia/New Zealand) by Demografix Pty Ltd. Handwriting fonts for your state or country. Trace shapes, numbers, letters and words, with or without audio. Teacher can create, save and share customised lessons

» **S** A M R
Sentence Builder by Abitalk Incorporated. Helps students create grammatically correct sentences, with or without audio

» **S** A M R
Subitising by Aleesha Kondys. Provides beginning counters the opportunity to practise and test their subitising knowledge using flash cards, dice, ten frames and number match

» **S** A M R
Teaching Number Lines by Aleesha Kondys. Introduces the number line concept for skip counting, sequencing, addition and subtraction

» **S** A M R **TJ's Picture Dictionary by UmaChaka Media Inc.** Easy to use picture dictionary to explore first words

Middle and Senior

» **S** A M R
ABC iView by Australian Broadcasting Corporation. Watch catch up TV such as children's programs and documentaries

» S A M **R**
Aurasma Lite by Aurasma. Augmented reality. Use it to create web pages, animations, 3D models and videos

» **S** A M R
Boggle by Electronic Arts. Word search

» **S** A M R
Book Creator by Red Jumper Studio. Create an iBook, send to a friend, sell in the iBooks store

» **S** A M R
Drawing Box by Nguyen Tan Hon-Hu. For drawing and painting using multiple tools, import, share, type and lessons

» **S** A M R
eClicker by Big Nerd Ranch, Inc. Create and deliver real time polls with instant results

» **S** A M R
Four in a Row Free by Optime Software LLC. Similar to Connect Four. Game only

» **S** A M R
Four Pics One Word by LOTUM GmbH. Guess the word based on pictures. Great for reading visual texts, making connections and expanding vocabulary

» **S** A M R
FreeSaurus by WeesWares Inc. Thesaurus

» **S** A M R
Google Earth by Google, Inc. Real time mapping tool in 3D

» **S** A M R
Google Search by Google, Inc. Fast search engine

» **S** A M R
iBooks by Apple. Buy and read books. Some free books

» S A M **R**
iMovie by Apple. Create and share movies and trailers. Good add ons

- **[S A M R]** **Jumbo Calculator by Christopher Weems.** Pretty self explanatory!

- **[S A M R]** **Jumbo Stop Watch by You Can Sleep When You're Dead Studios.** Can run in the background whilst using other apps. Easy to operate

- **[A M R]** **Keynote by Apple.** Create presentations, animations and videos. Import and export.

- **[S A M R]** **Math Evolve by Zephyr Games.** Practise maths facts, mental maths and number sense. Story or practise mode in arcade game style

- **[S A M R]** **Mathletics Student by 3P Learning.** Currently the online version is better than the app. Mathematics challenges, practise, tutorials and games. Worldwide challenges available

- **[S A M R]** **Montessori Place Value by Montessori Tech.** Learn and practice the decimal place value system by manipulation of numbers

- **[S A M R]** **Natural Dice by Nathan Hansen Games** Select many sided dice and eliminate noisy rolling in the classroom

- **[S A M R]** **Prezi by Prezi Inc.** Create mind maps and presentations

- **[S A M R]** **Quick Voice Recorder by nFininity Inc.** Easy to use. Excellent for children with disabilities and for both literacy and numeracy

- **[S A M R]** **Wikipanion by Robert Chin.** Quick access to Wikipedia allowing bookmarking feature

- **[S A M R]** **Whirly Word by Mighty Might Good Games.** Find words in the six letters. Similar to the TARGET 9 letter word

- **[S A M R]** **Word Salad by Libero Spagnolini.** Word cloud generator. Import, export or share options

Use this pad to record your own list of fantastic apps.

Website Suggestions

There are many ways to use websites in your classroom, both as a whole class and independently. The web gives an educator access to various teaching materials such as curriculum documents and strands, rubrics, lesson plans and teaching strategies. It provides students with excellent resources to discover and explore various topics in many different contexts.

Apart from the research and idea aspect for teachers, there are many brilliant websites to use in your whole class teaching. Videos, newspapers, games, educational sites and books bring the world into the classroom and help to provide a stimulating lesson. The list of websites listed below was current at the time of printing. Sites are divided into content areas, rather than age levels, as some sites are suitable for many abilities. It's best to explore them and decide yourself.

Numeracy

Count us In http://www.abc.net.au/countusin/games.htm Flash based online games for juniors.

Maths Drills - www.maths-drills.com/ Pdfs of all Mathematics curriculum areas. Save into Dropbox for annotating or print. Don't set them for homework!

Mathletics www.mathletics.com A subscription based website that covers all aspects of mathematics. Games, competitions and tutorials. Parents really love this site and in the classroom it can be used as part of a rotation.

Math Live http://www.learnalberta.ca/content/me5l/html/math5.html Outstanding Canadian maths interactives and manipulatives covering all topics. Fantastic for whole class lessons.

National Library of Virtual Manipulatives nlvm.usu.edu Brilliant site that uses manipulatives and concrete materials for renaming and demonstrating many operations. Great for whole class.

Rainforest Maths, part of the Mathletics site, available with subscription, by Jenny Eather. Covers most of the curriculum requirements for all Australian states.

Sumdog www.sumdog.com/ Similar to Mathletics but free. Available as an app too. Play maths games and challenge players.

Literacy

Reading Eggs www.readingeggs.com.au from Blake eLearning. Focusses on a core reading program of skills and strategies essential for reading success. Paid subscription but check out the two-week trial and download many of the resources for free.

Spelling City www.spellingcity.com/ Game based learning tool for vocabulary, spelling, writing and language arts.

Storyline Online http://www.storylineonline.net/ Books read aloud.

General

BBC http://www.bbc.co.uk/schools/0/ Clips, educational games and revision material.

Behind The News www.abc.net.au/btn A high energy and fun way for upper primary students to learn about current affairs and events in the world.

Google www.google.com.au Search engine.

Pinterest www.pinterest.com Heaps of ideas and resources on just about anything, particularly for juniors.

Teacher Tube www.teachertube.com An online community sharing instructional videos on just about any topic. Some clips suitable for whole class teaching.

Ted Talks https://www.ted.com/talks/browse Videoed talks on many topics.
Useful for both students and teachers.

Woodlands Junior School www.woodlands-junior.kent.sch.uk An extensive resource based website with lessons, games and activities for all curriculum areas.

Word Shark and Number Shark http://www.wordshark.co.uk/wordshark/wordshark-home-use.aspx Excellent for children with Dyslexia. You need to buy it but it's good to recommend to parents who are looking for extra assistance.

YouTube www.youtube.com

At the time of printing, all website and app suggestions were correct. If you are having trouble locating an app via the iTunes store, search for it through Google. This will then take you to the App store to download or purchase.

Use this page to record your own list of websites.

Web 2.0 Technology

The whole purpose of this type of technology is to allow a community of people to share information easily, collaborate, and connect with others with common interests.

Wikis

A wiki is a collaborative webpage with an edit button! The purpose of a wiki is to facilitate participation in an easy-to-use online environment by a community of people who care about the content because they have ownership of the process and the results. A wiki is pretty easy to use so is a good choice for the classroom. Use them for digital portfolios, group projects, and to demonstrate learning across a wide variety of subjects.

It's important to choose a wiki host that is free of advertising. Check this by looking into the support services on the site to see if it will allow you to create an educational version. Some good options are:

- Wikispaces
- PBWiki
- WikiFoundry

Before you begin using a wiki for the first time, search for some open educational wikis to get a good idea how they look and feel. To use a wiki for collaboration you will need to invite people. That's why it's important to use an education specific wiki, as they do not require children's email addresses. The web is also full of excellent lesson suggestions and ideas for how to use a wiki based on your selected topic area.

WHY WIKI?

Wikis are easy to create and are very student friendly. There are no geographical borders so students from around the world can collaborate on the same project. The applications are limitless within education.

WIKI TIPS

- Anyone can read a wiki therefore it's important not to use ANY identifying information
- They are not a reliable source of accurate information as anyone from within the wiki can edit
- Encourage visitors
- Make sure the content reflects the topic in a positive light
- Appoint roles for your wiki - Champion (trains others), Gardener (fixes typos and grammatical errors) and Designer (fixes format to make it look better)

Blogs

A blog is basically a journal available on the web with articles often displayed in reverse chronological order. The blogger posts an article, tags relevant words, includes relevant links and then individuals can comment on a thread. It lets people write, react and share, using the web as a participant.

WHY BLOG?

It encourages students to practise forming opinions based on evidence, canvas public opinions and to share information. Blogging is a great platform for teaching online ethics, Internet safety, and the responsible role of a digital citizen. Some teachers allow collaboration with other classes and as a motivator for writing tasks.

BLOGGING TIPS

» Bloggers must know their target audience

» Write catchy headlines

» Keep it short

» Anyone can read a blog, therefore it's important not to use ANY identifying information

» Use spam protection and moderation tools

» It's a good idea to choose an ad free blogging site, just to avoid any unexpected inappropriate ads popping up

Social Networking

Social networking allows an individual to create a profile for themselves on the Internet and share that profile with other users with similar interests to create a social network. In primary school there's no real need for students to be engaged in social networking for their learning. There are plenty of other viable platforms to use in the classroom that perform a similar function.

If you are looking to use social networking then there are a couple of options. Edmodo helps to connect learners. www.edmodo.com. It's a safe way for students and teachers to connect and collaborate. The teacher is at the centre of the network. It operates better as a whole school platform and is more suited to secondary schooling. Another option is 99chats. www.99chats.com. This tool allows teachers to create customisable chat rooms to blogs or a class website.

Social networking is the cause of many problems in school settings nowadays. Interactions throughout the day spill over after hours into one of the many networks children sign up to. At this stage, social networking in a primary school setting should be avoided.

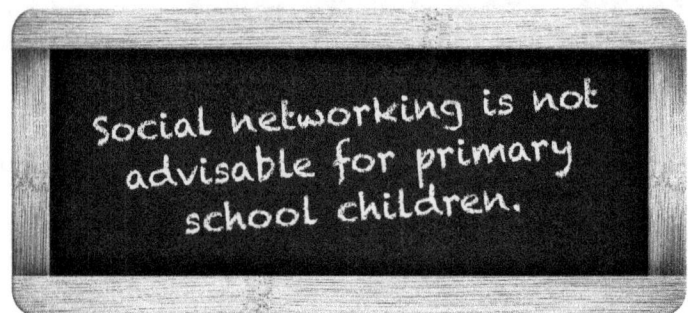

Virtual Worlds

A virtual world is a computer based simulated environment designed and shared by individuals. In an interactive 3D online community, users take the form of avatars through which they can interact with one another and use and create objects.

I have used virtual worlds in teaching on several occasions and have found it to be a stimulating and rewarding experience for the students, allowing them to redefine activities previously inaccessible to them. To use a virtual world in your school requires someone on staff with a deep understanding of the technical needs, in order to set up and manage the world.

Today's students are much more clued up about technology than their parents. In fact, you could probably call them a digital generation. Therefore, it makes sense to use this as part of their learning. One approach is blended learning where you mix computer-aided learning such as virtual reality systems with traditional forms of learning. This hybrid approach can meet the needs of all students, regardless of their learning style.

WHAT TO USE VIRTUAL WORLDS FOR

- » Problem based learning
- » Enquiry based learning
- » Game based learning
- » Role playing
- » Virtual quests
- » Collaborative simulations
- » Collaborative construction

WHAT WORLDS?

There are a few available that are suitable for education purposes, some free and some subscription based.

Second Life http://secondlife.com/

Active World www.activeworlds.com

Minecraft minecraft.net. The senior team at my school have used this platform every year recently for different integrated topics. It is extremely versatile, appealing to a wide range of students and the skills practised and learnt through using it are myriad. Search up any educational technology site for tips and ideas on how to utilise Minecraft and for the educational benefits.

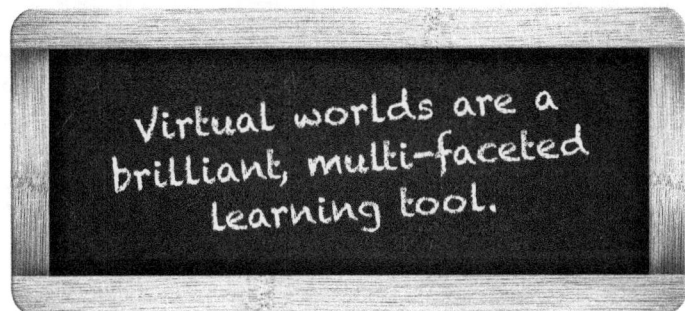

Email

To set up Google accounts, or to use some applications, children will require an email address. This should all be set up by the I.T. department at your school. Request a spreadsheet of all your student's addresses and passwords as it is difficult for them to remember.

As a teacher you may need to email your students or whole class for a variety of reasons. One of the many benefits of this instant communication is the ability to develop a rapport with a child in a different manner. The year I bought a Border Collie puppy I connected with a student in my class, via email, who was desperate for a puppy. I'd email him pictures of my dog doing silly things, and he'd email me pictures of the type of dogs he wanted. It progressed to me encouraging him to nag his parents for a dog with some good-natured ribbing. At parent teacher interviews his parents were so thrilled with our email interactions. It helped their child feel more connected to school. On another occasion, I received a very funny homework meme on a Friday night from a student who had difficulty controlling his behaviour each day. It provided the space for us to laugh together. I even printed it out and stuck it to a wall at school, telling the rest of the class who sent it to me and how funny it was.

Some students have difficulty learning appropriate etiquette regarding email and you will need to dedicate a lesson or two to this, prior to giving children access to this platform. See the cyber safety section over the page for more information.

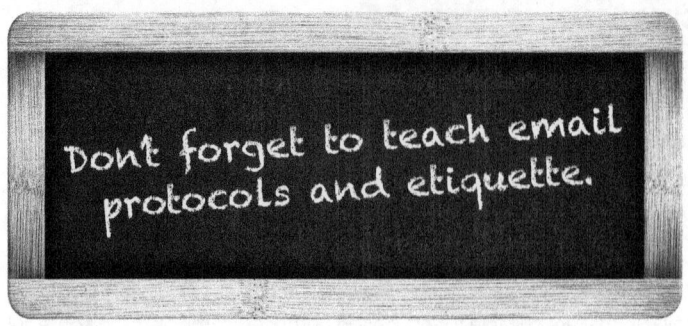

Cyber Safety

Finally, no information on technology is complete without reference to cyber safety. For children, this is of paramount importance and should be taught every year, including revisiting it throughout the year. Children spend increasing amounts of time collaborating and learning online so they need to learn to do the right thing by themselves and others. They will often be working independently and should understand their rights and responsibilities.

Your school will have policies in place that outline expectations for when children use digital technology and will also employ a filtered Internet service. An agreement between home and school on acceptable use is necessary. As a new graduate you will not be responsible for writing agreements or policies but you will definitely need to be intimately aware of their details in order to enforce them and maintain your student's safety. Sequential sanctions for breaking the I.C.T. agreement should be in place, with penalties such as a warning, two-week ban, further warnings or month long bans in place. For very serious or repeated offences then you may want to consider a permanent ban.

WHAT TO TEACH

- » Never give out personal details of yourself or others, including passwords, addresses, full names or other identifying information
- » Do not sign up for any social media that has age restrictions
- » Do not post images of anyone without their permission
- » Do not post images that contain identifying information or are inappropriate
- » How to recognise and avoid scams (click on this - you are the 1,000,000th visitor to this site!!)
- » How to recognise and avoid grooming
- » Never take a photo or video without the subject's consent
- » To not include people they don't know in chats or as 'friends', 'adds' etc.
- » To use avatars where possible and avoid using their own name
- » Remind students that whatever is uploaded to the internet is there forever and is public
- » Private messaging is not necessarily private. It can be screenshot and shared or forwarded to others. Never write anything that you wouldn't say in person
- » Not participate in online bullying and to be respectful. Encourage students to report to parents or teachers instances of bullying
- » No griefing or sabotaging of another person's work
- » Not to search up rude or offensive content or sites

> » What to do if they see or experience something they are uncomfortable with. On occasion the Internet filter service will experience a breakdown or get hacked. This has occurred twice whilst my students have been online, allowing them to click on or search up inappropriate content. The first time the male student told me immediately when up popped a naked woman accidentally. We were able to react quickly to prevent any further drama. I informed that child's parents after school what had occurred, to be proactive, and they were very relaxed about it as they also educated at home about what to do. The second time that a breakdown in the filter service happened, a male student searched inappropriate content and then showed it to a grade four girl. She handled it well, informing me immediately. When I updated her mother, out spills a remarkable tale. Was I aware of her daughter's previous porn addiction? Ummmm, she's grade four!! Lucky that wasn't my problem to manage. The Internet filter cannot block every single item of inappropriate content on the web. Children need to know the best ways to handle slip-ups

This is not a definitive list by any means and cyber safety resources will support and enhance your school's policy. Stay Smart Online is an Australian Government initiative promoting cyber safety tips for both home and school use. https://www.communications.gov.au/what-we-do/internet/stay-smart-online/youth. Cyber Smart is another Australian Government site, chock full of lessons and interactive experiences for children of all ages http://www.cybersmart.gov.au. Kidsmart http://www.kidsmart.org.uk and Think U Know https://www.thinkuknow.co.uk are both great resources to access from the United Kingdom.

Device Management

When children bring devices from home there needs to be secure and stringent management of them to prevent damage, theft or misuse. Hardware is expensive and parents, justifiably, get very upset if their child's device is abused or rendered unusable.

Non-school sanctioned devices such as M.P.3 players and mobile phones should be handed in to the office each day before school and collected afterwards, unless the teacher has a lockable drawer or cupboard. Leaving devices in school bags is extremely insecure and theft can occur. If the item is stolen you will have parents demanding recovery or replacement and it is incredibly difficult to determine who was the thief. You are busy enough without becoming a super sleuth! Directing children to store them in the school's office offers you freedom from the responsibility of securing the device. This is for primary school children only. Secondary school students tend to maintain possession of their phones all day.

Devices should not be used on the school grounds, before or after school hours. This time is largely unsupervised and the opportunity for abuse or misuse is high.

When a school has a 1:1 tablet program then it should have detailed management plans.

This should cover the following:

- Hard covers or cases for tablets are essential to protect screens
- Tablets need to come to school fully charged and ready for use. It's too difficult to manage charging at school
- Teachers should do spot checks on tablet contents
- Only age appropriate applications should be permissible
- Children should not message or email each other during school hours
- No passcodes
- Child's picture or name as their lock screen and home screen so anyone can identify the owner
- No other child should touch a device that's not theirs without permission
- At recess and lunch breaks, or when the students are outside, devices should be kept in a lockable cupboard or case
- Devices must be stored upright at all times to avoid pressure on fragile screens

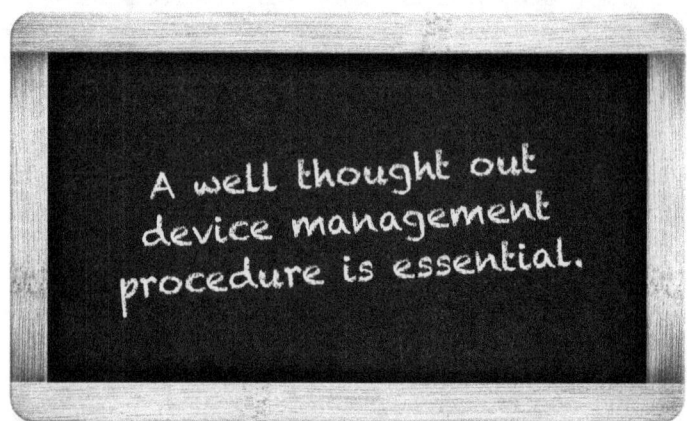

Username/Password Management

Many apps and websites that are designed for educational purposes require usernames and passwords. The I.T. department at your school will manage the big picture, in terms of signing up, syncing and possibly even password generation.

Junior school students often have difficulty typing in the correct letters, let alone recalling or finding their details to do so in the first place. There are a few options for managing this procedure:

- Post the usernames and passwords on the wall for them to copy from
- Copy them into the rear of one of their workbooks. If you ask them to copy down the details you may want to double check they are done correctly. Their handwriting or transcribing skills may mean difficulties when they try to re-log in
- Print and laminate individual cards for each student with their details on it. Collect after each session that they are utilised
- It's highly recommended for you to keep a spreadsheet with your entire classes' usernames and passwords in case of emergency. It's very frustrating setting a task, only to discover several students can't log in because they can't access their details

Middle and senior students have more maturity to be able to manage their usernames and passwords. Suggest they start a document or note on their device that contains all their log ins. Alternatively they can record them in the back of a workbook. Where possible keep whole class log in details yourself, such as for Mathletics.

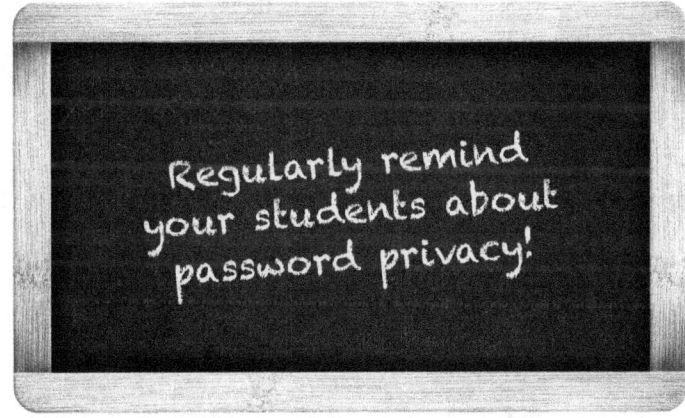

Regularly remind your students about password privacy!

Partnering Positively With Parents

Chapter Overview

- » Why a good relationship is important
- » What a good partnership looks like
- » How to establish and maintain a good relationship:
  - Communication
  - Aim for win/win outcomes
  - Establishing and maintaining boundaries
  - Easy relationship builders
- » Parent types and how to optimise your interactions:
  - Easy
  - Overly Assertive
  - Overly Controlling
  - Invisible
  - Vulnerable
  - Aggressive
- » When parents contact you

One of the most important aspects of teaching is that of the partnership between teacher and parents. It can also be one of the most challenging! A positive relationship is beneficial for all parties - child, teacher, parents and school. On the flip side, a difficult relationship can be damaging for everyone. Don't underestimate the negative influence parents can have on your career, or state of mind, so learning to be proactive and healthy in the early years of teaching can really minimise stressful situations for you.

Whilst writing this book I often posed questions on social media, to both teachers and parents, regarding a topic I was looking for feedback on. I asked this question, "Parents, what advice would you give your child's primary school teacher in order to have a great partnership?" The volume and depth of responses was amazing. This leads me to believe that it is a concerning and important issue for parents, one they are passionate about getting right. Of course, parents play a role in establishing and maintaining a good relationship with you, but there are many ways you contribute also. This chapter focusses on what YOU can do to foster a great partnership with parents.

Many of the examples and theories contained in this chapter are transferrable to other people in your workplace, not just school parents. Your interactions with colleagues, leadership and school children will all improve if you employ some of the relationship building techniques I write about.

I want to stress that the management techniques and suggestions outlined in this chapter are mine only. They are not theory based, they are experience based. (Although you will definitely find some of my techniques in behavioural theory). Through trial and error, as well as input from more experienced colleagues at the time, I have developed some actions to respond to parents, as well as learnt to change my own practices to avoid difficult interactions in the first place.

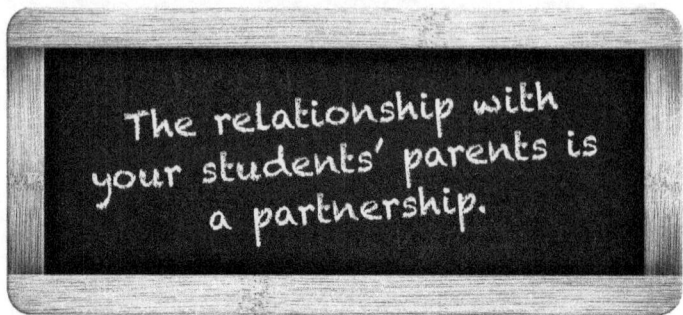

Why a Good Relationship is Important

The main aim when desiring a good relationship with parents is to view it as a partnership. When all parties contribute constructively then everyone benefits, especially the child. Advantages for the student may be increased motivation for learning, regular attendance at school, a positive attitude towards school and learning, and possibly even improved behaviour.

A good relationship with a parent paves the way for healthy and constructive interactions. They are more likely to speak positively and supportively about you, which has a flow on effect to their child. When a student observes their parents speaking encouragingly about a teacher they will naturally be more predisposed to desire a good relationship also.

A parent who is happy with their child's teacher and school is very unlikely to cause you trouble if an issue arises. You may have a student in your class that is difficult to manage, has learning issues or social problems. If the relationship you have with their parent is a good one you are more likely to be able to work together to improve the situation for their child.

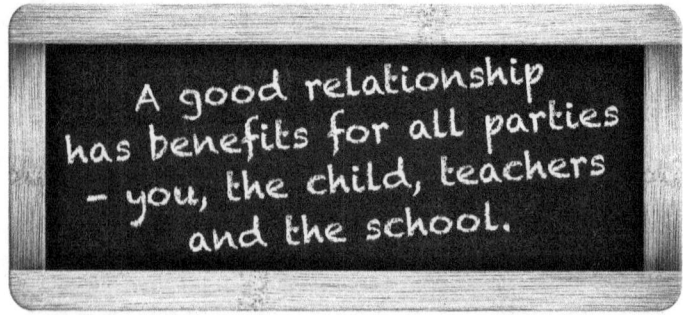

What a Good Partnership Looks Like

A partnership involves two or more people working together on a joint interest. In a school setting, an important partnership is between parent and teacher, where your joint interest is the child's wellbeing and education. There are other partnerships involved in education but this is the relationship this chapter focusses on.

You only have control over what and how YOU contribute towards an effective partnership. It is impossible to control the effort, frequency or style of the parent's input and futile to attempt to do so. You must responsibly maintain professionalism and courtesy at all times, especially when it can become a little more challenging.

A good partnership would look a little something like this:

- » Regular, clear and honest communication
- » Openness and willingness to **receive** constructive feedback
- » Ability to give constructive feedback
- » The child's best interests are at the forefront of all interactions
- » Respectful interactions
- » Meeting deadlines and following up/through on plans and suggestions

It must be acknowledged that in partnerships such as these, a parent will not always strive to contribute in the most pleasant or healthy manner. This situation will be addressed in more detail later in the chapter.

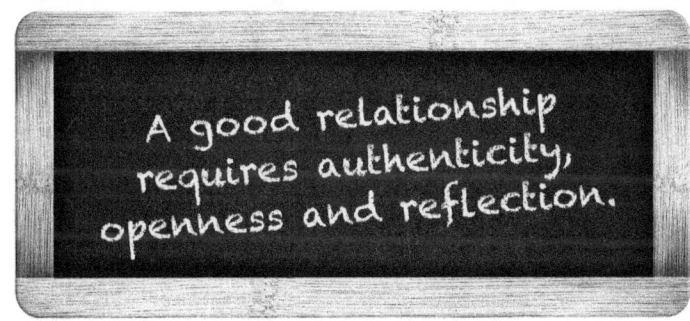

A good relationship requires authenticity, openness and reflection.

How to Establish and Maintain a Good Relationship

Whilst you may have twenty-five other students, for a parent, their child is your most important student. They want you to ensure their child feels safe, respected and positive about their learning at all times.

There are many ways for you to establish and maintain a good working relationship with parents.

Communication

This is the number one concern listed by parents in my very unofficial poll! What do they want? A whole lot more of it.

In preschool or childcare, a parent has daily access to their child's teacher and carer. They are receiving an update a day on events and progress made. It may be hard for parents to adjust to a school setting, where communication is less available and it is not possible to speak to their child's teacher every day.

As children progress through primary school it's natural to communicate less with parents as the years pass. Children grow more independent and often parents return to work or increase their employment hours. As a result, teachers can tend to 'forget' parents as we see them a whole lot less.

We can communicate in many ways with parents. However, just because we think we are communicating, doesn't mean it is being heard. Choosing a variety of methods will hopefully mean at least one style will connect with a parent's preferred method.

Outside presence: A very simple step is to spend fifteen minutes outside your classroom each day after the final bell. This way you can catch parents you need to talk to, and it allows parents to approach you if they choose. Doing this regularly sends parents the message you are approachable and accessible. Avoid always talking to the same parents or rushing back in after five minutes if no one approaches you. Use this opportunity to approach a parent or small group of parents and share what is happening in the classroom or what went well today. Junior and middle classes frequently have parents waiting outside for the child at the end of each day and so this type of communication is easy to establish. Senior classes rarely have parents waiting nearby after school so you can attempt this strategy or choose to communicate in a different way. It doesn't hurt to try this method and when parents learn you are regularly outside after school they may come over more.

Message boards: A large whiteboard attached outside the line up area or classroom blocks is another easy way to communicate with parents. When parents drop off or pick up their children each day they will see any signage or posters you have put up on the message board. Add reminders and requests for classroom assistance. Post samples of children's work or regular newsletters. Depending on the layout of your school this could work either for your own classroom or for the whole year level. You may have to check with your team leader or leadership before you proceed with this method.

Newsletters: Most schools send out a whole school newsletter on a regular basis. This does not guarantee parents actually read it however! Most parents enjoy receiving newsletters that contain information about their child's class or year level. A lot of principals request that they vet all written communication that is sent home to parents, so check the procedure at your school before undertaking any newsletter writing. If you get the go ahead, setting up a newsletter template is a good time saving device. Determine the content, method of distribution, frequency and dates of distribution. When you make it a regular occurrence, parents will look out for it.

Phone calls: If a parent is not a visible presence on the school grounds on a regular basis, it may be preferable to give them a phone call occasionally. How good does it feel to be contacted when the caller's sole purpose is to tell you something great about you? We all love to hear good news about ourselves. This also works the same way when someone tells you something fabulous about your child. It's such a simple and easy thing to do, yet we often only think of contacting someone when we have something to complain about. A five-minute phone call to a parent to share something noteworthy is priceless for both the child and parent and an awesome way to work on your parent/teacher partnership with minimal effort.

Sometimes you will be unable to catch up with a parent in person to discuss an issue. Rather than let it go, a phone call is the next best thing. If they are not able to meet with you face to face, then a phone call will suffice. Before I begin any phone call with a parent, when I know I will be communicating something difficult, I always jot down the main points I wish to get across and the outcome I'm looking for. This is to ensure I cover everything I need to and to have my aim clear. Parents can often take conversations off on another tangent if you have unwittingly triggered something for them, so having notes prepared allows you to gently bring the conversation back to the important points to cover. The section later covered in this chapter on 'Parent Types', will give you clear guidelines for successful interactions.

A good privacy measure is to never give out your personal phone numbers. Once your personal phone number is made public you have no control whether a parent shares your number or uses it to contact you inappropriately. Either use the school's phone to make calls, or block your number before you make any calls or texts to parents. Texts should be used sparingly, perhaps only when you are updating parents when requested. For example, I have taught a student with diabetes. Occasionally I had to message her mum throughout the day with her blood glucose readings. This was a more efficient system than a phone call or email.

When making phone calls to parents, it's important to stick to working hours when possible. Regularly making calls after dinner gives parents the impression you are accessible at all hours and this has the potential for unintentional abuse.

Hand written notes: Keep a stash of nice writing paper and envelopes in your desk at school so you can write a nice handwritten note to parents. Make a point of thanking parents for any extra help they have offered - manning fete stalls, being your parent representative, contacting books or sharpening pencils. It only takes five minutes to write a little thank you and this small gesture is a powerful one for developing and maintaining a great relationship with parents.

Communication books: Some students with disabilities or behaviour issues will require a communication book. (See Chapter 11 on Disabilities for more comprehensive information). These are rather onerous for teachers to complete daily, but can prove helpful. If the child has an aide, request that they complete these each day. An unfunded child means it's your job to fill it in. It may not be possible to do this daily, depending on the level you teach and what is timetabled towards the end of the day. Whatever system you settle upon, communicate clearly to the parents when it will, and won't, be used. Parents can misuse communication books by using them to whinge and vilify so be as brief as possible. Don't get caught up in any ineffective communication methods. Their child is their whole world and they can sometimes forget you are responsible for twenty-five, not just theirs.

Email: Email, as a communication device, can be efficient or a disaster. I've experienced both! The strongest tip I can impress upon you is to not put anything in writing. It's so easy to quickly type up a message and press send, before we've reflected carefully on the content. Emails are easily open to misinterpretation due to a lack of face-to-face contact to determine tone.

A good use of email as a communication device is to send out pre approved newsletters, minutes from meetings or notices via attachment. Never use email to attempt to talk to a parent about their child's progress or lack thereof. Face to face or phone call only. Once you put something in writing it is now in concrete form and you may experience repercussions for this. It may be tempting to think it's more efficient to quickly update via email than a phone call, but in the long term it's quite possible it will prove less efficient.

When you do choose to use email, check, check and recheck before you press send. Perhaps send it to a colleague to check. You can't take it back once it's gone! Always make sure you have used an address to send from that you are comfortable with parents knowing.

Blog/Website/Dropbox/Wiki: Some classes have blogs or wikis. These are great for communicating with parents by using students! Children can write and upload class information for parents to read and they also get to see samples of student's work. Dropbox is a way to add notices and newsletters into a folder that parents can access anywhere they have a device. No more lost notices in school bags or locker bays! Remember, it is public (for those with the log in details), so don't post anything personal.

Early intervention: This was really important to the parents I surveyed. They want to know when a problem arises with their child, not weeks or terms later. It really does make sense to talk to parents at the time of an incident. What you need to do is determine what is important to convey to parents and what is a normal part of school life and manageable internally. For example, if a student has trouble keeping their hands and feet to themselves, it is realistic and advisable to attempt management strategies at school. After a few weeks if there is no improvement and you have asked colleagues for ideas also, it is time to have a chat to parents about working together. If a student breaks a serious school rule, such as leaving school grounds or biting another student, then parents should be informed the same day.

Having concerns about a student's academic performance may take a term to clarify. You need to really get to know the child first and examine test results. Calling a meeting with parents should occur when you have enough information to make a clear presentation. Sometimes parents choose to deny or ignore a learning issue, but the point is that you have acted professionally and communicated concerns in a timely manner.

Raising Concerns: If you need to speak to parents about an academic, social or behavioural issue, it can be awkward at times. Here is a helpful step-by-step plan to make everyone more comfortable.

1 "I am seeing the following...." From the beginning of the conversation you are making it clear what the concern is. This can't really be debated as it is what YOU are observing.

2 "I'd like to chat with you about ways we can work together to help Xxx to..." (For example, participate more fully in class or feel more comfortable in certain situations). Here you are informing the parents that you want a partnership with them to assist their child. You are wanting a positive solution, rather than to place any blame.

3 "Do you see any similar behaviours at home? And if so, are there any particular strategies that you use that helps curb behaviour/ assist?" You are asking for advice and input as well as acknowledging that they are the experts on their child.

Document interactions: The final aspect of communication with parents is to record important interactions. This could be as simple as diarising, "Called Xxx parents. Left message and asked for call to be returned." The purpose of this is to have clear records if parents complain about a lack of communication or early intervention. Another form of documentation is to write notes (preferably digital), recording what was discussed in meetings and filing it for future reference. A copy can be forwarded to parents when an agreement was made or action is to be taken. Finally, if you suspect a meeting will be difficult or unpleasant, ask a more experienced colleague to sit in on the meeting to take notes.

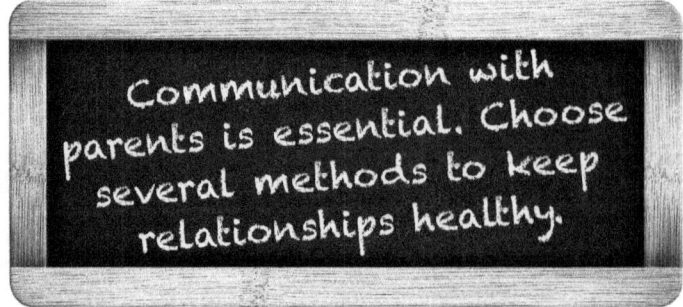

Communication with parents is essential. Choose several methods to keep relationships healthy.

Aim for Win/Win Outcomes

There will be many occasions when you will need to have a conversation with a parent that has the potential to be difficult or awkward. A win/win outcome is the ideal that you should always work towards to maintain an effective partnership with parents. This scenario proposes that both parties end up pleased with the outcome. Win/lose suggests that both parties have the mindset of 'winning' and have little regard for the outcome of the other party. Lose/lose is pretty self-explanatory! Let's not go there.

WIN/WIN NEGOTIATION SKILLS

Let's use the following scenario as an example of how to negotiate win/win with a parent.

> *A student in your class is a constant distraction to others, and to you, due to their talking. They talk during whole class instruction, when seated next to anyone else and during independent work. It has been an ongoing issue all year and it is now mid term two. You have tried several strategies with the child to curb their chatter and none are working. This includes moving, separating, warning, reminding, teacher to student discussion, a reward program, talking to previous teachers and suggesting/modelling self-management strategies. The reason it's time to talk to their parents is because it is now at the point where it is negatively impacting upon their learning and the learning of others around them.*

Before the meeting, jot down your optimal outcomes:

- » Parents understand and/or acknowledge that this is a problem that all involved parties have a responsibility to work together on
- » Parent, teacher and child develop a shared vision for a strategy that both are happy with
- » Goals for parent/teacher/child are realistic and attainable
- » Dates for updates are discussed

There are a few key aspects to remember and put into practise when aiming for a win/win outcome:

Focus on maintaining the relationship: you may really dislike their approach or their attitude towards you, however you need to separate their behaviour from the problem. Perhaps they disagree that it is a problem, or accuse you of not being able to manage the issue. Don't let the discussion descend into argument or blaming on your behalf.

"You've expressed your points very clearly and I can now appreciate your position. However..."

"It's clear that you are very concerned about this issue, as I am myself. Yet from my viewpoint..."

These statements show to the parent you still have a positive regard for them and lays the groundwork for continuing the discussion without blame. Remember, win/winners separate the behaviour from the problem. Your aim here is to avoid disagreements about issues becoming personal disagreements. That can get messy and nasty.

Focus on interests, not positions: this is not an argument to be 'won' by either side. There are no brownie points to be scored for negotiating a superior position for yourself. Instead, think about what the parent's interests may be. In our example, it is perhaps to help their child understand the importance of not talking during class and to be able to self-regulate. Same as your interest, right? Thinking about their interests may help you to take into account their needs, wants and worries.

So, what if the parent shows no real interest in helping to improve their child's behaviour? This is quite possible; sometimes they are either incapable or think it is your job only. Your positions may be opposed but you can still find common interests on which to build upon. Remind the parent that you like their child (even if you don't!), and that you are keen to help improve their learning outcomes. This is a negotiation process and you cannot force a decision in a win/win scenario.

Generate a range of options that both sides will gain from: you've already done some preparation here by listing the optimal outcomes before discussions began. The more options there are the more likely you will be able to find a win/win solution to the problem. Brainstorm together; remember the parent knows their child far better than you do and may provide an idea that you hadn't thought of.

Using our example of the chronically chatty student, some options for resolution that involve all parties are:

- Role playing at home and school
- Reward program at home based on measurable progress at school
- Regular check ins
- Non verbal signals by the teacher as a quiet reminder for the student
- Specific, special reward chosen by the student, on attaining small goals

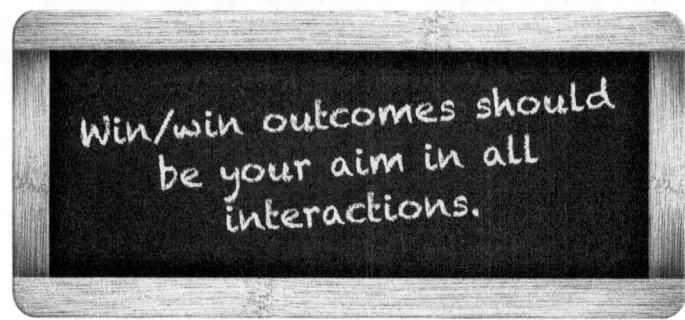

Establishing and Maintaining Boundaries

Boundaries are both physical and emotional. Establishing and maintaining healthy boundaries are very important in both your personal and professional life. A personal boundary is the guidelines, rules or limits that you create to identify what are safe and permissible ways for other people to behave around you, and how you will respond when someone attempts to step outside/inside of those limits. (See Chapter 19 on Boundaries for a much deeper look at how they work).

It is easy to go a little overboard with a needy parent. It's a natural desire in most of us to help where we can. A teacher's challenge is to be open and accepting, inviting communication, whilst being really clear about the boundaries of your responsibilities. You are professionally capable of offering advice on teaching, learning and social matters AT SCHOOL. It is outside the parameters of your professional expertise as a teacher to offer parenting advice, even if parents seek it out or even if you are a parent. Tactfully decline to offer your opinion or to get involved with personal matters.

There are many areas you could set boundaries with parents, in order to maintain a good relationship.

Email: Do you want parents to communicate with you via email? Will you email only during working hours? What types of interactions are you comfortable with via email? For example, sometimes parents have contacted me via my work email to ask about homework or an excursion. I'm happy to reply by email for these sorts of enquiries. However, if the email is regarding a concern, I will not reply via email. I call and ask them to come in for a chat. Likewise, if I am raising a concern about a child's behaviour or progress, email is not the forum.

Social Media: Will you allow parents to be your friend? Do you have enough privacy settings so parents can't see your personal posts and information? I cannot state this strongly enough - either never post ANYTHING controversial or concerning, OR, don't friend/follow parents and staff.

Phone: Will you give out your personal phone number? Will you communicate with parents using your private phone, or, work phone only? Will you take/make phone calls after hours? Will you block your number?

Friendship: Should you allow a personal friendship to develop with a student's parents? What will the possible ramifications of this be? There are pros and cons and I suggest you think very carefully about this. Considering you their friend can mean they expect inside information. As teachers we get asked often enough 'What grade are you teaching next year?' Or, 'What do you think of Miss X?' It's hard to deflect these questions when you are put on the spot. It's even harder if you have a friendship.

Meetings: How often are you prepared to meet with a parent on their instigation? Will you allow drop in visits that turn to meetings or only allow booked meetings? What are your off limit times?

Professionalism: Offer advice on school based issues, not home based problems.

Easy Relationship Builders

There are some pretty easy and simple ways you can contribute to a great working relationship with parents.

- » Show interest. This is so easy to do. You should make it a regular practice to ask children about their weekend on a Monday, their holiday plans, and their milestones. Talk to parents about their child's interests and achievements. All parents love to talk about their children with anyone and everyone! Realising their child's teacher knows about them is priceless. Celebrate with them and encourage them. (See Chapter 3 on Enjoying Teaching for more detail)

- » Be truthful. Don't dodge issues because it makes you uncomfortable. Parents respect tactful honesty but avoid controversial or extreme language

- » Thank them. Parents help out in many different ways in your classroom and at school. Make an effort to seek them out and personally thank them. This goes a loooooong way towards maintaining a great relationship for anyone in your life. Email, make a phone call, chat when you bump into them in the school grounds, or write a letter

- » Invite them in. Open your room regularly or make it possible for parents to assist in the classroom. They love to be involved

- » Believe in their children. Parents can tell when you don't think high achievement is possible for their child

- » Don't use teacher speak. All interactions with parents should be in language they can understand as much as possible.
- » Commit. When you say you will do something for either parent or child, do it
- » Don't judge. You have no idea how a family's experiences have informed their parenting style. Be compassionate and tolerant
- » Don't diagnose. This is really, really important to understand. Your expertise is education. It is not in diagnosing disorders, disabilities or syndromes. What if you are wrong? If you have concerns, your job is to raise them tactfully with parents and refer to specialists who will be better positioned to diagnose. (See Chapter 11 on Disabilities)
- » Respect official diagnoses. When a child has been diagnosed with a disability, by a professional, don't ignore or deny its existence. Perfect way to get a parent offside and cause yourself problems. Endeavour to make adjustments to lesson plans and expectations
- » Treat each child like you would want your own treated
- » Look out for the good kids. Because they are not a problem in the classroom, it's possible they may fly under the radar with academic issues
- » Offer concrete suggestions for how parents can assist their child academically at home. They don't really want to hear, 'Maybe it's a maturity thing.' Or, 'Just do more reading.' If you aren't sure off the top of your head when they ask you, tell them you will get back to them with suggestions after you do some thinking
- » Every child deserves your attention and effort. It's impossible to like every one and, like in all settings, some people in particular press our buttons. It is in your best interests to put on a pleasant facade when you have to talk to parents who annoy you
- » Answer parent inquiries/correspondence promptly, even if it means saying, 'I need a little time to think about this first,' or explaining that you will not be able to meet immediately but that you will get to it A.S.A.P.

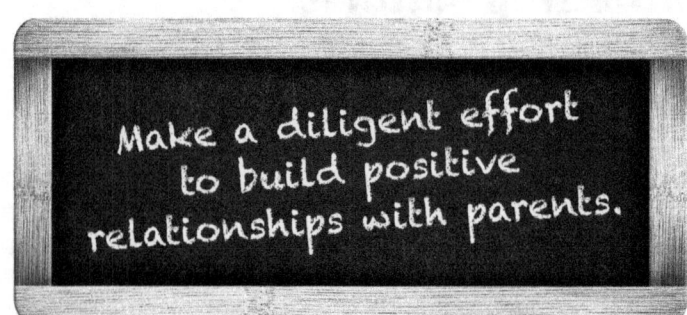

Parent Types

This section explores the types of parents you will interact with during your teaching career and makes helpful suggestions for optimising and dealing with difficult people. Why is it necessary to define parent types? When you are able to identify the type of parent you are interacting with, you are able to determine the most effective manner in which to speak and respond to them. This in turn optimises positive outcomes for all and minimises stress and anxiety for you. Of course, some parents are a combination of types so you may need to utilise more than one approach for effective management. I've often had greater insight into my students after parent/teacher interview night. The reasons for the child's behaviour is explained when I meet their parent/s.

The first four parent types identified are the most common types you will encounter. The final two are uncommon, however you will probably have one to two children each year with this type of parent. Overly Controlling and Overly Assertive parent types are both driven by anxiety, however they are exhibited through different behaviours.

Easy

If only our classroom was filled with students who have easy parents! They can also be defined as healthy parents. We would have very few behavioural issues and our gut wouldn't clench when we saw them at the door waiting to speak to us! An Easy parent has fostered and nurtured a secure attachment with their child, respects them and is self-reflective about their parenting. They spend quality time with them and help their child to become independent. These parents have not allowed their children to dictate to them and have set healthy emotional and physical boundaries. Easy parents will listen to your advice, be grateful for it and follow your suggestions closely.

IDENTIFYING EASY PARENTS
Some signs of an Easy parent at school are:

- Their child is well adjusted and is secure enough to transition from home to school each day
- They follow correct procedures for contacting you
- They speak respectfully to both you and their child
- They acknowledge when their child has contributed in a negative manner
- They are mostly happy and often willing to help out where they can
- Their child is independent and well adjusted
- You are happy and comfortable with all your interactions with them

DEALING WITH EASY PARENTS

Well, this is your easiest parent to interact with so not much needs to be said here. This parent type is your greatest ally. If you receive feedback from them that challenges you, it pays to listen to and hear their concerns, as they are not motivated to hurt you in a negative way. Remember to show gratitude for their efforts and continue to encourage the healthy parent/teacher relationship.

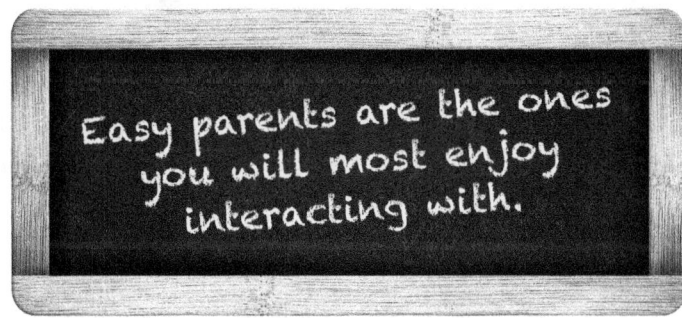

Easy parents are the ones you will most enjoy interacting with.

Overly Assertive

Society has seen a rise in the number of Overly Assertive parents over the past two decades, to the detriment of their children. These parents are pushy, overprotective, often anxious and have a strong need to be heard. Their anxiety may transfer onto their child, causing them to become anxious. They are often competitive with other parents about their child's achievements and want you to tell them their child is the next Einstein or Van Gogh. Children hearing often enough from their parents how much better they are than their classmates, can potentially become bullies in their attempt to fulfil their parent's delusions that they are superior to everyone else. The child can also be very unsure about themselves and lack confidence because they know that they'll never achieve the expectations set for them.

IDENTIFYING OVERLY ASSERTIVE PARENTS
Some signs of an Overly Assertive are:

- They want their child to be completing work far ahead of their abilities or for their age
- They often have no true idea of what their child's abilities are
- They will contact you regularly
- They will often attempt to disrespect your boundaries as they think rules don't apply to them
- They may complain often and loudly about your shortcomings as a teacher to both you and to others
- They believe their child is academically, creatively or physically gifted and that you can't see how special they are
- They frequently do not acknowledge their child can contribute in a negative way
- They will listen to their child's point of view over yours
- They will instantly believe their child's point of view regarding incidents and not question them about their contribution

DEALING WITH OVERLY ASSERTIVE PARENTS

The key here is to treat them just like you would treat demanding children. You must have strong boundaries and be fair but firm with them.

It is also helpful to remember that no matter how effectively you communicate with them or how much effort you put in, they may remain unhappy in certain situations. This will often be more about their anxieties and you must attempt to not take that on.

- Before all planned interactions ensure you have written a list of objectives and have a calm and clear headspace
- Ask a team member to sit in on meetings with you if you are nervous or worried
- ALWAYS take notes throughout meetings and forward agreements to parents and leadership
- Recap at the end of a meeting or phone call, "So, we agree that I will... And you will..."
- NEVER interact with these parents via email or message
- Document ALL interactions with parents in your diary or in a specialised app
- Discourage lingering goodbyes or visits to their child throughout the day
- Discourage regular contact with the parent; see them only when you think there's a genuine need
- Be clear what the curriculum covers for their child's grade

- Show them test results when necessary to confirm how their child is performing in relation to expected levels
- Don't show them another child's work to compare. Compare them only to the appropriate curriculum or rubric
- Slip into conversation some praise about their child
- Try to avoid playing into their hands by being intolerant, aggressive or nasty
- Read the chapter on Boundaries for great tips on maintaining yours in difficult situations
- Avoid emotive language and remain respectful whilst factual
- Show a lot of empathy to the child; imagine their stressful home life
- Encourage parents to involve their child in rich, interactive experiences at home

> Don't be afraid to ask for backup and assistance from other colleagues when dealing with Overly Assertive parents.

Overly Controlling

Parent involvement in their child's education includes participation in school activities as well as helping them at home with homework and tasks. This is healthy and welcome. Involvement turns to interference when they hijack activities and turn up announced or when inappropriate. Long term, interference hinders their child's development, the exact opposite of what they are aiming for.

IDENTIFYING OVERLY CONTROLLING PARENTS
When in the classroom 'helping' they may:

- Talk over the teacher in front of the students
- Stop the students from working in some way
- Change the task you have set to one they think is better or more appropriate
- Come in prepared with an activity they want to do, not what you have scheduled
- Be classified as a 'helicopter parent' by hovering over their child and attempting to do all their tasks for them
- Only help their own child
- Enjoy focus on themselves so will distract children from focussing on the teacher
- Try to talk to you about their child whilst you are supervising or teaching
- Pass judgement on other children

Other times may:

- » Turn up unannounced to 'help'
- » Begin volunteering even if the roster is full and they haven't been timetabled on
- » Drop their child off each day by walking them in and then staying too long and observing or interfering
- » Complete their child's homework for them
- » Book accommodation next door to the school camp to control their child's activities and collect them each night so they are safe (this really happened to me)
- » Attempt to convince you their child's grade/report needs to be changed
- » Question your decisions or lessons
- » Fill your inbox and messagebank with complaints and concerns

Dealing with Overly Controlling parents

- » Speak to the parent directly and outline what it is they are doing that is inappropriate or unhelpful
- » Request they cease the behaviour and suggest ways to be involved instead of interfering
- » Model appropriate ways to complete the classroom activities
- » Repeat and repeat and repeat the above three points
- » Don't use the term interfering! That will just make them upset or angry and you will find it difficult to communicate further with them
- » Be specific. For example, 'Xxx, I notice you are not rostered on to assist today. It can be overwhelming for students with too many adults during learning time and I have enough today. I'll see you on Wednesday when you are rostered on
- » Cease rostering them on if they continually display interfering behaviour
- » Enlist the help of leadership in speaking to them if they are not getting your direct messages
- » State that one of your tasks is to teach children independence and that having mum (or dad) there to help inhibits this
- » Point out that problem solving skills are important and that the child needs opportunities for independence in order to learn how to solve minor and major problems that arise
- » Reinforce that children need to be able to ask questions, advocate for themselves and speak up when they need something
- » Convey to parents that children need to experience consequences for their actions so that when they experience life outside of the classroom they are equipped to cope

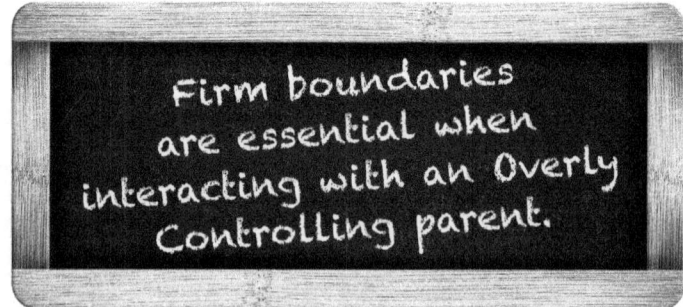

Firm boundaries are essential when interacting with an Overly Controlling parent.

Invisible

An Invisible parent or family show little interest in their child's education. They make few demands of their children and are often dismissive or indifferent towards them. Children of Invisible parents are often emotionally withdrawn, have poor attachment and can often feel fear, anxiety or stress due to their situation.

IDENTIFYING INVISIBLE PARENTS

Well, this is pretty easy, you never see them! Not to be confused with the parent who is really busy and works many hours, an uninvolved parent refuses to be involved in any way with their child's learning. They are physically present in their child's life, yet quite emotionally disconnected from them. Unfortunately, this leads to poorer educational outcomes for children.

An Invisible parent may exhibit the following behaviours:

- Will not attend parent teacher interview days, no matter how many times you contact them or how flexible you are with arrangements
- Chooses not to support camps and excursions
- Will not answer phones or return calls
- Refuses to visit the school if an issue needs to be dealt with
- The child has to get to school by themselves from a very early age
- Don't support their child to do home reading or homework
- The parent/s most likely had bad school experiences or interrupted schooling
- The child often doesn't come to school in appropriate attire for free dress days or bring money for donations or events. Not because the parents cannot afford it, but because they don't read notices and possibly don't care if their child has good experiences at school
- Will often talk to their child about how school is stupid or put down activities/events the school organises
- Will never volunteer at school
- May have a physical or mental illness preventing them from involvement. (Note; some physically, mentally or physically impaired parents are very involved)

DEALING WITH INVISIBLE PARENTS

Invisible parents are usually not difficult to deal with, as you never speak to them! Your main focus here will be supporting their child in a way other children don't need to be supported.

- Don't rely on past teachers telling you the parents are uninvolved (even if they definitely are). Attempt to establish a good working relationship with them, as you would with all other parent types
- Phone the parents when necessary and leave messages
- Check with leadership if permission for excursions is acceptable via a phone message
- Make sure you phone to share good news too
- Continue to send home all notices, even if a child tells you their parents don't read them
- When there is an upcoming excursion or camp, allow plenty of time for negotiations to take place between the parent and school
- Investigate if there are funds available at your school for children in this situation
- Make appointments for them for parent/teacher interviews, even if you know they won't show up. Consider conducting an interview over the phone

The Essential Teacher's Guide

- » Younger children may feel really left out of dress up days and special events, so perhaps thinking of how you could support them on these days would be a kind thing to do
- » Provide a safe, predictable and consistent environment for the child and use a lot of modelling of appropriate behaviours

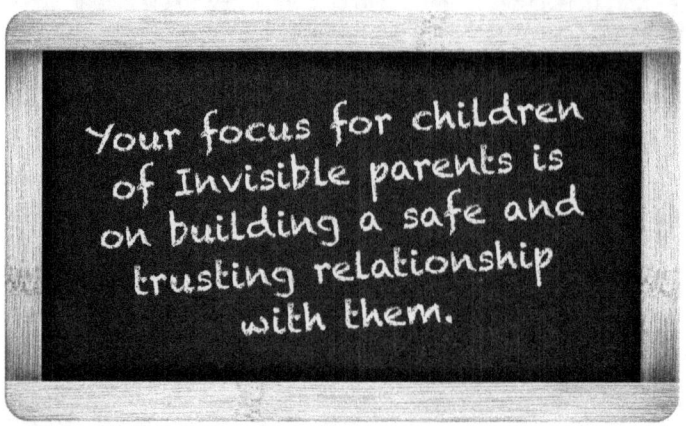

Your focus for children of Invisible parents is on building a safe and trusting relationship with them.

Vulnerable

Vulnerable parents are incapable in some way of looking after their children to meet society's standards. Neglect can be either physical or emotional, or both. The reasons for neglect may be, but are not limited to, drug abuse, mental illness or low I.Q.

IDENTIFYING VULNERABLE PARENTS

As with Invisible parents, you will not sight Vulnerable parents very often. They have similar traits to Invisible parents, however their children may present differently. It's easier to identify Vulnerable parents through their children.

- » Children may often come to school without food or with poor food choices, such as a large packet of chips for the entire day
- » Children often have personal hygiene problems
- » Don't underestimate how important these first two bullet points are. They can often communicate to you a lot about a child's parents
- » Children often appear very dirty or bedraggled
- » Clothes and uniforms are often ill fitting, wrong or inappropriate
- » Be on the lookout for children who don't present as neglected (clean clothes, good hygiene etc.), yet may be emotionally neglected or psychologically traumatised. You may observe children who are overly anxious or who cry easily
- » Fees, excursions and camps are usually not paid for
- » It's highly likely you will never meet with or even see Vulnerable parents
- » There's a chance they may be volatile or aggressive if they turn up at school
- » Children are unsupported for special days at school and with homework
- » Children may present with difficult social/emotional

DEALING WITH VULNERABLE PARENTS

It's important to tread very carefully here as Vulnerable parents may potentially become Aggressive parents (see section on Aggressive parents on the next page).

- » Vulnerable children will have large student files for you to read through regarding past interventions or interactions with parents. It's imperative you read these thoroughly before taking any action

- » Vulnerable families often have a support team with government agencies and negotiations and meetings may need to be held with them present

- » Heed the advice of past teachers and leadership on the best way to communicate with these families

- » If you are concerned about volatility or aggression when a meeting is planned, request support from senior leadership

- » Encourage your class to show tolerance of unusual behaviours or hygiene issues as much as possible

- » Any hygiene issues are most likely long term and extremely difficult to address (see Chapter 12 on Student Hygiene for suggestions on talking to families). Extreme hygiene issues need to be dealt with immediately, such as soiled underpants or lice. Either yourself, or leadership, should call the parents to ask them to collect the child and return when they are clean or treated

- » As with Invisible parents, think of how you could support vulnerable children to attend camps/excursions and to participate fully in school life

- » If you suspect abuse, or have abuse disclosed to you, you must do a mandatory report. Seek experienced advice before you do this. Each state has their own procedures and guidelines to adhere to

- » Adjust your expectations for vulnerable children. For example, can homework be completed at school? Can you find five minutes everyday to hear a child read regularly? Can you provide supplies for projects yourself? These children will most likely not appear grateful for your extra efforts. They are used to being let down so will not show appreciation or excitement. However, having a person show care in a gentle way will have a huge impact. Don't underestimate the effect this can have on a child's sense of worth

- » Regular, unexplained, non-attendance at school needs to be monitored and reported. Seek advice from leadership as all schools will have different policies and follow up procedures. Often government agencies are involved for this issue too

The most important things you can do are to display compassion and a lack of judgement.

Aggressive

Let's begin by establishing that anger is separate from aggression. Anger is a healthy emotion that we all experience on occasion. It lets us know that we are experiencing something we are uncomfortable with or are upset by. This is perfectly normal. How we respond to our anger differentiates emotionally healthy people from those who are unhealthy. Aggression is an unhealthy response to feeling angry. It is hostile and violates another's rights, even if not done intentionally.

There are a few types of Aggressive parents (and people) you may encounter, however, we will only look at the two main ones - Openly Aggressive or Passive Aggressive. Both are tricky to navigate.

OPEN AGGRESSION

Experiencing open aggression is unpleasant and it will be immediately obvious that they are being aggressive towards you. They may shout, swear, finger point, clench their fists or get too physically close. As a response, your heart may begin to beat harder and faster, you may flush or break out in a sweat or get very nervous. I've known teachers and/or schools who have had to take out restraining orders against Aggressive parents. One year a very young mum raced into my classroom just after school started, very distressed. Her partner was physically abusive and had kept her and her son up a lot of the night terrorising them. He'd dropped them at the school gate, remaining in his car. However, when she returned to get into the vehicle, he made threats to her life and she'd raced away petrified. We had to lock down the classroom and call the police. Whilst this wasn't originally a school matter, the awful aggression had spilled over into the schoolyard, having an impact upon students and teachers. I was relieved it wasn't directed towards me, but still frightened that he may try to get in!

IDENTIFYING OPENLY AGGRESSIVE PARENTS

- » They may contact you more regularly than is justified
- » They are quick to pass blame onto the school and teachers
- » They NEVER admit fault or apologise when in the wrong
- » They are often under a great deal of stress and are incapable of handling it healthily
- » You may witness them verbally abusing their children by making threats, swearing at them, calling them stupid etc.

- » You may witness them physically harming their children by smacking, yanking, pinching etc.
- » They may yell at you or get up close and in your face
- » The behaviour is usually intentional
- » They may try to assert dominance over you
- » They may try to threaten or intimidate you
- » They may shout or swear at you

DEALING WITH OPENLY AGGRESSIVE PARENTS

It can be very challenging to react well when someone displays aggression towards us. Depending on our backgrounds we can react in one of three ways - aggressively, submissively or healthily. Before you read further, think of some times when people behaved aggressively towards you. Can you identify how you reacted? I have experienced all three reactions in myself. Originally I would react aggressively, then for many years I'd just go quiet and finally I now react in a healthy way (most of the time!) It's been a long but good emotional journey!

Responding to aggression with aggression:
If this is the way you have commonly reacted it can be challenging to change. A helpful tool for change may be to acknowledge this and make a conscious effort to be aware of acting differently. Self-reflection is your only hope of change.

- You will have zero chance of a positive outcome
- It is unprofessional
- A win/win situation, described earlier as optimal, is impossible
- Will possibly inflame the situation to a dangerous or risky level

Responding to aggression with submission:

- You will have little chance of a positive outcome for yourself
- A win/win outcome is unlikely as submission doesn't allow you to put your needs forward
- Submission may dampen down aggression for the short term or until you have the opportunity to process what just occurred and determine a healthy way forward

Responding to aggression in a healthy manner:

- You have a high chance of a positive outcome
- A win/win outcome is more likely
- It is the most professional response to aggression
- Requires you to remain calm and think quickly on your feet
- Requires you to not react to the emotional triggers the aggression causes (this is hard!)

Suggestions to respond to aggressive behaviour:

- Be conscious of your body stance. Make it as non threatening as possible
- Keep your physical movements calm
- Maintain eye contact
- Listen to what they are saying and make empathetic statements where possible – "I can see you are really upset." "That must be very difficult for you…"
- Avoid any expression of power, such as, "You must calm down." Instead you could say something like, "I am uncomfortable with the tone in which you are speaking to me and I think it's important to try to come to a common understanding and keep the best interests of Xxx in mind"
- Avoid blaming
- Encourage the aggressor to take responsibility for their own behaviour. "Perhaps you could make a formal complaint, or write a letter"
- Maintain self control to avoid escalation of the aggression
- When you have a scheduled meeting with known Openly Aggressive parents, don't do it alone. Enlist the support of leadership. This is important for your own safety and for legal reasons
- If you have been physically threatened, assaulted or traumatised by an Openly Aggressive parent, it is your right to refuse to meet with or contact them again. Sometimes you may need to seek legal advice

> » After an aggressive interaction with a parent you need to have some time to calm down and rest. If you still need to teach for more of the day, ask another teacher or leadership to take over for awhile. If it's at the end of the day, don't leave without debriefing with colleagues and documenting the interaction to the best of your recollection
>
> » Making your phone number or email address available is strongly discouraged
>
> » When calling Aggressive parents, the only message you should leave is for a call-back. Don't leave any details

A colleague shared this experience with me about an Openly Aggressive parent:

"One parent I had was particularly aggressive. She believed that I was neglectful of her son's educational, physical and emotional needs. Most interactions or communication ended in her suggesting she would call the department of education and sue the school. Meetings, in the end, were held with the principal, vice principal, myself and a psychologist from the D.E.E.C.D."

"Maintaining a confident and professional manner was extremely challenging and I needed a lot of support from leadership both to stay sane and also to make sure I was legally covering what I needed to. Acknowledging her concerns and presenting factual evidence of the contrary was the only way forward and it was essential that I was very well prepared for meetings with assessment data, work samples and examples/evidence to back up any suggestions. Such evidence will not make such parents happy but even parents as unhappy as this one, cannot argue with evidence that you are supporting their child. It was also important for me to recognise her unhealthy approach to 'supporting' her child and to acknowledge (to myself) that I was not at fault and that no amount of stress or worry on my part was going to make her happy – some people will never be happy - but it's important to maintain a professional manner and remain focussed on how you wish to conduct yourself."

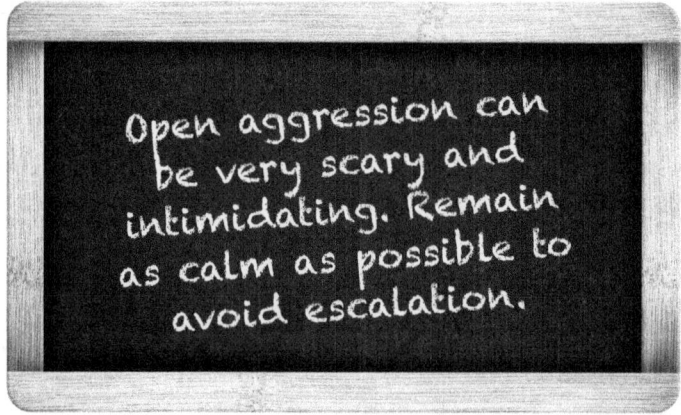

PASSIVE AGGRESSION

Passive aggression is a defence mechanism that allows people who aren't comfortable being openly assertive to get what they want under the guise of still trying to please others. They want to get their way but still have everyone like them. It's an indirect expression of hostility. This may be experienced through procrastination, sarcasm, deliberate and repeated failure to accomplish required tasks or avoidance.

IDENTIFYING PASSIVE AGGRESSIVE PARENTS

It's harder to identify passive aggressive people, as generally, you take people at face value. When people are pleasant to us, we don't usually expect an ulterior motive, especially if we don't know them really well. It may take you a while to figure out who is being passive aggressive.

- » You will think you have settled on an agreement and then the parent does something completely different to what you agreed upon
- » They will be nice to your face or in meetings but you may uncover evidence of nastiness behind your back
- » They may try to play you off against other teachers. For example, slander a previous teacher whilst praising you

DEALING WITH PASSIVE AGGRESSIVE PARENTS

Too often passive aggressive people get away with their behaviour, as it's harder to recognise when it is happening. The first couple of times you can dismiss it as perhaps you don't know them well, or maybe misunderstood or misread. When you are able to recognise passive aggressive behaviour, then it's time to act.

- » Avoid 'tit for tat' behaviour. It's tempting to want to get them back for their passive aggressive behaviour when it directly impacts upon you, however no good will come from this
- » Confront them with facts. For example, if a parent regularly promises to make a meeting time with you to discuss their child, yet repeatedly avoids doing so, it's appropriate to confront them. It's reasonable to speak to them by saying, "I have asked on three separate occasions for you to make a meeting time with me to discuss your child. It's really important that we meet. Is there any reason you are avoiding making a time?" You have avoided emotive statements, you are not making accusations, you have presented them with facts and you are requesting honesty
- » Remember, they want to be-seen-to-be-liked. When you confront passive aggressive behaviour, they will most likely refute it by making excuses, denial or finger pointing. Before you confront, make sure your evidence is clear. Factual evidence cannot be argued with as it's not opinion based
- » Sometimes people are passive aggressive as they don't believe they have a 'voice'. Allow them input. "I'd really like your input. What suggestions do you have to manage the situation?"
- » Formalise all interactions. Do this by writing minutes of meetings and providing a copy for all involved. When actions to be taken are clearly written down, excuse making becomes harder
- » It's not your job to try and change them. They will only change when they mature or become more self-aware
- » Keep your distance where possible. If there's no need to interact with them, don't. Just remain pleasant and professional
- » Set limits. If a parent is constantly late for meeting times, tell them you are only available until a certain time, and then follow through on your limit
- » Don't take it personally. Their passive aggression stems from their own background and life situation and therefore is not your responsibility
- » Show empathy. An empathic response may disarm them. "It seems like you are frustrated by the circumstances. That must be difficult."
- » Keep your boundaries firm. Passive aggressive people seek out people with flimsy boundaries, as their behaviour is most effective with them

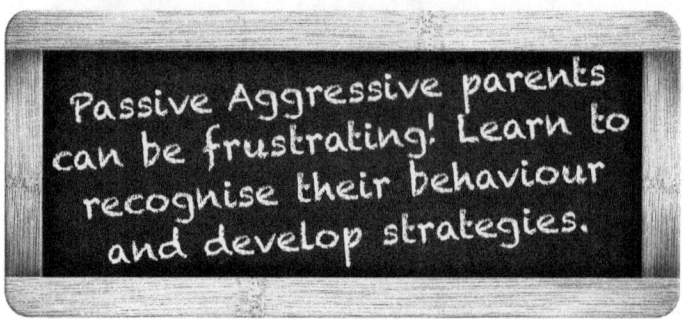

When Parents Contact You

There will be times when a parent wishes to meet with you to discuss a concern they have with either you or their child. The worst thing you can do is be defensive as this makes it seem like you have something to hide. Try to listen to what they have to say before you react. Maintain eye contact, keep your face pleasant and nod when appropriate. A lot of the time their concerns are just misconceptions or miscommunications. Clear these up in a calm and professional manner, even if they have spoken aggressively towards you. A lot of the time parents just want someone to listen to them.

When a parent raises a concern directly about you then it's more important than ever to listen and remain professional (99% of the time they are not strong enough to actually approach you directly, they will go over your head). Repeat back to them what you think their concerns are. This is to establish a shared understanding of the issue and to also help them feel heard. Best practice here would be to suggest another meeting time with your team leader or someone from leadership. That way you have support and time to plan your approach.

In some circumstances you may feel quite shaken when you are questioned or criticised. This is normal. What you need to work hard to avoid is slipping into a negative headspace or to allow their feedback to affect your self-esteem. They do not have the power to diminish or destroy your career; that will only happen if you give them that power. Seek affirmations from your colleagues and try to keep at the forefront of your mind that you are a good teacher and worthwhile human being, doing your best to educate the next generation. It's very important to continue to treat their child respectfully and kindly, as you would all other children in your class. It is not the child's fault they have difficult parents!

BUT!!! This is a brilliant opportunity to self-examine. Does what the parent raised have any validity at all? If you put aside the manner in which they spoke to you, are you left with a hint of truth? It is sometimes hard to admit that this might be the case, however, a mature person striving to be the best teacher they can be will look at how they can grow, change and learn from any feedback. If you don't do this, you will continue to make the same errors and find yourself in similarly uncomfortable situations.

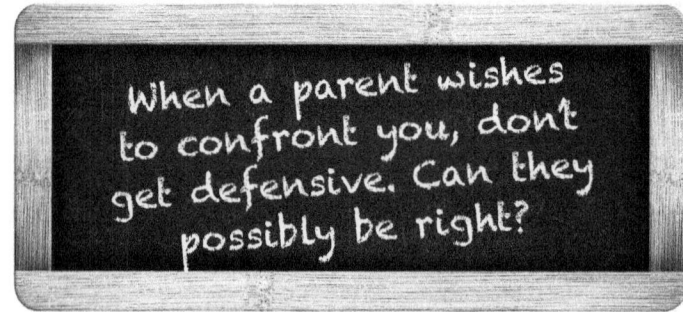

Final Word

Whilst I was an integration aide, I was introduced to the term 'Carpark Mafia.' Once I understood the meaning I realised it was perfectly true. The Carpark Mafia are parents who stand around in the school yard, long after school begins and ends, and gossip. No topic is off limits and one of their main gossip topics is that of the school and teachers. They criticise, slander and seek to uncover as much 'dirt' as possible in order to assert their social position.

When I was a parent in the schoolyard myself I witnessed it occurring often, and, most likely, was drawn into it on occasion myself. A girlfriend described to me once the full on Carpark Mafia at her children's school. She witnessed very nasty negativity directed towards a teacher and, when the ringleader attempted to draw her in, she declined. It was social suicide in the school yard, but really, what was she missing out on? Nasty, small minded and selfish women, fostering a toxic atmosphere. I know the type of people I'd rather hang out with.

When teachers witness the Carpark Mafia (C.M.) in full swing, we like to say that it's time for them to return to work and worry about real problems, rather than go searching for non-existent ones. The C.M. can have a real impact on teachers. Non-factual gossip spreads like wildfire and then parents question teachers on why this or that is happening, when none of it is true. It's frustrating having to devote time to dispelling rumours and myths.

Once I experienced reverse C.M. "I've been asking other parents about you. The reports are good. I'm glad you have my son next year." Umm, what the?

The point to all this is that some parents will gossip, fabricate, promote rumours and slander you and your school. It can be incredibly disheartening, especially when you put so much effort into their children. This sense of deflation is valid, however there's nothing you can do about it and not worth worrying about something you have no control over.

Working Effectively With Colleagues

CHAPTER 16

Chapter Overview

- » Why you should identify personality types of teachers
- » The identification process
- » Identifying and coping with challenging teachers
    - Externalisers
    - Passive Complainers
    - Resisters
    - People Pleasers
    - Pessimists
    - Experts
    - Fence Sitters
- » School politics

The focus in this chapter is on identifying seven personality types of teachers, gives you examples of expected behaviours so you can identify them, and some helpful coping strategies.

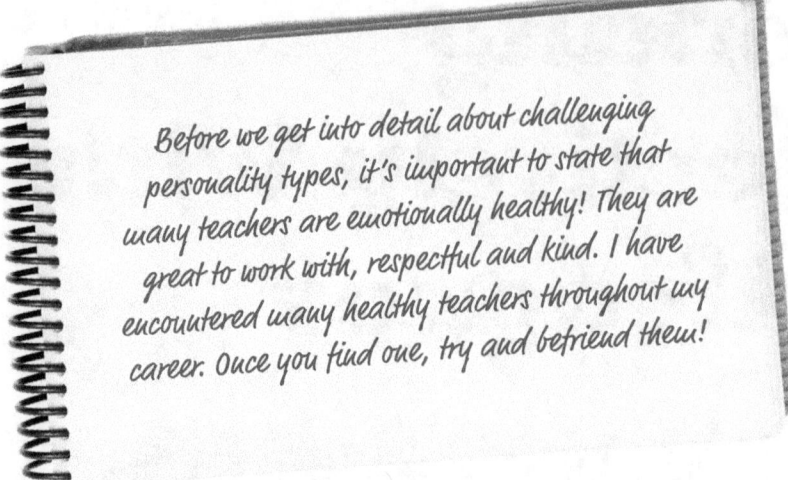

Before we get into detail about challenging personality types, it's important to state that many teachers are emotionally healthy! They are great to work with, respectful and kind. I have encountered many healthy teachers throughout my career. Once you find one, try and befriend them!

Why You Should Identify Personality Types

In all workplaces you will encounter a variety of people from many different backgrounds. Therefore you will encounter a variety of different behaviours from teachers in a school, some helpful, some unhelpful and some, downright difficult. This chapter is intended to help you identify and label the challenging behaviours you will experience in the workplace and to equip you with a healthy response so you are able to continue functioning well. We are not labelling as a form of judgement, but as an explanation of why people might act in a certain way. It helps you work with them positively and also helps them, so you have a mutual way forward.

The difficult behaviours identified are through a combination of my own experience and research. The coping strategies are transferrable to other areas of your work and life - students, parents, friends and even your own family.

The identification process is as important as the coping process. Don't expect a quick fix to your problems, as sometimes it takes quite a bit of practise to identify what behaviour the difficult person is exhibiting that presses your buttons and causes a reaction in you. That process in itself can be a major breakthrough. Spend some time thinking about someone currently annoying you and see if you are able to list what they specifically do or say that ticks you off or stresses you out. There are usually one or two personality types that annoy you more than the others. For me, I struggle to respond appropriately to Externalisers. Their behaviours always tap into some childhood stuff for me, and this is the personality type I have to work hardest at not attacking back and maintaining clear thinking whilst interacting with them.

The chapter on Parents (Chapter 15 – Partnering Positively with Parents) has a large section devoted to establishing and maintaining good relationships. It's really worthwhile reading this now, as all of the guidelines discussed are as relevant with colleagues as they are with parents. Clear communication and win/win outcomes are the main ideas.

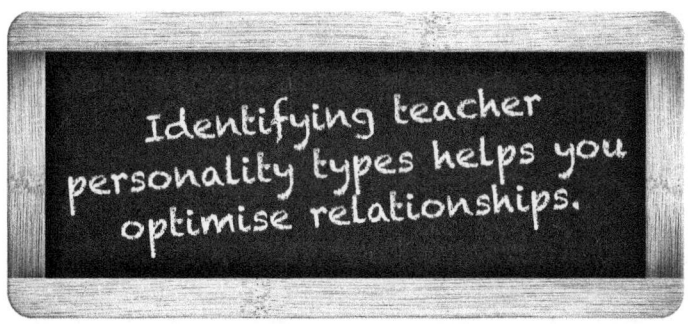

The Identification Process

You are experiencing difficulty with a colleague. What should you do? Jot down what it is about them that is upsetting you or causing you problems. Compare their behaviour to the seven different difficult personality types listed on the following pages. Does their behaviour fall into one or more of the types? No person fits neatly into one category or has ALL of the behaviours listed. Just look for a type that the colleague most fits into.

If you are having problems with a particular teacher (or two), then it's a great opportunity for some self-evaluation. How are you contributing to the problem? Don't kid yourself that you are blameless, relationships are a two way street and you will be making a contribution in some way.

Next, look at the list of possible coping strategies. Are any of them applicable to your situation? Do you think any of the suggestions look plausible for you to implement? If so, match up the solutions to the symptoms you listed and decide what you would like to address first. Don't try and do too much when you begin to make changes to the way you interact with peers. Even making one small change to the way you approach a colleague can be daunting or tricky, so start out with baby steps. Add more changes as you experience some success.

A further suggestion for coping with challenging colleagues is to talk to a sympathetic teacher who knows them too. Be very cautious about who you choose to confide in as you need to be confident they won't gossip with others, will be helpful and is not aligned with the teacher you are experiencing difficulty with. Talking with an experienced teacher can be really beneficial and they may give you insights and suggestions for managing interactions with a specific colleague.

A word of warning here - don't become a gossiper where your aim is just to bitch or moan. When talking about challenging colleagues you should focus on strategies to improve communications, rather than just becoming a difficult person yourself.

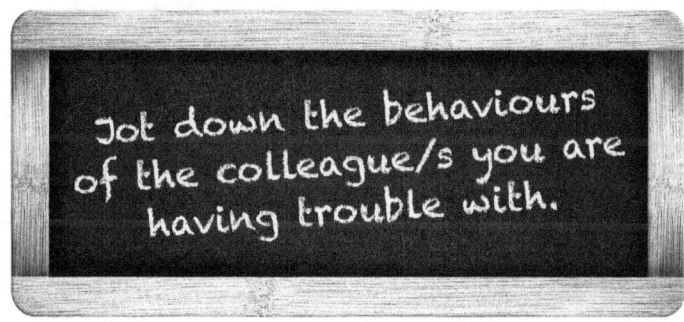

Identifying and Coping with Challenging Personality Types of Teachers

Externalisers

Externalisers are people who can display aggressive behaviours when under pressure. They have strong needs to prove to themselves and others that their view of the world is always right, and the only view. They have a strong sense of what others should do, coupled with forcefulness and confidence. Externalisers often have an arrogant tone and when criticising something you've said or done, they seem to attack not just the particular behaviour but you. They are contemptuous of their victims, considering them inferior people. When they feel threatened, they attack.

Externalisers actively seek the dominant or superior position in any relationship, they abhor submission to anyone they might perceive as being authoritarian, they can be ruthlessly self-advancing, generally at the expense of others and they lack internal brakes. That is, they are going to mow you down when they are attacking. People often feel devastated by an encounter with an Externaliser.

Phew! That list is a little scary, and justifiably so sometimes. As with any personality trait there is a continuum. Some attackers will be more aggressive and forceful than others. It's no surprise then psychopaths and sociopaths are Externalisers. Not that I'm suggesting your colleagues are psychopathic!

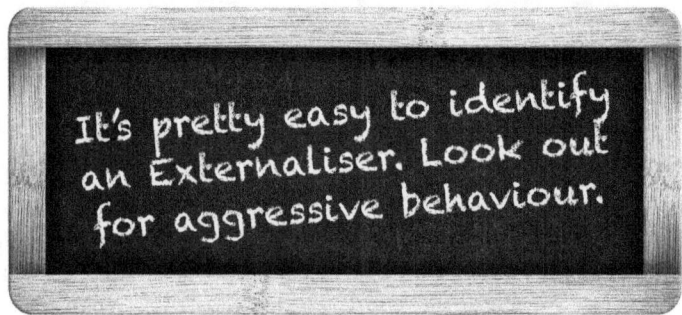

IDENTIFYING EXTERNALISERS

VERBAL CHARACTERISTICS:

- » Put downs
- » Use of threats
- » Boastfulness
- » Opinions expressed as fact
- » Threatening questions
- » Emphasising blaming words
- » Sexual/racist remarks
- » Tone sarcastic, cold or harsh
- » Often shouting, voice can be strident

NON-VERBAL CHARACTERISTICS:

- » Crossing arms
- » Scowling when angry
- » Striding around impatiently
- » Staring the other person out
- » Intruding into personal space
- » Gestures such as pointing and fist clenching

COPING WITH EXTERNALISERS

Your aim is to stand up to Externalisers but not personally defeat them. It requires you to avoid an open confrontation with them over who is right. They may resort to nasty tactics to prove themselves in the right and you will only end up hurt or damaged. Some of the following suggestions will be helpful when faced with an Externaliser.

- Stand up to them. If you don't, you will feel overrun and give them license to repeatedly behave aggressively towards you. The last thing you possibly want to do is stand up to them, however it's really important you do so

- Separate the person from the issue. "I want to talk with you about what's on your mind, but I can't whilst you are yelling." Statements such as these help to establish yourself as a good problem solver. It's also beneficial because it lets the attacker know they are yelling (sometimes they don't realise) and states your acceptable conditions for communication

- Put the spotlight back onto them. Their focus is typically on you, rather than the issue. The easiest way to address this is to ask questions. "If you continue to treat me with disrespect I'm not going to talk with you anymore. Is that what you want?" "Have you given clear thought to what you actually want to do?"

- Recognise that feeling fear and confusion, as a response to being attacked, is normal

- Give them time to run down. They will run out of steam eventually. This is then a good time to jump in

- It may be necessary to interrupt in order to stand up to them. Do this only after you've given them 'air time'. If they interrupt you, firmly tell them they are interrupting you and continue talking. Repeat as necessary

- Try to get them in a seated position. Most people behave less aggressively whilst seated

- Only speak from your point of view. Use lots of 'I' statements

- Talk about how you feel. This cannot be debated. It may allow some aggressive people to realise how their behaviour is impacting others. Some will fail to understand their impact, however

- Avoid a head on fight. Don't fight aggression with aggression. If you are not naturally an Externaliser personality you will have no chance of a reasonable outcome as this type of behaviour is not your natural reaction and you are not as experienced at attacking type behaviour. If you are an Externaliser personality, and you choose to employ this behaviour with another Externaliser, it will end in tears

- Some Externalisers, when stood up to, but not defeated, may make friendly moves towards you. This perhaps happens as they see you in a different light and might respect you a little more

- Standing up to Externalisers can be a daunting prospect. It's worthwhile practising some statements beforehand

- Pick your battles. If you have very little to do with this staff member on an ongoing basis, might be best to just avoid them

- Try to put yourself in their shoes for a moment. Internalised statements such as "It must not be easy to deal with her difficult students," or "It must not be easy to work for such a demanding boss," help you to empathise. It does not excuse their unacceptable behaviour, but helps you to understand that their behaviour is due to their own issues.

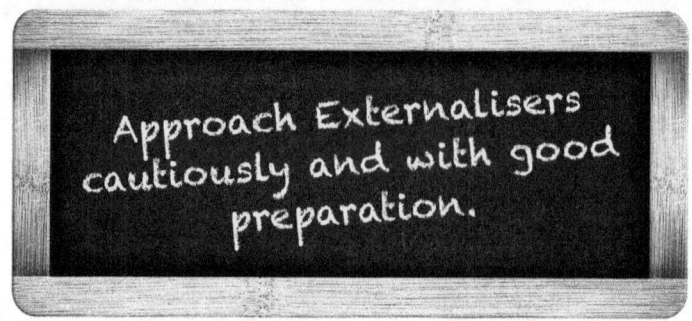

Passive Complainers

Passive Complainers are those people who manage to find fault with everything. They have a negative outlook on life and find it difficult to find any positives. The disguised message behind all the whining is that YOU should be doing something about them. You find yourself automatically placating them or becoming defensive, even if you've done nothing wrong! These types of people can be exhausting to be around.

IDENTIFYING PASSIVE COMPLAINERS

- » Don't often realise they are chronic complainers
- » When you point out they are chronic complainers you are met with an assurance that the problem is real
- » Often sit down - they are keen to have all their complaints heard
- » Feel powerless in the management of their own lives
- » Attribute things that go well to good luck
- » Persist in their behaviour as it keeps them looking blameless and perfect, at least to themselves
- » Gain validation for themselves twice. They have brought an issue to your attention, so therefore it's now your responsibility to deal with it and they become self-righteously angry at you for not doing your job
- » Are hard to ignore
- » Get attention, but seldom action
- » May appear patronising or impatient
- » Aren't looking for solutions. They just want someone to validate their hurt, anger or confusion

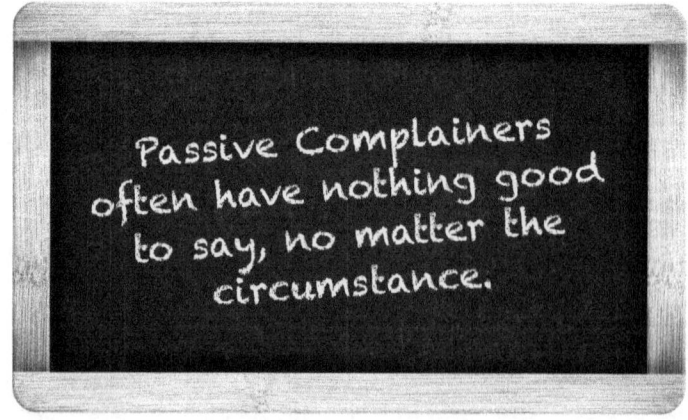

COPING WITH PASSIVE COMPLAINERS

» Recognise that you cannot change their feelings. Until they develop some stronger internal strength they are trapped in their whining misery

» Set firm, clear limits on how long you will listen or how you will help them. "I know this is really bothering you, unfortunately I cannot sit and talk with you any longer. I have to get back to work."

» To break the cycle of complaining, at first you must listen attentively. This is a necessary first step. It provides them the opportunity to let off steam, it can lessen the experience of being 'dismissed' which increases feelings of powerlessness, and it allows you to gather enough information for the next coping step

» Acknowledge what they have said by paraphrasing back

» To acknowledge you may have to interrupt

» Passive Complainers love words like **always** and **never**. Attempt to pin down specifics, which usually dispels the 'always' theory

» Don't agree with their complaints about you. Acknowledging conveys understanding, however agreement confirms to the Passive Complainer that you are responsible. It may dissipate the complaining but it does not lead to problem solving

» If the complaining is directed at you, don't accuse back as a defence

» Pose specific problem solving questions to them. "Are there times when the problem doesn't occur?" "What specific things tell you it is getting worse?"

» Expect some frustration. They aren't used to problem solving and want either air time or you to solve it

» If all else fails, and you have tried all the above tricks, try commenting on the interaction. "By the end of recess, where do you want this discussion to have gone?" It might help find a resolution quicker and also help them to recognise their long-winded road to a solution.

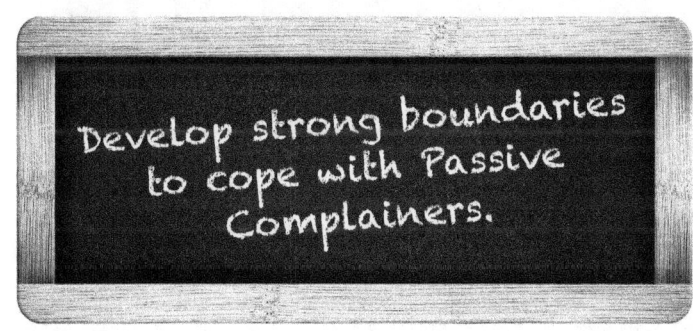

Develop strong boundaries to cope with Passive Complainers.

Resisters

Resisters refuse to communicate or cooperate. They are often silent and unresponsive at the times when you need a response. Their main purpose is to escape accountability and to avoid revealing embarrassing information. In a school setting you may encounter them when you need backing up on an issue to other staff or leadership; instead you find yourself hopelessly alone.

Resisters remove themselves mentally from any conflict by retreating into themselves. They think they are being neutral, when in fact they are conveying a powerful message that speaks of disapproval and smugness.

As a new graduate, it is unlikely your superiors will be Resisters. Perhaps you will only encounter them in other teaching staff and you can only guess what their motivation is about.

IDENTIFYING RESISTERS

- » Eye rolling
- » Most typically are men
- » May offer monosyllabic responses such as "Yep," "Nah," or "Whatever"
- » Having to make decisions with Resisters can be maddening
- » Not to be confused with the quiet person
- » Refuse to give you a response or decision when you are specifically searching for one
- » It can be difficult for you to understand what the silence is about.

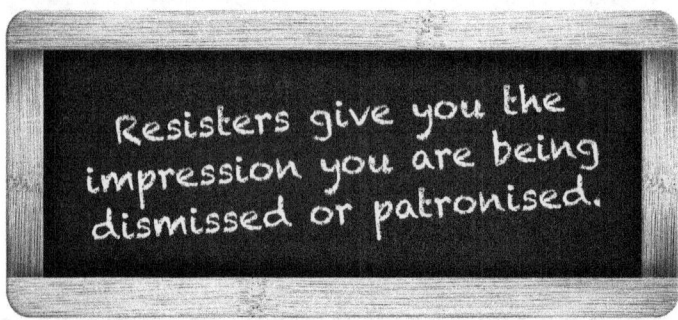

Resisters give you the impression you are being dismissed or patronised.

COPING WITH RESISTERS

They only way to manage Resisters is to attempt to get them to talk. No easy task if they are refusing!

- » Ask open-ended questions. "What is your response to what I have outlined so far?"
- » If you get the "I don't know" answer repetitively, try asking "and what else?"
- » Provide space. Silence works wonders. Ask an open ended question and then just wait. It's natural for people to want to fill it. Even if you ask a simple question that requires a little more than a yes or no response, it is still reasonable to allow a period of time for them to answer. The longer it goes on, or the more you do it, the more uncomfortable it makes them feel so they are more likely to respond
- » Employ the friendly stare! Whilst you are waiting for a response, look at their face with a non-threatening look on your face. Maintain this past your own feeling of discomfort. It lets the Resister know you are expecting a response

» Keep quiet. It's really tempting to jump in and fill silences. This only serves to keep the Resister quiet

» Bring it out into the open. You've done all of the above and got no response. So say, " I'm expecting a response to my question and you're not saying anything. What does that mean?" Either they will request you ask the question again, or respond

People Pleasers

A People Pleaser is one of the nicest and most helpful people you can know. They never say no! You can always count on them to help you out and usually can get both their own and your work done. Their need to constantly please others is rooted in either fear of failure or fear of rejection. It's easy for others to take advantage of super agreeable people and this in turn creates negative consequences for them if they are unable to manage their behaviour.

People Pleasers always tell you things that are gratifying to hear. So intense is their need to not be the source of irritation to anyone that they go to great lengths to please everyone around them, usually at their own detriment.

IDENTIFYING PEOPLE PLEASERS

This is tricky! It will probably take you quite awhile to identify a People Pleaser.

» Agree with your point of view always

» Agree with your suggestions and lesson plans always

» May agree with you to your face and then quietly do their own thing

» If you ask their opinion will most likely be non committal, unless someone has already stated their position, in which case they will agree with that

» May rebuff genuine compliments

» Will be quite skilled in avoiding giving you their opinion, especially if they are the first one to be asked

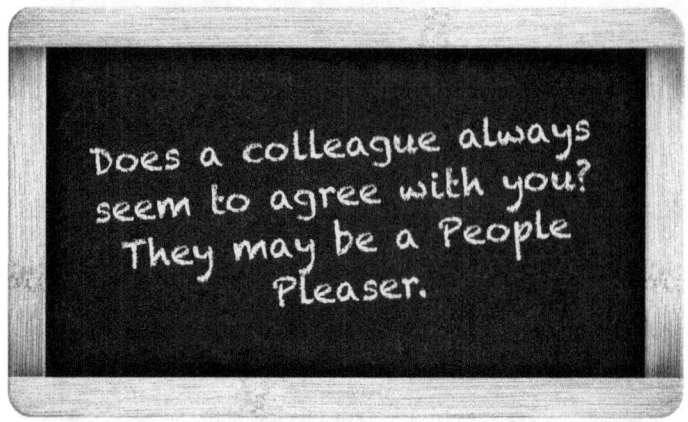

COPING WITH PEOPLE PLEASERS

There's not much to cope with here! If you wish to be a kind and respectful colleague and teacher, then perhaps you should aim to not take advantage of People Pleasers. Their need is so strong to avoid anger and frustration that they will say yes or agree with everything you suggest. This can be quite gratifying at first, and on the surface easy to work with, but it can create an unhealthy working environment. We all need to hear occasionally that our idea is stupid or destined for failure. It keeps us level.

I dated two People Pleasers many years ago. At first it was GREAT! They'd do anything I said! Go anywhere I suggested! Buy anything I wanted! BUT.... my respect for them eventually wore off as they were unable to tell me what they wanted and the relationship felt very biased towards my needs and not mutual.

- » Encourage them to speak up where possible
- » Don't overload them with work or take advantage of them
- » Ask their opinion first before other opinions have been made known
- » Display lots of patience

Pessimists

Doom and gloom! Everything will fail. Pessimists can have a profoundly detrimental effect on the workplace. They potentially impact us all as their behaviour and mood can tap into our own negative side. Pessimists are constantly negative and never look happy. It's really important to be able to identify a Pessimist in the workplace (or in your personal life) to avoid them having a negative impact on your mindset.

Pessimism is the often sub-conscious belief that undesirable outcomes are inevitable and that hardships and setbacks outweigh the positives in life. Gee, I feel a bit sorry for people with this outlook on life. It's a hard life to live.

As a new graduate it is really, really important to be able to identify a Pessimist quickly. Unfortunately, they often seek out newbies to offload their negativity onto. You're new, trying to be polite to everyone and less likely to tell them to rack off. It's very important that you pay no attention to negative people when you are starting out. Try to surround yourself with positive and kind teachers. You do not want to be drawn into the fold of the Pessimists and tainted by their negativity.

IDENTIFYING PESSIMISTS

- Generally they are not intentionally being obstructionist
- See obstacles as insurmountable
- Have little power in their own lives
- Will become irritated with you if you persist in attempting to solve a problem
- Love to trash talk any new initiatives or changes
- Constantly find things to complain about - the amount of yard duty required, a change to the roll taking system, their students, their parents, their furniture...
- Seek out newcomers to indoctrinate with their pessimism
- Will try to get you to say negative things about any situation they are stirring the pot about
- Usually unhappy
- Fail to thank others or show gratefulness
- Regularly feel others have wronged them
- Often hold grudges and have difficulty letting things go
- Fear change

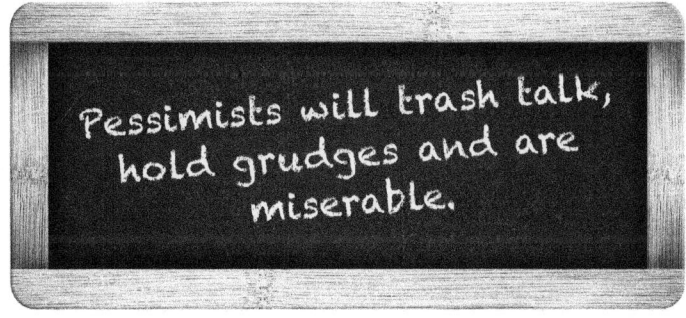

The Essential Teacher's Guide

COPING WITH PESSIMISTS

- » Avoid befriending them
- » If possible, avoid them. This is hard to do if they are in your team or on leadership. If you are aware that hanging around negative people can have the tendency to bring you down a little, avoid spending time with them. I have to be conscious of this as it's easy for negative people to taint me with their pessimism
- » When you have a fresh new idea or approach, share it with like-minded people first for feedback
- » Acknowledge their point of view by using active listening skills
- » Keep an open mind and try to be objective about what they say
- » If you think a negative comment lacks foundation, bring it to their attention
- » Question their statements, "The Principal will never approve that idea." Ask them to explain why and what you or the team can do to avoid this problem
- » Flip their statements around. "You've given me some good reasons why this excursion isn't a good idea, now give me some reasons why it IS a good idea."
- » Many pessimists say, "I can't." Ask them to tell you what they CAN do
- » Resist the desire to make the Pessimist's day sunnier. A Pessimist doesn't want to take on your optimism
- » Stay positive. Look for some good in everything and remind yourself that everyone can find flaws in any idea or plan if they look closely enough. Nothing is 100% perfect
- » Look for the Pessimist's good qualities. Everybody has something good!

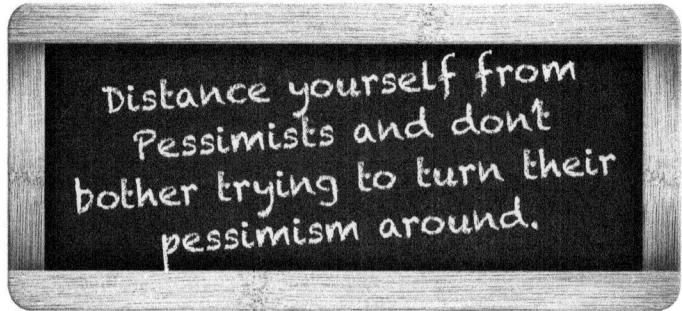

Distance yourself from Pessimists and don't bother trying to turn their pessimism around.

Experts

Experts convey a belief in their own superiority that often leaves teachers feeling humiliated, immobilised and helplessly angry. They communicate with others as if they know everything there is to know. Sometimes they do know a lot, however they feel the need to bash you with their superior knowledge, even if they actually know nothing about a topic. Frustratingly, presenting an Expert with concrete evidence is not enough to dissuade their attitude. I have regularly heard, "The rules must've just changed!" Experts are not to be confused with teachers who are accomplished and knowledgeable. They are gracious and kind in sharing knowledge and assistance.

IDENTIFYING EXPERTS

- When speaking they use a tone of absolute certainty that often, without conscious intent, leaves others feeling like objects of condescension
- They can often turn out to be right, sometimes leaving you feeling inept or stupid
- They leave little room for other's creativity or judgements
- When they come up with a plan it's virtually impossible to dissuade them
- If things go wrong it's not their fault; it's the fault of the incompetents, namely you!
- Always looking to pass the blame
- You will be left with a feeling of never being listened to. This is because an Expert doesn't need to listen to anyone else. They know-it-all!
- They are often swift or fast talkers, able to dump multiple facts on you if you question them
- Operate with the idea that if you speak with enough authority you know what you are talking about
- It's very difficult to win an argument with Experts
- They can tend to monopolise conversations and make decisions without all the facts to hand
- They speak more than listen
- Are often close minded
- Their behaviour can be construed as bullying

COPING WITH EXPERTS

The main coping strategy with Experts is to get them to consider alternative ideas whilst carefully avoiding direct challenges to their expertise. Otherwise, they will see your challenge as a personal attack on them.

- Pick your battle. Can you let it go?
- Don't take it personally. Their attitude often implies they are right and you are wrong. Comfort yourself knowing they didn't single out you - they do it to everyone
- If you decide to challenge them you MUST be prepared. Research and plan with back up material and be able to present your facts in an orderly and unemotional way. You will be dismissed if you fail on this point
- Question Experts firmly but don't confront. Use a questioning format rather than a statement format. For example, "I'm having a little difficulty seeing how changing bell times so that recess and lunch times are the same length benefits teachers. Can you explain that to me?"
- Ask questions that extend a concept. "How will that look in practice?" Or, "Can you tell me how you envisage that program looking in a year from now?"

- » You can always work wonders if you can make an Expert convinced that your fabulous idea is their fabulous idea
- » Flatter them. Experts thrive on self-importance. "I have an idea I'd like your opinion on..." whether you really want their opinion or not
- » Avoid being a counter expert. You'll probably end up engaged in a futile struggle. Be the bigger person by being aware of their personality and strategising around it
- » Avoid Experts if possible. They are pretty grating

Preparation is key to dealing with Experts.

Fence Sitters

A Fence Sitter is someone who is annoyingly indecisive. You know, when you get to the end of a conversation and you still have no idea of the plan? This can be quite frustrating when you are needing to know the lesson plan or a firm decision needs to be made that effects you. When you depend on others to make decisions it is maddening when they cannot make up their minds. As a new graduate you are frequently at the mercy of decision makers, until you gain enough confidence and experience (or authority), to make more decisions yourself.

IDENTIFYING FENCE SITTERS

- » They are often very nice people, striving to avoid disappointing anyone, thus avoid making polarising decisions by sitting on the fence
- » They are not actually interested in making a decision
- » They frequently have high standards and find making a decision that may compromise these standards difficult
- » Cannot make rapid decisions or respond quickly when a dilemma arises
- » Are accomplished at fobbing you off, in order to avoid decision making
- » Respond to questions that need decisive action with, "I don't know", "Maybe", "I'll think about it", "I'll decide later." These statements all avoid inflicting direct distress on anyone and also stalls for time
- » They are pretty masterful at indirect communication, using hints and vague allusions, leaving you confused
- » Fence Sitters often don't get ideas or projects off the ground
- » In meetings and communication, a Fence Sitter is non-committal about any new initiative, often considering pros and cons in great depth

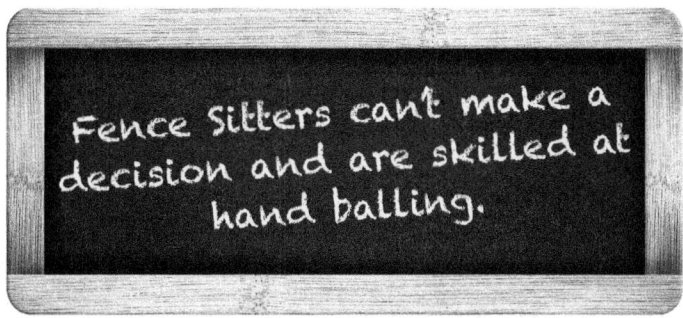

COPING WITH FENCE SITTERS

- » Don't count on them eventually being able to make a decision
- » Try and determine why they are sitting on the fence. Is it an ongoing character trait or appears every now and then? Is it when high risk or ground breaking decisions need to be made? Is it with particular people?
- » Be clear that you need a decision. "I'm teaching Maths today at 11am and I need the lesson plan you said you'd provide. When can I expect it by?"
- » Start to wise up to their stalling techniques and get in early. "As I need to get resources ready for the Maths lesson you are providing, and I have yard duty and a parent meeting, I'd like the plan by 5pm today so I can prepare early tomorrow morning."
- » Help them to make decisions - sift through the road blocks they will spout to avoid disappointing anyone and be specific. "I'm not sure I'm clear on what you have decided. Can I take my class to the local shops, yes or no?"
- » Put things in writing after a decision is made, just to confirm and remind the Fence Sitter that a decision has been made
- » Split the decision if possible. "How about I plan Maths and you plan Reading?"
- » Try not to rely on them
- » Have a back up plan ready if they fail to make a decision that effects you
- » Limit the options to narrow the frame of decision-making

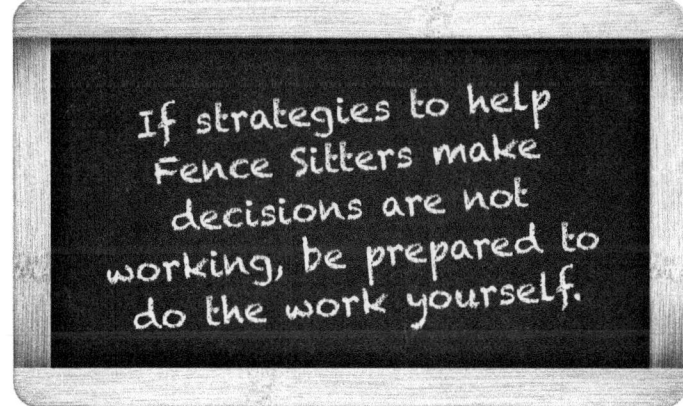

School Politics

When you are a new graduate you are beginning work in an established working environment where some staff have worked for many years. There will be allegiances and alliances that you unknowingly step into. Some will be welcoming and some not. Your first term or two you need to focus on your own teaching and classroom management, whilst avoiding getting involved in any politics.

An unkind teacher once specifically went out of their way to speak to two new graduates, not in their team, to warn them against the other teachers in their level. The purpose was to try and get them aligned with them and turn them against members in their own team. It put these new grads in a tricky situation. Wisely they chose to wait before making up their own minds about the teachers they worked with. It's sad that people feel the need to behave so immaturely. Outwardly it looked like they were being 'helpful and kind' by warning, but what they were really doing was trying to meet their own needs.

In staff meetings and the staffroom it's wise to keep your cards close to your chest in the beginning terms. By all means ask questions, but avoid putting your opinion forward, especially when you haven't been specifically asked. This is recommended to allow staff to get to know you, judging you on your classroom teaching and behaviour management, as opposed to your opinions and views. You have no idea the background to some decisions made prior to your appointment and not enough information to form a considered opinion on lots of topics. A new staff member I know loved a particular teacher and kept raving about them in the staff room, whilst having no idea that leadership had been trying to get rid of them for years for incompetence. You can end up looking a little silly when you don't know all the facts.

The chain of command is not always clear in schools, and can differ between schools too. Ask your mentor or team leader for guidance about who to approach for different things to avoid stepping on toes.

One thing that may surprise you is the way teachers talk with each other about students. I remember being shocked on rounds to hear teachers talk about kids in a negative way and vowed to not do it myself. Hmmmm, that vow didn't last long. We really do love children and have their best interests at heart, but teachers love to let off steam about those kids or parents who are pressing our buttons. Just check who is around before you decide to do it. Parents are everywhere...

Final Word

Now that I have scared you with all this negativity about your new teaching colleagues, let me assure you there are many fabulous people in the teaching world. You'll meet great people with similar ideology who could easily become life long friends. Share your ideas and resources with each other, whilst bouncing ideas off them too.

Use this page to document the characteristics of teachers you find challenging and list ways to improve outcomes.

Homework

Chapter Overview

- School policies
- How to deal with parent complaints
- What to set
- What not to set
- Managing homework

School Policies

Arrrghhhh! Homework. We hated doing it at school and now we have to set it AND mark it AND chase it up. If you are lucky enough to teach at a school with a no-homework policy, then big high fives to you! You can sit back smugly whilst your friends at other schools moan about it.

School homework policies differ wildly and some schools seem to set unrealistic amounts. Personally, I think it is unnecessary for primary school children, apart from regular home reading, as children are often wasting their time practising known knowledge or ploughing through work without the appropriate support. If you teach at a school that endorses homework, like I do, then you just gotta do it. Hopefully if you work in a great team you can share the burden of setting it. Just make sure you know the expectations of the level or the team.

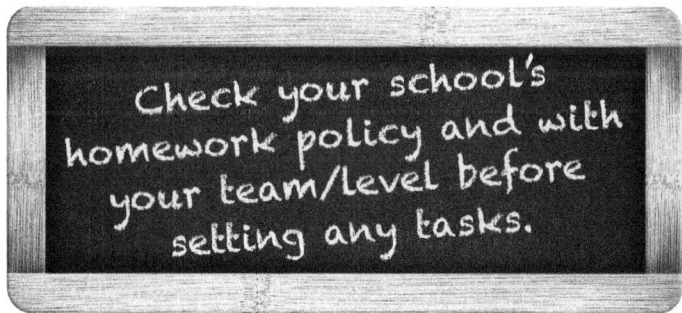

Check your school's homework policy and with your team/level before setting any tasks.

How To Deal With Parent Complaints

You will NEVER please parents with homework. If you set the same amount or task week after week, some parents will complain it's too much, whilst some will complain it's not enough. Some will complain about the type of homework. Some will complain it requires too much of the parent.

If a parent wishes to talk to you about homework, set a time to meet with them. If it's possible, ask them to come in to meet, rather than handle it via email or phone. Email is a very bad idea. Never do this! The phone is suitable if they cannot make it during school hours.

Any amount or type of homework should be able to be justified with a purpose. If you can first explain the purpose behind the set task then this might be enough for the parents to realise the intention with which it was assigned. They often don't have the full picture or understand how homework fits into the program. Prior to the meeting, make sure you have a notepad and paper to take notes. This is for two reasons. It will help you remember later on and it also helps the parents think you are listening and responding. Start off by asking them what their concerns are. Then empathise by feeding back to them what they just said. "I'm sorry to hear Xxx is finding the homework too time consuming. I'm glad you have made me aware of your concerns." The next step is to ask them what they think is a realistic expectation/solution and jot down their thoughts. Here is the tricky part. Don't promise anything at the meeting unless you think it is really doable. This is the point where you say that you will think about it for a couple of days, talk to leadership or colleagues and then phone them back with a response. Give them a day you will call and make sure you write it down AND make sure you call them. Did you notice I used the word response? That was very purposeful. Saying you will call with a solution can cause you further problems as your idea of a solution may be very different to theirs. For example, if they want their child to have no homework and the school's policy is children must do it, then you can't agree to that. They have opted to send their child to a school WITH a homework policy so they can't realistically expect their child to have none.

When you have come up with what you feel is a suitable outcome you can call the parent. On your notepad make sure you have the most important points you want to convey. This is why it works best in a phone call - you have had time to think about a response, you don't have to have another meeting (that can drag on) and you can refer unselfconsciously to your notes. Before you ring, make a clear decision about what you expect the outcome to be. Ensure that if challenged, you know that leadership will back up your position. (See Chapter 15 on Partnering Positively with Parents for more information on how best to cope with different parent types).

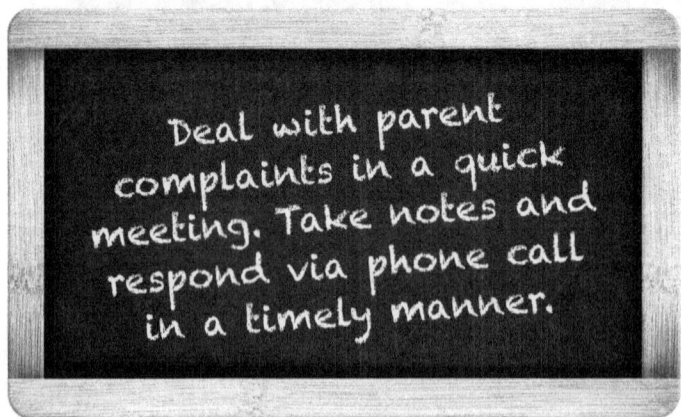

Deal with parent complaints in a quick meeting. Take notes and respond via phone call in a timely manner.

What To Set

I'm always astounded to see what homework my friend's kids are assigned. There are a lot of lazy teachers out there! Meaningless tasks don't benefit anyone. Allowing for guidance from your team/school, this is a healthy homework policy:

- Homework should consolidate concepts learned in class
- Junior classes should have daily reading or learning sight words
- Middle classes should have daily reading, learning multiplication tables and another small task
- Homework should be given out once a week and handed in the following week. i.e., a full seven days. (Some schools require a higher frequency than this. Unless directed by authority, keep homework tasks to once a week, apart from reading)
- Senior classes should have daily reading, learning multiplication tables and another task or two of greater depth

TASK IDEAS:

- Interviewing and recording data
- Basic investigations
- Using graphic organisers
- Using recipes
- Creative/artistic tasks
- Outdoor activities
- Basic research
- Mind mapping
- Sourcing examples
- Measuring in real life
- Philanthropy

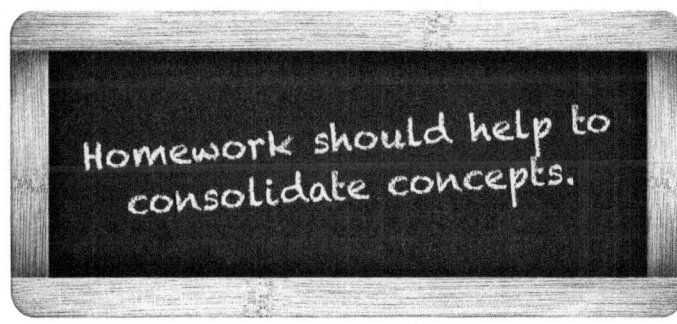

The Essential Teacher's Guide

What Not To Set

» Sheets of maths equations should NEVER be given. Why? Quite often children need concrete materials or copious amounts of modelling and repetition in class. If they haven't consolidated the concept then there's a big probability that parents will teach their child the wrong process or strategy. Approaches to teaching Mathematics develop and change over the decades and you can guarantee the process parents were taught is different from the way we teach their children nowadays. When children are confused at home then it makes sense that their parents will assist and teach them the way they were taught and confuse the child even more. Everyone thinks the way they were taught to do formal algorithms is the 'right' or 'best' way. If you take no other advice from this chapter, please, please take this advice. Don't send home Mathematics worksheets full of algorithms!

» Anything that requires too much parent participation

» Mindless busy work

» Sheets

» The same thing week after week

» Anything that requires too much time consuming marking

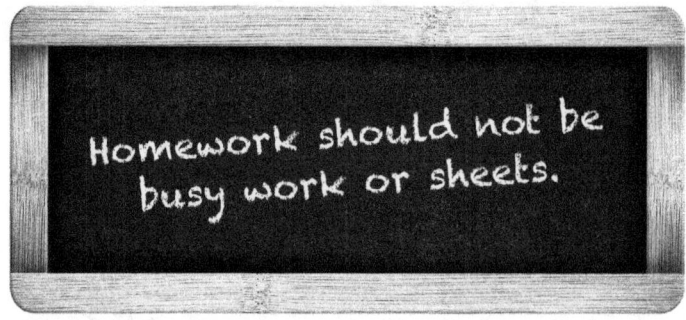

Managing Homework

Middle/Senior

Pick a permanent day that homework is handed out and due. Due in on a Wednesday is good as it gives you a couple of days earlier in the week to remind children. Handing out new homework on a Thursday gives you twenty-four hours to mark the previous week's tasks.

If you choose to hand out paper copies of homework then add to the booklist for the year a dedicated take home book or folder. An A4 spiral bound book works well, or an A4 display folder with clear pages, is good too. Ask children to paste or slip in that week's homework in the book (after you have explained it) and then put it straight into their bags.

Alternatively, you can manage homework digitally. There are a few ways to do this, depending on the software and apps available to both you and your students. One option is to prepare the homework and save it as a pdf. Place it in Dropbox in a dedicated Homework folder. Children can access the task/s at home on a tablet or personal computer. Using an iPad, the student would open the pdf in Goodreader and annotate it. It can then be either emailed to you directly (with the task named in the subject line) or saved into an Evernote (or similar app) Homework Folder. Check that families have computer or Internet access at home and if not, provide a paper copy and comparable activity.

It's important to keep track of homework completion. Prepare a template consisting of a table with each student's name in your class down the left hand side. Across the top will be due dates. Mark a Y for Yes, N for No or L for Late. Keep on top of your marking and give feedback. This type of documentation is excellent come reporting time.

Offer incentives to encourage the regular completion of homework. The type of reward depends on whichever system you choose to run in your class for reward. House points, free time minutes, points towards an activity or game etc. I use free time minutes - ten minutes extra personal free time on a Friday if you hand it in the same week, five-ten minutes if you do an exceptional effort, and subtract ten minutes for late or non completion. Never accept late excuses, as you have no way of knowing if the child has actually done the homework or is pulling your leg. Definitely chase up the late homework though! Children need to learn accountability, responsibility and time management. Regular homework completion does encourage this.

Always follow up when a child doesn't do their homework. I have a cheeky folder on display on a shelf or window ledge to encourage children not to forget. The front cover states, in large and bold font, "I'm sorry Nadine, I didn't do my homework. It won't happen again." Inside this folder there is a plastic pocket for each child, containing a template to include their name at the top, the date and room for them to take ownership about their homework. (See Templates in Chapter 26). Children must write the reason why they didn't do their homework. I never accept a lack of time as a reason. In seven days, everyone has time. I will then put in a quick call to their parent to inform them of the situation. This is done for a few reasons - often parents don't know their child has homework, let alone not doing it, they may be surprised at the reason their child gave for not doing the work, it encourages parents to take a more active role in their child's learning and there will be no surprises for parents come interview time. Having a piece of paper with the child's handwriting and reason is quite powerful viewing for parents.

Another system you might like to trial is to allow one 'grace' per term, where homework doesn't have to be returned (they may have forgotten to bring it back or been extra busy that week). However, once a 'grace' is used, that's it for excuses for the term. They will then need to complete their homework either during free time or Friday lunchtime homework club. If students haven't used their grace by the last week of term then they have a homework free week. This system works really well - the conscientious kids who have genuinely forgotten to hand it in for a week can cope without a complete meltdown that they've forgotten their homework (they never forget twice) and kids who have to go to homework club go more willingly because they recognise they have already been given a chance. If children hand in their homework each week then they can look forward to a reward at the end of term - no homework for the week!

If you are using homework books, provide a large labelled tub or box for children to place their completed homework in. They should have access to this anytime throughout the week. Doing a little bit of marking everyday helps to ease your burden so grab them out daily. Sometimes it only takes a few minutes to mark whilst children are working independently.

Besides the task you set each week, children should be doing daily reading for extended periods. At home, it doesn't matter what they read, as long as they are reading. Prepare a reading log template (or see Chapter 26, Templates) that allows students to record the date, the book, the amount of time they read for and a space for parents to sign. This can either be pasted into the rear of their homework book or saved digitally in Dropbox. Children then open it in Goodreader, enter their daily data, parents sign, then they email to you or you can view it on their iPad. It's a good idea to keep track of who does and doesn't hand in their log each week. Follow up those kids who don't and, if necessary, speak to parents.

If you have children in your class with special needs you will need to adjust homework tasks for them. They should still be required to complete homework, however the tasks can be formed in conjunction with the integration aide (if there is one) or taken from their Learning Plan. Be aware of children in your class who don't have funding, yet will still need adjustments to homework tasks. It's up to you whether you talk to parents or not about the differences - some will be pleased whilst others may be in denial that their child requires adjustment. Tread carefully! Sometimes it is best to wait until either a parent speaks to you about their child's difficulties, or it becomes apparent to you the student is not coping.

In my experience, parents really appreciate being updated about their children and are usually more than willing to step up. Occasionally this isn't the case. Recently I taught a student who comes from quite an unorthodox background. His mother rang to inform me that she doesn't agree with homework for primary school children and her son is not to do it. Of course, her son was the type to quite benefit from regular routine and time management practise. Predictably, he returned to class the next day gloating to his friends that he didn't have to do homework anymore. His friends were agog and plotting how to get out of homework themselves. I nipped it in the bud quickly by proclaiming that he still had to do homework, just during the class free time period. That took the gloat right out of him! To his credit, each week he completed his homework before embarking on free time.

Junior

For junior students, add to the booklist a reading folder. This can be either a foolscap size zipped plastic case or document wallet. Middle students may still require this type of homework transport case.

Take home readers: There are a couple of systems that you can trial and select the one you find most beneficial.

> » Send home ONE reader with the children EVERY night and swap the next day.
>
> » The children swap TWO readers ONCE a week. The second system may minimise the time taken out of the day to day classroom program and hopefully allow children to develop deeper comprehension, success and fluency in their reading at home.

In the reading folder you can send home:

> » A laminated cursive name sheet for the children to practise writing their name and forming their letter correctly using a whiteboard marker
>
> » A reading log sheet parents sign after they have heard them read (see Junior Reading Log in Templates chapter)
>
> » Take home reading information for parents –one book each night or two books per week (see Reading at Home With Your Child in Templates chapter)

Another homework reading option is for students to use a subscription reading app such as P.M. (Nelson) ecollection. This provides all students with a user name and password and allows access to Levelled eBooks. Teachers manage and select appropriate levels for individual accounts/students. This is utilised in classrooms with school iPads and for students who B.Y.O.D. (bring your own device). It's also accessible at home on a family iPad.

N.B. this is just an addition to the take home reading program, not the core element by any means. This is the website if you'd like to check it out further: https://cengage.com.au/pmecollection.

A colleague, very experienced in the junior school, has had many parents over the years ask for more readers. If they want more, suggest borrowing books together from the library, reading shopping lists or playing board games. She has also had parents justify why they don't read with their child every night. Let the parent know it's okay to skip every now and then, as it's their job to determine what is too much or too little for their child.

About half way through the year, or a bit before (depending on the students), send home sight word check lists for the children to practise reading/writing with their families. An excellent sight word list to use is the Oxford H.F.W. lists: 16 most common, 24 most common, 68 most common, 100 most common.

Finally, if your school subscribes to Mathletics, students have access to this at home- this is not set homework, only if families/students choose to utilise it. You will need to send home their usernames and passwords.

Displays

Chapter Overview

- » Personalising your space
- » Using anchor charts
- » Creating posters with your class
- » Create areas within the classroom for specific purposes

Personalising Your Space

Ahhhhh, displays. You either love to create them or shudder at the thought. Luckily we are beyond the days where student teachers were marked on their chalkboard displays. That would be incredibly stressful for me as I'm a pretty lame drawer. And, frankly, I have better things to spend my time on at work that actually directly benefits children. However, some displays and anchor charts are essential and stimulating for students. A classroom needs to be warm and inviting, with an encouraging learning environment. Displays help provide this atmosphere.

At the beginning of the year our classrooms can look a bit barren, before we've had learning time to create any posters. Prior to the first day, display number and letter charts, and grammar posters around your room. These can be pricey, however the Internet is gold for freebies. Search for what you want, print it in colour and laminate if possible. Try to personalise your room also. What is unique to you that will prompt discussion from the children? A footy team poster, old photos of you, items from holidays or posters of people you admire are great additions. Can you hang things from the roof or from the roof trusses? (But make sure you follow O.H.S. guidelines!)

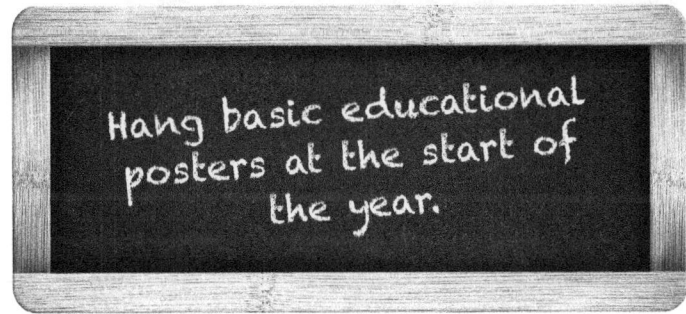

Pinboards can look so bland and bare at the start of the year. Some options are to staple large coloured pieces of poster paper in a pattern, or tack up some material that posters can be pinned over. Create borders using tapes or wide ribbons, or you can purchase custom made borders. I was gifted a few packets of these before I started teaching. Most capital cities have an educational supplies store to visit where you can buy many classroom supplies. Alternatively, you can buy them online.

Using Anchor Charts

Anchor charts work best when they are created together, are simple and easily readable and are referred to often. There's no point spending hours creating a gorgeous poster, tacking it up and then just expecting students to absorb the message by osmosis. Think about the purpose of the poster and the information you wish to convey in the plainest language possible. Keep that in mind as you create the poster together. Afterwards you can add an attractive border or decorative heading. In subsequent lessons, always recap what you have previously covered and quiz children on their recall. Remind them to look at the poster and even move to stand near it as you discuss it.

Creating Posters With Your Class

Another option is to have children create posters and/or anchor charts for the classroom. Be clear on your expectations and ensure spelling, grammar and the purpose are all correct before hanging them. Children are more likely to recall a concept if they've had to create something associated with it.

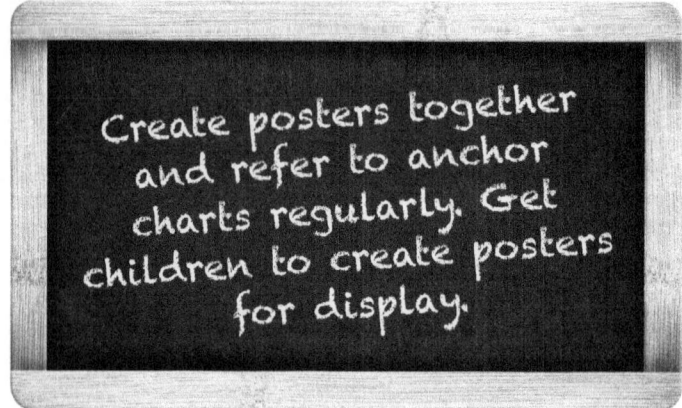

Children love to see pictures of themselves. At the start of the year you can use photos for the children to create information posters about themselves. (See Chapter 4, First Few Days for more ideas). Display photos throughout the year of children at work, with an explanation of the task they are undertaking. This is really for parents who visit the classroom! When you display any work created by children, ensure you have a written explanation of the task posted alongside it. This is mainly for parents or visiting teachers. Make yourself look smart!

At the end of each term take down student created posters or displays and send them home. If they are jointly created, they may need to play Paper, Scissors, Rock! Children want to take home everything, especially in the junior and middle years. Take advantage of this so you can rotate your displays regularly, helping to keep your classroom space fresh and relevant.

Create Areas Within the Classroom For Specific Purposes

Literacy, numeracy and the unit topic should all have equal prominence given to them for display. I have been in classrooms where there are no displays at all for numeracy. Mathematics is as important as literacy and children need to create and read displays on this topic too. Students always notice when you begin to work on a display area in preparation for a new topic. It creates a little buzz and anticipation of what is to come. My most favourite topic to display is sexuality education. Children are often agape at what I'm prepared to put on the walls. Puberty changes, self-drawn bodies with penises, vaginas and breasts, leaflets children create on body changes, and the life cycle of sperm. When the principal brings a tour around of prospective families it always creates some interesting discussions!

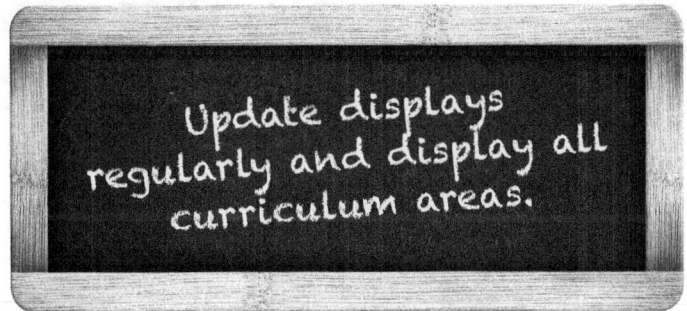

Boundaries

Chapter Overview

- » Physical boundaries
- » Why teachers need physical boundaries
- » Physical boundaries teachers need
- » Emotional boundaries
- » Why teachers need emotional boundaries
- » Emotional boundaries teachers need
- » How to set boundaries
- » Seeking assistance

A personal boundary is the guidelines, rules or limits that you create to identify what are safe and permissible ways for other people to behave around you, and how you will respond when someone attempts to step outside/inside of those limits. Put another way, boundaries are the limits we set in relationships that allow us to protect ourselves from being manipulated by, or becoming enmeshed with, emotionally needy others. Children can often be emotionally needy, particularly those raised in dysfunctional families. Everyone's boundaries are different based on personal experience, opinions, attitudes and social expectations. As a teacher it is essential that you have strong personal boundaries, both physical and emotional, with children and colleagues.

Every state and territory in Australia has a teacher professional code of conduct. It is worth downloading these to read through them. They refer to respecting children's privacy, modelling and engaging in respectful language, actively aiming to increase a child's self worth and protecting yourself from physical intimacies, to name a few.

> *Personal boundaries are both physical and emotional and are essential to set for yourself when working with children.*

Physical Boundaries

A physical boundary is how close you allow children to get to you, in relation to touch and physical proximity. It includes your body, personal space and privacy. I never really thought much about physical boundaries when teaching full time in my own classroom. These were set subconsciously and therefore I was happy with how little or how much I let the children touch me and thought it was appropriate based on my life experiences and attitudes.

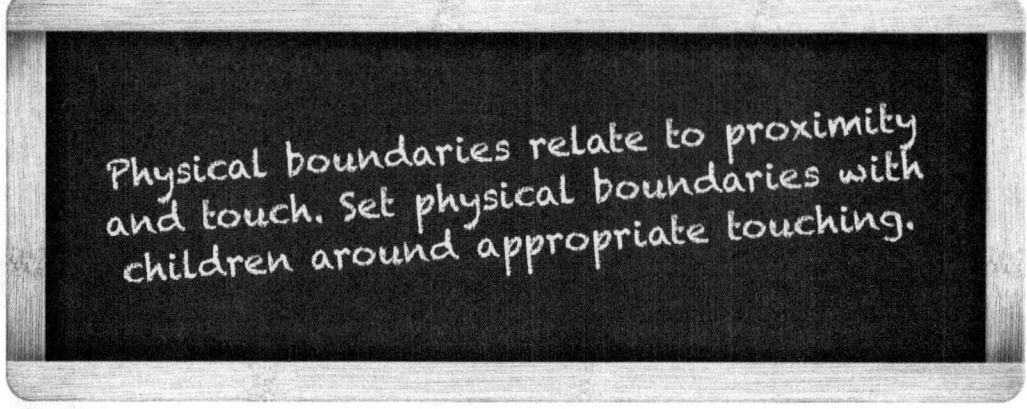

Physical boundaries relate to proximity and touch. Set physical boundaries with children around appropriate touching.

It wasn't until I stepped into the role of Casual Relief Teacher that it became noticeable some teachers had very different personal physical boundaries with children than me. I knew this based on how the children in some classes attempted to interact with me, theorising that how they wanted to touch me was how they were allowed to touch and interact with their usual teacher each day. Some classes had children who maintained what I felt was a respectful physical distance, whilst others had students who constantly wanted to touch me or drape themselves all over me.

I'm not saying that there's no role at all for physical touch. Sometimes that can make all the difference to a child. High fives for congratulations and encouraging back pats are awesome! A hand on a child's shoulder can convey care or show you empathise. Every now and then every child will require comforting and empathising of some sort. When I was teaching Prep, a sensitive young boy wasn't coping with how his own mother was coping with the sudden death of her father. For a week he was distressed. Not crying, but withdrawn and hurting. Once or twice a day he'd curl up on my lap and tuck his head under my chin and just sit quietly. I would continue to teach or interact with students, not really interacting with the boy, just allowing him to take comfort from me in a way he normally would with his mother. Ten minutes later he'd hop off my lap on his own accord and feel rejuvenated emotionally, enough to get back to work. I never picked him up and initiated it, never encouraged it, but allowed it as I knew it was an unusual circumstance and unlikely to be a long-term behaviour. The following week, with his mum a bit more responsive to him, he no longer needed me in that way. It's important to stress that I was not the initiator AND it met no emotional need in me.

Societal norms support general physical touching of a caring or comforting nature between a female adult and child. Unfortunately, the response is often open to more judgement or suspicion if a male is in the adult role. The boundaries that are discussed in this chapter are equally relevant to male and female teachers. Your gender should be irrelevant. However, even if it is unfair, males should be prepared for possible closer scrutiny.

Why Teachers Need Physical Boundaries

- It's emotionally healthy
- To protect yourself from claims of inappropriate touching
- To keep children engaged and focussed on their learning. Whilst you are attempting to teach, do you really think the children you are allowing to stand behind you and massage you are engaged with your lesson?
- Due to the power imbalance. The relationship between a teacher and student is, by definition, one of power. In a child's life, not many people have more power than their teacher. The child has limited power and will find it difficult to enforce boundaries. It is up to you, the adult and the one holding the power, to set appropriate limits
- To be consistent. Some days you won't feel like having children draped all over you. How do you manage it when they are used to doing it and you want to push them away? How do they cope? Consistency helps create a safe environment for children
- To demonstrate and model to children, especially those with social disorders, appropriate expectations within society of physical proximity and touch
- Lacking a bit of physical touch in your life outside of school does not legitimise children fulfilling that need
- It is a professional expectation

Physical Boundaries Teachers Need

Spending some time reflecting on what your physical boundaries will be is essential. Doing this before you start teaching is ideal, however sometimes you need to experience a classroom environment to determine what you are comfortable with. Below are some suggestions for emotionally healthy physical interactions between teachers and students.

Don't encourage children to touch you. This includes massages, foot rubs, leaning all over you or your lap and hugging you. Some children, particularly younger students, will throw their arms around your waist (usually as you are trying to walk somewhere!) Simply disentangle yourself from them by gently grabbing their wrists and bring their arms back to their sides. Say simply, at the same time, 'Please don't hug me, hugs are not for school time."

As a rule, **don't initiate** physical interactions with children. This includes hugging them, picking them up, kissing them or any physical games such as wrestling.

Are you reading this and thinking, "I'm a touchy feely person, I don't agree with this advice"? I can understand that adults who feel very comfortable being physical with others would want to ignore setting firm physical boundaries. However, I challenge you to examine your motives behind the desire to touch your students. Why is it important to you that you allow children to give you physical comfort? If you were to cease all physical interaction, what would be the consequences for you? Try to think of appropriate touch - high fives are great, so is a pat on the back. Remember, at school, you are a professional and must keep within professional boundaries.

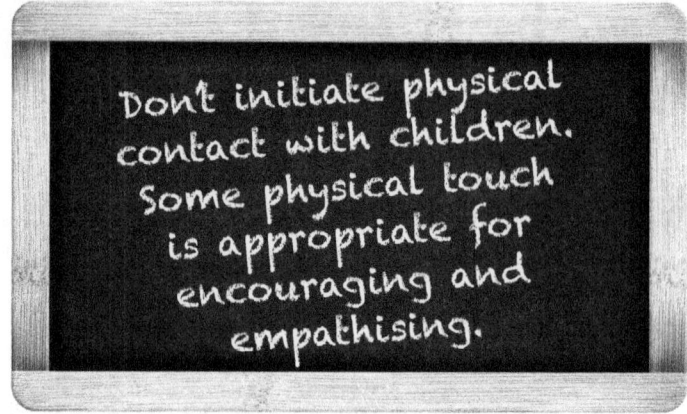

Emotional Boundaries

Emotional boundaries protect your sense of self and ability to separate yourself from others. When you have weak emotional boundaries you expose yourself to being greatly effected by others' words, thoughts and actions and can end up feeling bruised and battered. Setting emotional boundaries is as important with students as it is with co-workers and parents.

Let me make this very clear. You are there to teach. Children are at school to learn. It is not the child's role to provide you with an ego boost, physical touch, attention or love. Generally you must find that from within yourself or from outside the workplace. It is emotionally dysfunctional to consciously or subconsciously source that through children, especially those that are not yours. You will sometimes naturally receive an ego boost through your teaching when a child or parent compliments your teaching, but you should not rely on these as a source of emotional pleasure.

That sounds quite harsh and I bet you are most likely thinking that you would never do that, discounting that you would ever engage in this behaviour. I implore you to withhold your self-assessment until you have read further. Some honest self-examination is essential.

It seems obvious that no one would want their boundaries violated. So why do we do it? Or why do we allow it to happen to ourselves? Some reasons could be due to fear of rejection, confrontation or guilt, or because we weren't taught healthy emotional boundaries as a child. Also because for many, teaching feels a natural part of who they are, and separating the teaching self from the emotional self is difficult!

> Emotional boundaries are to protect your sense of self-identity and to take responsibility for your emotions and actions.

Why Teachers Need Emotional Boundaries

Establishing a strict set of emotional boundaries seems contradictory to the teaching process, where we are encouraged to foster personal connections. Strong connections are one factor that assists students to learn effectively. However, having healthy emotional boundaries means taking responsibility for your own emotions and actions, while NOT taking responsibility for the actions or emotions of others. This isn't contradictory to the work of a teacher at all! So why wouldn't you strive to have strong emotional boundaries?

When we have healthy emotional boundaries we are better able to communicate with others and have more stability and control over our lives. Modelling this to your students is extremely beneficial. Don't underestimate the quiet impact this could have. It's also good for you!

Emotional Boundaries Teachers Need

- Recognise that students are not your friends or peers, in any way. You can be friendly and helpful, but not a friend

- Never discuss highly personal subject matter with students. Students are not your friends. When I was a classroom helper many years ago I observed a teacher sharing to a classroom full of six year olds, intimate details about her pregnancy complaints. So many things wrong with this!

- Do not encourage conversations with students where the student is sharing personal information that does not benefit the student. Don't dig for gossip or to find out gratuitous information for your own personal gain or pleasure. Sometimes children will share personal information for attention seeking reasons. (See chapter on Behaviour Management for more background). If disclosure is of a concerning nature, see the next point

- Maintain confidentiality. The exception to this is if you believe a child's physical or emotional wellbeing is unsafe. Under Australian law, teachers are required to make a mandatory report if they suspect abuse of some sort. Your principal will guide you through this process

- Recognise that students' needs and feelings are not more important than your own. Most people would think intellectually that they already know and practice this. In reality, however, if you are constantly seeking to solve children's problems, are hyper vigilant of what you are saying to students in order to protect their feelings and find yourself exhausted by doing these things, you are most likely not putting yourself first. Do this all the time and you will be heading towards exhaustion very quickly. By looking after your own feelings and needs first (in a healthy way), then you are equipped long term to look after students' needs and feelings

- Identify when you find a students' actions or behaviours unacceptable towards you. Don't just accept it due to worry about upsetting them if you speak up or because you fear confrontation. Tell them calmly what was inappropriate and why, and request they desist. Repeat and repeat as necessary

» Don't expect children to fulfil your emotional needs. Only you are responsible for this. Boosting your self-esteem and making yourself happy is your job, not that of your students. At times my own emotional boundaries have not been firm enough or clear enough to myself. That has resulted in the confusing and dysfunctional desire to have students meet my self-esteem needs. When I was teaching Prep in my first year, I found myself see-sawing emotionally throughout the day or week; how I felt about myself was dependent upon how well I thought things were going in the classroom. When my lessons and preparations were going to plan and the children were engaged my self-esteem was high. Yet when teaching was challenging and the children weren't engaged, I was very hard on myself.

How To Set Boundaries

» Determine healthy boundaries for yourself. Sit down and make a list of both physical and emotional boundaries that are suitable and that you are comfortable with

» When you have identified a boundary that needs setting, do it firmly, clearly, calmly and respectfully. For example, you have let children stand behind you and massage you whilst you are teaching and you wish to change that. After the children enter the classroom in the morning, get them seated on the floor as usual but do not sit down yourself. Say good morning and then gently inform students that they aren't to stand behind you and massage you anymore. For the next several transitions from desks to floor, remind children of the new boundary. Some children will still try to do it, because it was meeting a need in them too. Just gently remind them of the new rule and be consistent

» Do not justify, get angry or apologise for the boundary you are setting. It is your decision what your boundaries are with your class. When children try to ignore those boundaries don't take out your frustration on them with anger. There is nothing you need to justify about or to apologise for. It is what it is

» You aren't responsible for the other person's reaction to the boundary you have set. You just need to be respectful in the way you communicate it. A change in boundaries, particularly emotional ones, could be challenging for young children. For example, if you begin to verbalise and respond more firmly when children's behaviours or actions are unacceptable to you it will be confusing for them at first. A change in a previously held behaviour pattern usually is. The more consistent you are the easier it will eventually become. Until that point, however, students may attempt to ignore or escalate their undesirable behaviour. Their reaction is not your responsibility

» When you change the boundary from a previously held one, prepare for manipulation or testing of it. If they are upset, it is their problem. This is a natural response that both adults and children experience. Some children will attempt to find a way around or through your boundary. Be alert for attempts and respond firmly and fairly. When they discover they can't manipulate it they may either accept it or their behaviour may continue to be undesirable to you in a different way. Identify what they are doing and examine whether you need to set a new boundary or not

» Be consistent. Changing the boundary you have set too often is confusing for all. This is why it's best to start with one boundary change at a time. Once you are very comfortable at maintaining it from manipulation or testing you can look at setting a different boundary

» Learning to set boundaries is a process. It takes time. Don't be hard on yourself as you grow and learn through this process as it's not an easy task to change well established patterns of behaviour

» If you find yourself feeling anger or resentment, or find yourself whining or complaining, chances are you need to set a boundary. Set aside some purposeful time for self-reflection to determine what you need to say or do and then communicate that assertively. Sometimes this is too hard to do by ourselves and a friend or mentor might help you work out what boundary you need to set and how to do it

» It takes practice to set boundaries without feeling selfish or guilty or embarrassed. Keep practising, as it will eventually become natural and easy

> Self-reflect and assess the current state of your emotional boundaries. Only you are responsible for your boundaries and for maintaining them.

Seeking Assistance

If learning about boundaries is a relatively new concept for you then you may benefit from some extra reading on this topic. I can highly recommend books by Drs Henry Cloud and John Townsend. In my early twenties I read this book: http://store.cloudtownsend.com/books/boundaries-softcover-book.html and found it totally life transforming. The follow up book to this was specifically for boundaries with children http://store.cloudtownsend.com/books/boundaries-with-kids.html. These books are Christian based, however the religious aspect can be ignored if this is not relevant for you. Many friends of mine, both Christian and non-Christian, have read these and found them very beneficial.

Sometimes a few sessions with a trained counsellor may help you to fine-tune your own boundaries for both at work and in your personal life. Reading the books and other information was fantastic for me, but it was more beneficial to talk to someone trained in how to set and maintain boundaries. Chatting about specific challenges I was facing allowed me to come away with personalised action plans and areas of personal growth.

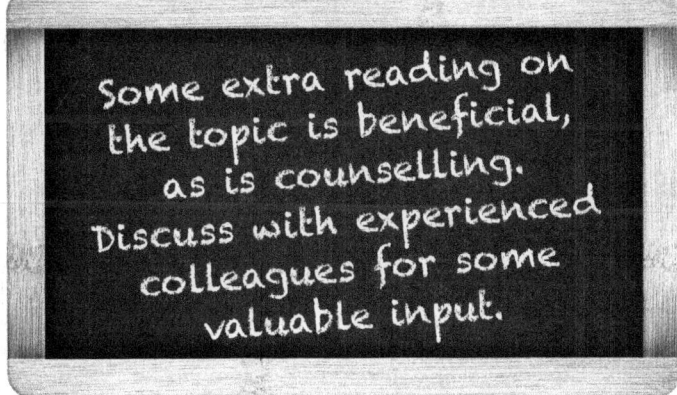

> Some extra reading on the topic is beneficial, as is counselling. Discuss with experienced colleagues for some valuable input.

The Bits That Don't Fit Into Another Chapter Neatly!

Chapter Overview

- » Social media
- » Yard duty
- » First aid
- » Staff meetings
- » Dress code
- » Expenses
- » Staff room
- » Extra responsibilities

Social Media

It is easy nowadays to get yourself into trouble on social media. Believe me, I've done it a couple of times, even when I thought I was being careful. Our private lives are less private now and principals are quick to intervene and discipline in an area we once could have considered private.

I teach cyber safety to all students. The same rules and information applies to teachers. Whatever you put on the Internet is there forever. Even if you delete it, I.T. savvy people can find it, or it can be screenshot and shared prior to deletion. Think twice before you share or upload anything, about the possible ramifications.

The following guidelines might seem overly strict, however following them should guarantee you avoid any problems.

- Ensure you have very secure privacy. If I was to search for you I should only see a profile picture
- Never 'friend' a current student. Why would you anyway? They are twelve and under and you are at least in your twenties. Do you really have anything in common? There's no need for you to be 'friends' with a student
- Never 'friend' a current parent. It doesn't matter if you have a good connection with them or think they are 'safe'. Even if your privacy is quite good, any time you comment on their feed it will allow their friends to see it also or possibly gain access to your profile page. The carpark mafia (parents!) just love an opportunity to gossip or dob you in to leadership. I know this sounds harsh but it is a realistic concern
- Consider very carefully about which staff you 'friend'. Several years ago I just added anyone I worked with but this backfired spectacularly on me. A teacher at my school reported me to the principal for a comment I made on another teacher's feed. The comment was factual and not nasty but it was regarding a volunteer at the school. I spent an anxious few days waiting to hear from the principal about whether there was going to be any disciplinary action or a permanent 'mark' in my personnel file. Luckily I got the all clear but I sure learnt my lesson. I immediately deleted all colleagues from my social media and now only add staff who I trust
- Don't post pictures of students online
- Do not discuss or name students in any public online forum. I would go so far as to suggest not even in private messages or email if you are going to slander or gossip. You have no control over other people and they may choose to share inappropriately
- A good rule of thumb is if you wouldn't say it in person, don't say it online
- Be careful about your online image. Potential employers nowadays may do a background search on you prior to interview or do random spot checks whilst you are employed
- Where possible, do not allow people to tag you in check ins or photos until you approve them
- The workplace is not the time to spend on social media. After hours only

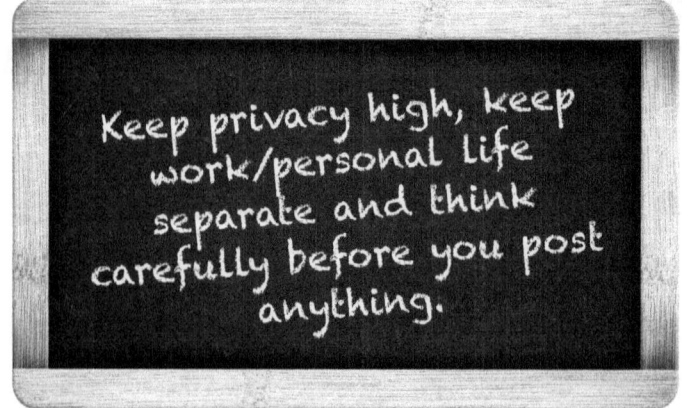

Keep privacy high, keep work/personal life separate and think carefully before you post anything.

Yard Duty

You will most likely be required to undertake yard duty several times a week. The purpose of yard duty is to ensure the safety of the children for the periods where they are outside. Before you begin the school year, read up on your school's rules for outside play and the conflict resolution process so you are clear on the procedures. Check out the gear you will need to carry so you know what it contains in case of an emergency, and where it is located. Bags may contain bandaids for minor scratches, tissues, a walk talky, an inhaler or Epipen, behaviour management forms and possibly jelly beans for diabetic students. What is the procedure to follow if there is an emergency in the school ground and you need assistance?

It's really important you diarise when you are rostered on, and also ensure the diary is updated when changes are made. Teachers are legally responsible to supervise students at all times and if you forget your duty and an incident occurs you may find yourself in a tricky situation. Plus, forgetting to relieve a teacher on duty so they can have their break is pretty poor form.

Each state or territory will have an employer agreement with their education department, stating clearly the conditions surrounding yard duty. If you suspect you are being given too much then see if you can check out the agreement before raising your concerns with the appropriate person in your school.

Some children like to walk with you if they are feeling a little lonely or find friendships difficult. This is okay occasionally but if the same children want to do it day after day you should flag this with their teacher. They may need some help with social skills and encouragement to approach people to play with them.

A popular game to play is Teacher Tiggy. It makes your duty time go quicker and keeps you amused. Ask children if they want to play, and once they've played it once or twice, they will be asking you! They just need to hide somewhere in the schoolyard and on your wanderings if you spot them then they have to complete a challenge. I get them to pick up five pieces of rubbish and if none is around then ten star jumps or they have to sing me a song. You'd think this would all be punishment but the children love it.

Don't forget it and find out where the areas and equipment are located.

First Aid

Some schools require all their staff to be first aid trained. It's helpful to have as many staff as possible trained to assist in emergencies. If training is not mandatory, volunteer to undergo training if it is offered. A first aid course can be expensive so if you can complete one whilst your employer is paying, go for it! You never know when you will face an unexpected medical emergency either in your classroom or school grounds, so feeling slightly more prepared if this occurs is ideal. Plus, having first aid qualifications may set you apart from other job applicants.

If your school has no nurse employed to administer first aid (and most don't), you may be able to go on a roster for first aid, instead of yard duty. This gives you the opportunity to practise many of the theoretical components you learnt during the first aid course.

Every classroom should have basic supplies of first aid - latex gloves, bandaids and tissues. O.H.&S. guidelines prevent any other supplies such as antiseptic or ointments. If you cannot locate these in your classroom, ask your mentor to point you in the right direction. When administering first aid to students, always glove up if you will be coming into contact with blood or other body fluids. If the cut or graze is minor, get the student to wash away the blood and grit with water and a tissue before you apply the bandaid. Try to deal with all minor medical complaints yourself rather than sending them to sickbay.

Children who bump their heads must attend sickbay and the office or nursing staff are required to phone their parents. Always err on the side of caution with head injuries, no matter how minor. If you are required to assist with an injury or illness that you feel totally out of depth to deal with, send a child to grab another teacher to help or call the office. When a very serious injury occurs, rest assured, staff will come running from everywhere to help. I have had to manage several very badly broken arms that ended up requiring surgery and assisted with some pretty nasty cuts that required stitching. There's always someone to help you. Helping with a serious medical issue can leave you a bit shaken afterwards so make sure you take some time for yourself to breathe and recover.

You will need to familiarise yourself with students at your school with medical plans or allergies. Usually, their plan and picture will be displayed in a prominent place as well as sick bay, and it is the responsibility of all staff to read through them and to recall those children in case of emergency.

If you have a child in your class with a serious illness or condition you may be required to undergo additional training. Epilepsy, diabetes and allergies are all very serious conditions and need to be managed closely. Ask their parents for resources and up to date management plans. It may be enough for a parent to train you in how to best handle their child's condition. Other situations may require the school to send you for professional training. Keep any notes and documentation easily accessible in your classroom and make sure it's clear for any relief teachers to see. Don't forget to take plans and medications when you have excursions or camps for these students.

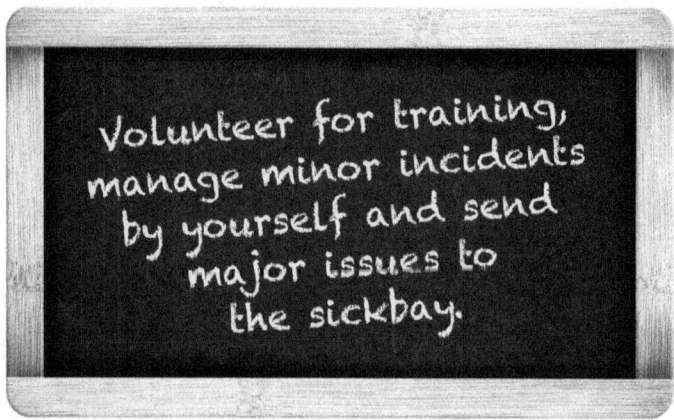

Staff Meetings

All schools have staff meetings that are compulsory for you to attend. Your mentor or the leadership team will let you know when they are. If for some reason you are not able to attend a meeting, you need to get this cleared with leadership so they are aware that you will not be present and why.

During the early days of teaching I found staff meetings incredibly overwhelming as there is so much assumed context based knowledge. I had no idea what the acronyms all stood for and spent many meetings feeling stupid and stressed. Being put into small groups to work on plans or strategies sent my stress levels sky high. I felt internal pressure to contribute but mostly didn't know what to say!

Some strategies to help you in the first year or so for staff meetings:

- Sit next to someone in your team, or your mentor, who you can whisper questions to if needed
- Find out where the minutes are filed so you can reread if necessary afterwards
- If you are not sure if the topic being discussed is something that is relevant to you, ask. I found it helpful, after I discovered it wasn't applicable to me or my level, to tune out
- Put the meeting dates in your diary so you don't double book or forget
- Occasionally you will be asked to pre-read documents prior to a meeting. Make sure you do this
- Make notes during the meeting on anything you need to follow up or new dates for your diary. Do this in a place you will remember to check - a scrap piece of paper is not ideal
- Everyone is usually tolerant and understanding of a new graduates' lack of experience and so you probably won't be called on to contribute to tasks outside of your ability
- Visit the toilet before the meeting. It can be a bit awkward to knick out!
- Put your phone on silent. Really, put your phone on silent. An incoming call or text during a meeting is embarrassing. The principal death stare is to be avoided. Or worse, a public dressing down
- Don't be annoying. Everyone wants to get out of meetings as soon as possible. There are some people who seem to love the sound of their own voice. Don't be one of them!

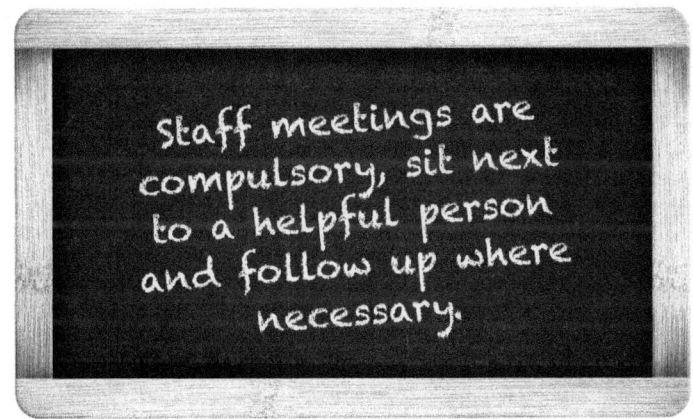

Dress Code

You are a qualified professional so you should dress like one. Before you begin at the school, ask the principal if there is a specific dress code or if neat casual is sufficient. Some schools require men to wear ties or ban denim. If there is, then it's important to adhere to it. (See Chapter 2 on Interviews for more pointers about dressing appropriately).

When neat casual is the go at your school, there are still a few guidelines to adhere to:

» Dress for your position. That is, wear tracksuits by all means if you are teaching Physical Education. Classroom teachers should not wear tracksuits, unless undertaking some athletic or sport training throughout the day

» Dress for comfort. That doesn't mean sloppy, just think about all the activities you will be involved in throughout the day. Most days I end up standing on a chair to put up a poster or to display some work. Everyday I spend some time sitting on the floor with groups of children or squatting to talk to students

» High heels are okay but think about how much of your day will be spent standing or walking. Pretty much every time I've worn heels my feet are tired by the end of the day. Perhaps throw some flats or sneakers into your bag in case you end up on yard duty or taking some sport unexpectedly. A previous assistant principal of mine wore very high stilettos every day. I don't know how she managed!

» Avoid items of clothing that are special and you don't want to ruin (not that you want to ruin any clothes!) Somehow, even if you are not scheduled to use paint or glue that day, you can guarantee you will have that smeared on you when you wear something special. I have a pen mark on a pair of tan boots from a grade five student and a new winter coat has glue on it from a prep

» Butt crack is to be avoided at all costs! You do not want to be the cause of sniggering and jokes when you squat down to help some children or to pick something up off the floor

» There's a difference between clothes you wear to impress on nights out, weekend casual, and clothes you wear in the classroom. Don't confuse them.

These should never be worn:

– Tight mini skirts that are more than slightly above the knee. Ditto for shorts

– Anything sheer or that gapes where underwear can be seen. My grade five teacher was pretty sexy and regularly wore tops where you could see her bra when she leaned over to help you. I remember having no idea what she was talking to me about! I was just focussed on what I was unexpectedly seeing!

– Low cut tops where your breasts threaten to spill out

– Clothes that expose your midriff or abs, even if you are ripped and proud of it

– Anything backless or strapless (my principal sent me home to change once for wearing a strapless summer dress, even though I had a cardigan over the top)

– Anything stained, ripped or past its use by date. Not clothes out of current style, but clothes that should really be binned (that same principal has sent home a colleague to dress more professionally)

– Any item that has an offensive slogan or image on it

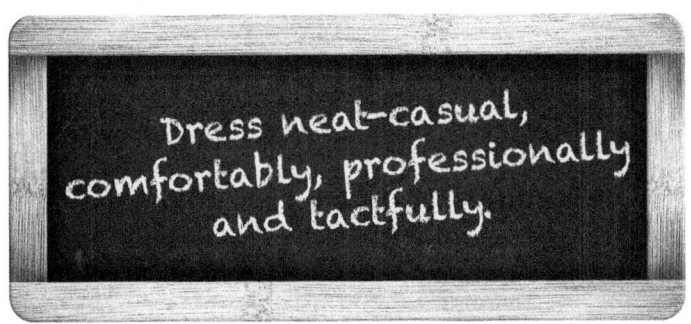

Dress neat-casual, comfortably, professionally and tactfully.

Expenses

Spending your own money on classroom supplies is pretty unavoidable in the field of education. Perhaps if you are in a well resourced private school you won't have to dip into your own wallet, but public educators usually have to. You can minimise your costs by purchasing second hand books at markets, printing and laminating your own posters and repurposing items from home where possible. If you choose to purchase items for your own benefit or for your classroom, then keep your receipts for the taxman and claim all you can.

Many schools request you contribute towards staffroom supplies in the form of tea money. I don't tend to use these supplies so have been able to negotiate a cheaper yearly rate, as I still have to contribute towards dishwashing supplies and the occasional morning tea. Make an effort to pay your bill in a timely manner.

Teachers require a laptop or tablet to perform their duties. In the public school system, one will most likely not be provided for you. You choose whether you buy one privately or opt to lease one through the department or school. If you choose the lease option then the fortnightly payments will be deducted from your salary. When you lease you will receive support and maintenance to a certain extent. There are lots of pros and cons to weigh up regarding personal purchase or lease. Ask the office manager or I.T. director at your school for advice.

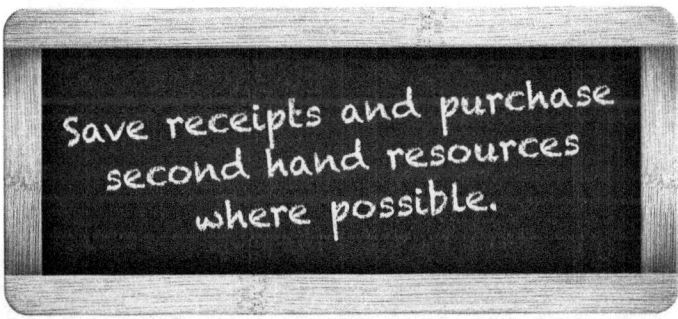

Save receipts and purchase second hand resources where possible.

Staff Room

It can feel a little intimidating going into the staff room when you are new to a school. It's really important that you spend time in there regularly, however, as it is the best way to get to know other staff. Informal gatherings are great for sharing suggestions and asking for ideas. Spending all day in your classroom can send you a little loopy so having a break in the staffroom, even if only for ten minutes helps to break the monotony sometimes.

You may be required to be on a roster for staffroom duty. This could include dishes, tidying up or restocking coffee and tea supplies. If this is the case, put it in your diary so you don't let others down. Being a teacher sure isn't just about teaching!

Don't hibernate in your room! Meet staff and share ideas.

Extra Responsibilities

Every teacher is required to undertake some extra responsibilities, based on their experience level. In your first year or two those jobs may be very minor such as ordering staffroom supplies or purchasing flowers when required. All are necessary jobs of course, but a bit of a drag. There will possibly be a job description, but if not, ask your mentor if they can either give you a bit of a rundown or point you in the direction of the person who most recently did it so you can ask them for advice.

At some schools you will be able to select the tasks you'd like to do, whilst at others they may just be allocated to you. All jobs have to get done so don't be surprised if you end up with a job you didn't request.

As your experience grows, so too will the amount of extra responsibilities you must undertake.

Here are some of the tasks that staff may be required to do for a school to run smoothly:

- Camp coordinator
- Transition coordinator
- Managing sports equipment
- Organising and running whole school special events such as Harmony Day or athletics carnivals
- Ordering supplies
- Fundraising
- Parent committee representative
- Marketing
- I.C.T. coordinator
- School council representative
- Managing reporting timelines and software
- Literacy and/or numeracy coordinator
- Social events

Extra responsibilities should be matched to your level of experience. Check out the role allocated to you with a mentor.

Use this page to document ways to improve your online security and privacy.

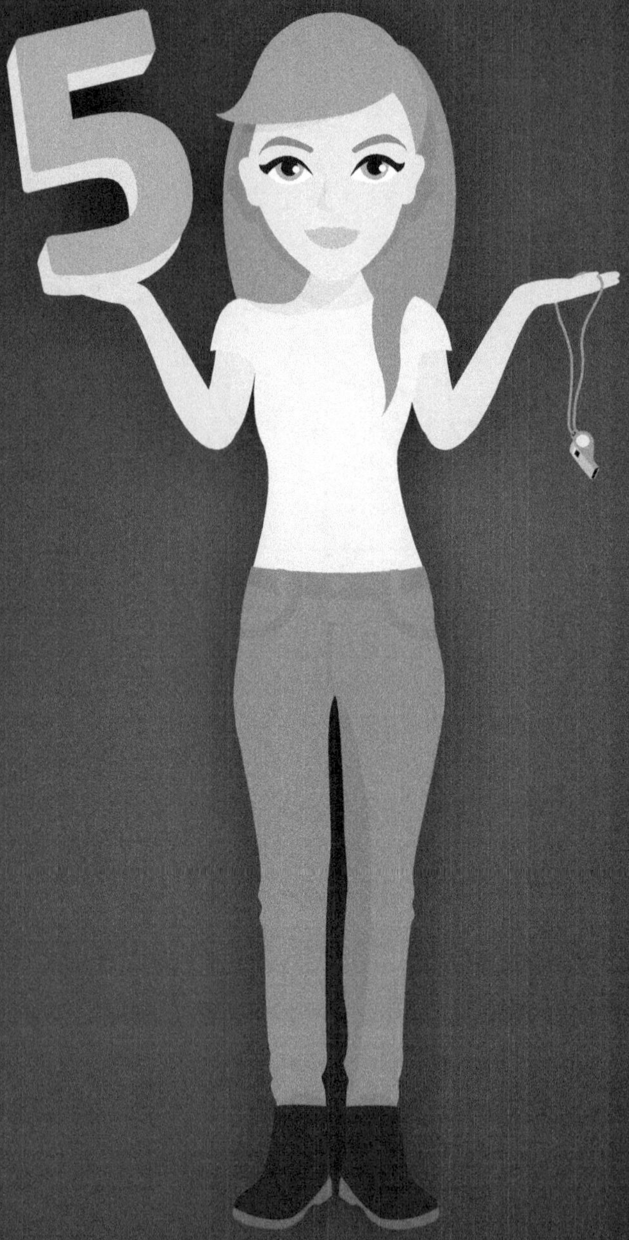
5

Five Minute Fillers

Chapter Overview

» Bank of five minute fillers for all age groups

Bank of Five Minute Fillers

The first year I taught I had a class of twenty-five Preps. One of the things I struggled with the most was how to fill those unplanned for five and ten minute gaps before a bell or between lessons. Over the years I have discovered many great activities through the generosity of my colleagues and there's plenty of ideas on the Internet to find too. Sometimes your students will teach you a game they have played in an earlier grade. I always challenge my class to attempt to beat the teacher, just to up their enthusiasm and drive. If they happen to beat me then there's usually a whole class reward of some sort - perhaps lunch five minutes early, listening to some music, showing me a YouTube clip they have found (this is a big favourite!) or a quick ball game outside.

Many of these activities can be adapted down or up, depending on what grade you are teaching. In time you will also put your own spin on them. They're also useful to use in conjunction with a particular topic you are teaching. For example, Buzz is great for skip counting, or Wipeout is good for subtraction. It's important to model these games and activities the first time you use them.

The five-minute fillers are in alphabetical order.

Thanks to my teacher friends who contributed ideas!

Legend: [J] Junior [M] Middle [S] Senior

[M][S] ATTRIBUTES
Make a set of attribute cards. For example, pointy, found outside, blue, squiggly, has the letter M in it, is cold. Put them into a box and children draw out one or two. They must think of as many things as they can that have both attributes. For a really hard challenge, use three cards.

[J][M] BRAINSTORM
This is similar to the game Scattergories. Give the children a topic - cakes, colours, animals etc - and five minutes to write down as many different types they can think of. Anything food related makes me hungry! You can alter this activity by writing a list from the chosen topic that all begin with the same letter. Countries - A - Australia, Austria, Afghanistan, Albania...

[J][M] BUZZ
This is a skip counting activity. Kids stand in a circle. You tell them what they are counting by and the BUZZ number. If you are counting by 2s then you might pick 10 as the buzz number. Students go round the circle one by one, calling out the next number in the counting sequence. When you get to the buzz number, that student yells out buzz and sits down. Counting begins again with the next student, from the start of the counting sequence, until there is one person left standing. This can be modified in a few ways. When the next person calls buzz, the previous person who buzzed can stand up again. You could also change direction.

[J] CAT AND MOUSE
Best played outdoors, this game is fast and fun. Choose a cat and a mouse. The rest of the class form a circle and link hands. The mouse stands inside the circle and the cat stands outside. The aim of the game is for the mouse to get outside the circle and to avoid being caught by the cat. The cat cannot come into the circle but can reach in to grab the mouse. The mouse must keep moving and exit the circle every ten seconds. The circle players try to keep the cat away from the mouse by holding up their arms and letting the mouse out and creating a barrier for the cat. If the mouse is caught it becomes a new cat and a new mouse is chosen.

[M][S] CONNECTIONS
Using your cards from the Attributes game (nouns), students pick two cards randomly and must make up a connection between the two objects. For a harder challenge set a time limit and play 'Hot Connections'. If a student can't think of a connection within three seconds then they are out.

[J] COUNTING FROGS
Students form a circle and crouch down in the frog position. The teacher chooses and announces a number. It has to be slightly less than the number of children playing. Any student can start off and call out 'One' whilst hopping once like a frog. Another child calls out 'Two' and hops. If two students hop at the same time they are both out. If any student didn't hop before the magic number is reached they are out too. Repeat with a new magic number until there is only one student left. You can use skip counting also.

[M][S] CURRENT AFFAIRS
Australia has a fabulous current affairs program aimed at children, www.abc.net.au/btn. Besides using it as a great resource in your curriculum, sometimes it's good to watch during lunch eating time.

[J][M][S] DATE ADDITION
Write the day's date on the board. For example, 12-9-2014. Challenge the students to find as many equations as they can, using the numbers in the same order. They can use any operation they choose.
$1 + 2 + 9 - 2 + 20 + 14 =$ or $12 \times 9 + 20 - 14 =$

J M DEAD FISH
Students lie on the floor. One student is the fisherman/woman. They wander around the room 'fishing' by trying to catch the fish moving. Fish need to keep as still as possible. If they are 'caught' the student must sit up and remain silent and they are out. Breathing allowed!

J M S DICTIONARY RACE
This is best played when you are teaching dictionary skills. You will require one dictionary each, or one between two. This won't work using an online dictionary. The teacher either calls out a word or writes it on the board. First to find it is the winner. You can decide the reward!

J DOGGY DOGGY
One child is chosen to be IT and plays the role of the dog. They sit in a chair with their back to the group. An object representing a bone is placed under the chair. The teacher taps a class member to steal the bone. They take it back to where they are sitting and hide it under or behind them. Everyone then sings "Doggy, Doggy, who's got your bone? Someone stole it from your home!" The dog has three chances to guess who took it. If they guess it they get another turn as dog. If not, the person who stole the bone gets a go as the dog.

J M S DOWN DOWN DOWN
Students begin the game tossing and catching a tennis ball between pairs. When a student drops a ball they go down on one knee. Throwing and catching continues. When the next ball is dropped the go down on two knees. This continues with both elbows and then chin!

J DUCK DUCK GOOSE
This can be played either inside or outside. Children sit in a circle. One person is IT and walks around the outside of the circle, carefully tapping the head of each child as they walk and calling out 'Duck'. Eventually they select one child and name them Goose. The aim is for the IT child and the Goose to race around the outside of the circle to be the first back to the Goose's spot. If the Goose doesn't win, they become IT for the next round. If the Goose wins they sit in the middle of the circle until they are replaced.

J M S HANGMAN
We all played this as kids. Great to play using unit words, spelling words or when investigating word origins.

M S HOMEWORK EXCUSE
Make a set of picture cards of different objects (nouns). Students select a card and then have to come up with an excuse for not doing their homework that involves that object. Students sit in a circle and begin individually to say "I'm sorry Mr/Miss/Mrs/Ms..., but I couldn't do my homework because..."

J M S HUMAN NUMBER LINE
Hand out number cards to some students. The value on the cards will depend on the age level and the numbers you are working on in class. This works for single digit numbers through to millions and decimals. Choose five students at a time to come out and order themselves from smallest to biggest, or vice versa.

J M I'M GOING ON A...
Children all sit in a circle. You begin a sentence that children need to complete. Examples can be, I'm going on a holiday and I'm going to bring... Or I'm flying to the moon and I'm going to bring... Prior to sending the sentence around the room you will have chosen a secret strategy that the kids need to work out as they go. It might be all words starting with M, double syllables, oa words etc. "I'm going on a holiday and I'm going to bring my mum." The next child repeats the sentence and adds on their choice. If it starts with M tell them they can come but don't tell them why. If it doesn't start with M then they cannot come. Go around the circle until someone works it out. Sometimes it helps to repeat all the successful words, or to write them on the board.

J **IPAD**

Apps can be used by the children independently but are also great for the whole class if you connect your iPad to the big screen. Subitising, Friends of Ten and H.F.W. (high frequency words) are a few examples. If you can't find them through the App Store, then search for them through Google, which will then link you back to the store. They are either free or very cheap. (See the Technology chapter for more ideas).

J M S **LAP SIT**

The whole class stands in a circle with shoulders touching. Everyone turns to the right and takes a step towards the interior of the circle. On the teacher's count, students gently sit on the lap of the person behind them. The group should be able to support themselves without falling over.

M S **LATERAL THINKING**

The Internet is awash with great lateral thinking exercises. After doing a few in class your students will get the idea and their lateral thinking skills will improve quickly. Find some you think are appropriate and retype them onto a document to display to the whole class, with the answer on the second page or revealed later. I accumulate a digital folder in preparation for that five-minute filler. Kids love them!

For example, can you name three consecutive days of the week without using Monday, Tuesday, Wednesday, Thursday, Friday, Saturday or Sunday? Yesterday, Today and Tomorrow!

Or, a murderer is condemned to death. He has to choose between three rooms. The first is full of raging fires, the second is full of loaded guns with assassins, and the third is full of lions that haven't eaten in three years. Which room is the safest for him? The third. If lions haven't eaten for three years then they are dead! I'm sure you get the idea...

M S **MAD LIBS**

This is a very popular game and a great way to revise nouns, adjectives and verbs. Mad Libs are short stories where key words have been omitted. Children must write down a list of words that will fill the gaps, prior to knowing what the story is about. A random and hilarious activity! There are many templates on the Internet for you to use, there are apps available and you can even purchase Mad Libs books via Amazon.

M S **MAN VS CALCULATOR**

A great game to develop mental maths. Choose two students to run the game. One has a calculator to check answers on, the other keeps a score of who won each round. First to five wins. Choose two students to play. One has a calculator, the other just their brain! The leader with the calculator calls out an addition equation. The players battle it out to be the first with the correct answer, one calculating it in their head, the other on the calculator. The winner selects a new person to challenge them. This can be as easy or as difficult as you'd like. 10 + 5 or 167 + 23 etc.

J M S **MASTERMIND**

Numbers can be big or small to play this game. Play it on the board or on scrap paper in pairs or groups. This is great for place value. Think of a number - this is dependent upon what you are working on in class. Junior classes may only need Units and Tens whilst senior classes can do millions or decimals. Draw a table on the board using place value headings only, depending on how many places you have chosen. Children can take it in turns to guess a number and you write it up. If the digit is in the right spot then tick it. Wrong spot and draw a small circle. Not in your number, then give it a cross. The next guesser uses the information gained from the last go to guess a new number until the class work out the correct number. You can use zeroes and the same digit twice. Once children get the hang of this game they can play amongst themselves or as a numeracy rotation during place value lessons.

J **MEMORY**

Select five objects, place them in a set order, then ask the class to memorise the objects and their location. The students turn around and you remove an object or two as well as shuffling the remaining objects around. When the children look again at the objects they need to determine what is missing and where it is from. This can be played in small groups too.

J M S MR SQUIGGLE
Mr Squiggle had a self-titled show on the A.B.C. for over forty years! He was a marionette puppet with a pencil for a nose. His off-sider, Miss Jane, helped him draw pictures from just a squiggle. This activity springs from him! Draw a squiggle on the board. Children copy it onto a mini whiteboard, a piece of paper or an iPad drawing app. They need to add details to turn it into a picture. Add challenges by turning it sideways or adding another squiggle or two. Prepare in advance some squiggles on paper and photocopy them ready for early finishers. Alternatively, do it all digitally and save them into an accessible folder in Dropbox for the children to access.

J M S NUMBER HEAD
Choose three to four students to sit out the front. On post it notes write a number and stick them on the children's foreheads. They have to work out what number they are by asking the class questions. The class can only answer yes or no. If it's your turn to ask questions, you ask until you get a 'NO' answer. Then it's the next person's turn. Sample questions to ask are: Am I a two digit number? Am I odd? Am I a decimal? Am I a prime number?

J M OBSTACLE COURSE
Set a course around your school's playground. Nothing too sophisticated, as the purpose is really to have a quick break from the classroom.

J M S PACMAN
Children stand all around the room so that when their arms are outstretched they do not touch another child. You call out times table questions. Choose the kid who shot their arm up to answer first. If they are correct then they take a giant step in any direction. If they can touch another child then they sit down and are now out of the game. This continues until the last person standing. Alter this game by using tens facts, larger addition equations or subtraction.

J M S RUN!!
21st Century children are more sedentary then ever before. It's good practice to get them moving regularly. When they need a break or breather, challenge them to run around something outside, be that the oval or the whole school. Keep an old pair of runners in your classroom so you can join in too. Aim to have no child behind you as you urge them on!

J M S SILENT BALL
Class too noisy and your ears are ringing? This game is your solution. I discovered this when I had a boisterous Foundation class. I was pretty dubious that it would work, but it does! The class spreads out around the classroom. They toss around a ball or beanbag. This is done in total silence. Anyone who makes a noise sits down. Drop it? Sit down. Sometimes it's too easy so mix it up a bit. Catch with one hand, stand on one leg, make it a hot potato etc.

J SINGING
Here's a few to get you started. Lyrics and tunes easily found on the Internet if needed.

| Hokey Pokey | Twinkle Twinkle Little Star | Ten Little Monkeys |
| The Ants Go Marching | Five Little Ducks | I Can See a Rainbow |

J M S STORIES
Even senior students love stories read to them. An engaging chapter book is ideal. Picture storybooks are fabulous in all levels. http://www.storylineonline.net/ enables you to have the story read on your interactive whiteboard or television. Some even have signing for the hearing impaired.

M S TARGET WORDS
How many words can you find? Templates for these can be found on the Internet. A nine square grid has a letter in each square. The centre letter must be used in all words found. The letter cannot be used more than once. There is at least one nine-letter word to be found.

J M S THINKING OF A NUMBER....
The teacher thinks of a number. How large depends on what grade you are working with. If you chose 587 you would tell the class you have thought of a number between 500 and 600. When individuals guess a number you tell them higher or lower. Don't forget to use decimals for a good challenge!

M S TIMES TABLES
There really is no other choice but to rote learn tables. Formal division algorithms become laborious without quick recall of times tables. There's many ways to have five minutes practise:

M S PLAYING CARDS
In pairs, with a pile of playing cards each, face down. Turn a card over at the same time and first to say the answer of the two card values multiplied together gets to keep them. Before beginning, remove the jacks, queens and kings.

M S ONLINE GAMES
Such as Mathletics or Math Evolve.

M S SONGS
YouTube is a great source for this.

M S CHALLENGE
I have had a whole class times table challenge for years. The kids love it and usually they improve their quick recall. On the board, in a ladder format, place a name card for each student in the class, in any order for the moment. Choose two students fairly low on the ladder. Either the teacher chooses the times table or the higher placed person does. Call out the times table chosen in random order, keeping a count on your fingers of who yells out the answer first. First to five is the winner. If they beat someone above them on the ladder then they swap the names around so the winner is now placed higher. Winner then chooses someone higher on the ladder than them to challenge. They cannot select the same times table, unless you have chosen for the whole class to focus on a particular one for the week. The aim is to be the times table champion. Champions can only be challenged once per day, then they are safe! Students high on the ladder who know their times tables well may elect to have random tables or division facts instead. A champion may elect to challenge the teacher. Bonus house points or free time allocated if they beat you. I've never been beaten yet!

M S WIPEOUT
This is a place value subtraction game for pairs. Each pair has a calculator and puts in a three-digit number. Take turns to ask the partner if they have one of the digits in their number. If they do have the digit they tell you the place value. For example, if the digit they have is a 5, they tell you if it is 500, 50 or 5, and you can subtract that amount your own number. If they do not have the digit that you asked for you add that number of ones to your own number. Partners take turns to ask each other for digits and add and subtract that number as necessary. Winner is the first to zero. Make it harder by starting with larger numbers.

J M S WORD WITHIN A WORD
Challenge your class to find more words than you can. Write a large word on the board and give the children five minutes to individually (or in pairs) find as many words within that word. Letters can be rearranged but not duplicated. Spaceship is a great word to use!

J M S YOUTUBE CLIPS
Many times children will come and tell you about a funny clip they want to show you or the class. Check them out first! Cats and dogs doing silly things are always a winner. Creative stop motion videos are also good fun.

List your own 5 minute fillers here.

Report Writing

Chapter Overview

- » **Before Writing**
  - Assessment
  - Curriculum
  - Time management
  - Determine format

- » **During Writing**
  - Numerical marks
  - Comment database
  - What to write when
  - Word limit
  - Word choice
  - Siblings
  - Disabilities
  - Extension
  - E.A.L. or E.S.L.
  - Future comments

- » **After Writing**
  - Editing
  - Proofreading

The task of writing reports about your students, at least twice a year, can be angst ridden. It's very baffling that universities do not cover report writing in the final semester of the degree. In my first few years of teaching I felt so overwhelmed and anxious about what I was writing and it took me forever. Since those early days I've developed some strategies to make the process smoother, quicker and easier. These strategies are a guide only; as you become more experienced at report writing you will develop your own. No two teachers prepare and write in the same way. The guidelines will help you get started and feel less stressed about the whole process.

Before Writing

Assessment

Assessment is ongoing throughout the year. When you write a mid year report, how are you going to remember what your students did in week four of term one? At that stage you may have assessed angles in numeracy, a topic that does not typically get reviewed again. My brain certainly cannot recall those facts! The answer is to get organised and keep records of all your assessments, both formal and informal.

At the start of the year, create a template with each of your student's names on it. I typically use Word on my laptop but you should use whatever you are comfortable with. There are a number of applications you can install on your tablet that perform a similar function, such as Teacher Notes by Gerrard Apps. This link http://www.educatorstechnology.com/2014/03/the-best-ipad-note-taking-apps-for.html provides you with a list of other digital options. Play around with them until you find the best one for you.

Any time you make an observation about a child's development or knowledge, record this in your template. Add in test or project results or even pictures if they are relevant. Don't worry about the language you use to take those notes, as long as you understand what you meant when you return to it months later. After marking work, remember to make comments in your template or app before you hand back work to students. This is especially important if you are assessing work completed digitally by them, where they just show you on their own device. Not all apps are capable of exporting. If this is the case, record that you viewed it on their device.

If you prefer to not use technology for observations, purchase a spiral bound notebook that is always left on your desk. Dedicate a page for each student and anytime you observe something of concern or something they are doing well, record it in the book. When it comes to report writing you will have a bank of observations to choose from. You won't necessarily need to use them all.

Having concrete notes on each student about what they have achieved, both academically and socially, is fundamental to the report writing process. When you sit down to begin writing, everything you need should be easily accessible. When questioned by a parent or leadership about what led you to make an assessment, because you documented all observations and results, you have concrete facts to back up your assessment. That's why you should note if you sighted a task on the child's device. Extra back up for you if necessary!

Curriculum

Prior to writing you will need to be well acquainted with your state or nation's curriculum documents. During planning for lessons you will be accessing them already. Download the documents for all the subjects you are required to cover from your state's assessment and reporting website. Either store these in an easily accessible folder on your laptop, or print and slip into a display folder. You will need to refer to these constantly throughout the report writing process.

When you begin writing, ensure you are not referring to skills and concepts that are not applicable to the year level you teach, unless you have a student who requires extension. If this is the case, you need to have specifically taught these skills, not just theorising that they would be able to do it. Remember, you need evidence!

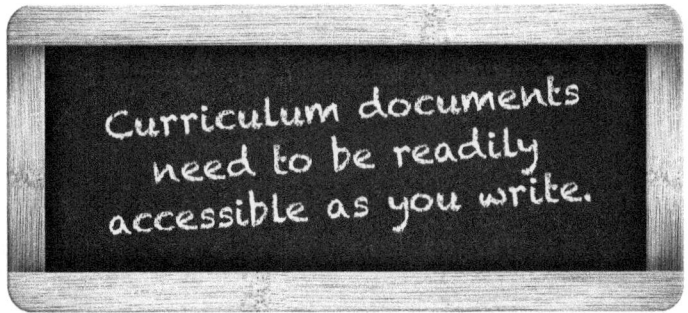

Time Management

Managing your time is fundamental to the report writing process. Speak to your mentor about timelines and ask for suggestions of when you should start writing or assessing. Each school will develop a timeline unique for them, that specifies when drafts and edits need to be completed by.

Once you know the timeline, put the dates in your diary. Everyone differs on how far out from delivery they choose to begin writing. My preference is to start about six weeks out, get them completed in about three and have some time up my sleeve for fine-tuning and editing. Others prefer to work under the pump.

Writing a little bit each day is one strategy, but not how I manage it. I work better if I dedicate at least half a day over three consecutive weekends to work uninterrupted in a huge block. That way I feel like I get in the zone and have better continuity. It's also not consuming my entire life for six weeks either. I mark it on the calendar so my family know not to book me up with social activities.

During the writing period you still need to plan lessons and teach. Reports need to be written around this and so a fair bit of your own time will be taken up with writing. Teachers, justifiably, get many extra weeks leave compared to the average worker. It means your term time is full on but you get more than adequate recovery and restoration time. You are just going to have to put up with the extra hours required during report writing time.

Determine Format

Every school has different expectations around format and content with regards to reports. Ask your mentor for a list of guidelines (hopefully the school have published expectations). Do this before you begin writing as it's quite dispiriting and time consuming to have to do rewrites.

Find out the answers to these questions:

- What sections are on the report? For example, what the student can do, areas for future learning, what the school will do, what the parents can do
- Is the report broken up into different sections for literacy, numeracy, social, general? Or is it all together?
- Are line spaces between paragraphs needed? Try and avoid these if possible as they take up valuable writing space
- Can you see some sample reports from previous years to get a good idea of format and content?
- How many words or characters are required as a maximum for each section? This is important! It's a tough job to slash if you've written too much, not to mention a waste of your valuable time
- What platform/software does the school use to write reports?
- Can I copy and paste from word processing software into the report writing software? I do this for a couple of reasons. I use Apple software, yet the report writing software I have to use is designed for P.C.s, and because I'm much more comfortable using software I know well I prefer to copy and paste
- Can you use dot points in any section?
- What are the punctuation expectations?
- Are there any particular words or phrases to avoid?
- Do I use a particular font or font size or does the software adjust it for me?
- Do I need subheadings?
- Who will proofread my draft?
- Does the school use a particular comment database or can you use your own?
- Do students who do not have English as their main language have a different report format or curriculum documents?
- Can you start sentences with verbs?
- For words that can be spelled in two ways, is there a way the school prefers? For example, focussed and focused
- Can I refer to a child by their nickname? For example, Nick instead of Nicholas? Do this if you can to save characters!
- If you have a funded child in your class, do you write a report with the aide or by yourself?
- What content areas are actually being assessed this semester? For example, Chance and Data in numeracy may not have been covered in semester one. Check with your team to know exactly what you are reporting on
- How do you use the report writing software? Each one is unique, not always smartly designed, and you may need some guidance or a tutorial by a more experienced teacher

During Writing

You've had all your questions answered, so now you are well prepared to begin writing. Set aside a block of uninterrupted time to have a good go at it, especially if it's your first time. Get everything you need close to hand. Wine, tissues, the remote control... if only! It's amazing how clean and tidy your house can become during report writing season, and the gourmet food that comes from your kitchen; yummo! In all seriousness, don't procrastinate, find a good comfortable spot in your house where you won't be interrupted, have water and snacks close to hand and begin writing.

When writing your first set of reports it's a very, very good idea to write a couple, or some sections, and then get your mentor to check how you are going. It takes practise to get into the swing of how to phrase your writing effectively and in a succinct manner. Many times I have seen distressed beginning teachers with a seemingly insurmountable task of changes and edits to make on their first few attempts at report writing. Having an experienced eye to read your initial efforts will save you a lot of angst in the long run. I cannot stress the importance of this more highly!

There's a few ways to tackle reports, as there's quite a bit to include:

Numerical Marks

A numerical mark (or progression point) will be assigned for each content area based on curriculum documents and assessment. You can complete these bit by bit as you write, all at the start or all at the end. My preference is to fill them all in prior to beginning any actual writing. The reason I do this is I have a clear 'mark' in front of me to guide my comments. Other teachers I know do it at the end.

You will require your state or national curriculum documents nearby and any assessment of individuals that relate to the progression point you are marking.

Obtain a copy of the previous semester's marks for your class and use these loosely as a base for how you assign marks. You will not agree with all the marks assigned by the previous teacher and if you think the child needs to be marked backwards you will need to be able to justify this when questioned. Generally children progress each semester, however development and maturation occurs at different rates and times. It's appropriate sometimes to keep children on the same ranking if your assessments have shown no growth. Again, be prepared to have evidence.

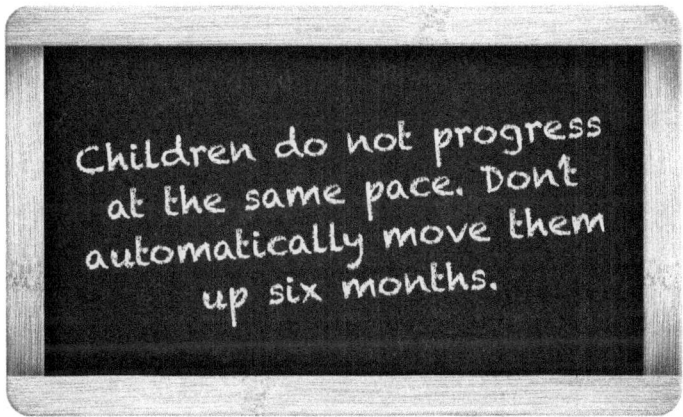

Children do not progress at the same pace. Don't automatically move them up six months.

Comment Database

If you have read some previous reports you will know the school's expectations. Using a good quality comment database is helpful, especially as you write reports for the first time. The report writing software that your school uses may have a database or another teacher may have created their own that they are willing to share. Alternatively, searching the Internet for good comments may assist. You can also write your own!

When you use a database you have to pay close attention to tailoring the comments to fit the child and your writing style. It can end up very disjointed if you are doing lots of copying and pasting. Beware also that comment databases often use 'teacher speak', which has been frowned upon in recent years. Another factor to consider when using a comment database is to ensure that the writing flows and that sentences don't all start with a child's name or he/she. Using a database should just be for inspiration and as a starting point.

I have created my own databases from comments I have used over the years. To do this I choose well-constructed comments that I have written and then file them in the appropriate template - Mid Year or End of Year. I have one each of these for junior, middle and senior. Within the template I have a table with the headings Literacy, Numeracy and General. Subheadings of high, medium and low for each heading complete the table. You can also include a section for comments regarding what the student needs to work on in the future. The sentences you insert in the database work best if they have no space for pronouns.

Initially, creating your own database can be a big task, however it will assist you long term to become more efficient at report writing. Your store of brainpower will thank you come the next report writing season!

Here are some sample sentences for a database:

- » She uses reading strategies such as clarifying the main idea, visualising the story and evaluating the main idea
- » In reading groups she offers considered opinions and responds to texts orally and in writing
- » She has written some excellent persuasive pieces that include multiple coherent arguments to establish a single point
- » He can estimate, measure and record formal units of measurement
- » He is able to explain and use mental and written algorithms for the addition, subtraction and multiplication of whole numbers

Alternatively you may be able to create your own comment database from within the report writing software. Just beware that the software your school uses may change and the new software may not be compatible with the old and you may lose all your comments.

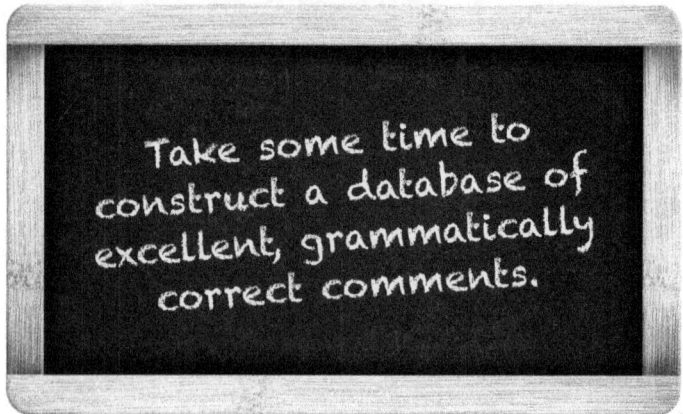

What To Write When

Do you write a whole child's report from start to finish before starting on the next student? Or do you write the literacy comments for all students before returning to write all the numeracy comments? Again, this is purely personal preference. I use the second option, simply because for me it is more efficient. When writing a numeracy comment for a student, it may be just as relevant for two other students in the class, so I copy and paste into their reports. As no two students are the same you will need to tweak the copied text to suit that individual. Don't get lazy!

Word Limit

Word and character limits guide how much writing you will need to do. As you write, check often that you are within these limits. It's annoying ditching well-crafted sentences because they don't fit. You will get to know what your word limit looks like as a block of text as you become more practised.

Word Choice

This is the most important part of a report and it's imperative you get it right. You do not want to be making massive revisions because your word choice was poor. As you write, check back with these guidelines regularly.

- State what the student CAN do. This seems obvious but you need to be specific. The report section that covers what was done for that semester should only contain what that student did. Avoid comments that refer to anything in the future. For example, 'is working towards,' 'when he matures he will'

- Avoid teacher speak. It's tempting to dazzle parents with all your intelligent curriculum knowledge. (If you feel the need to dazzle someone, dazzle your colleagues and boss). Try to write comments that are simple and that a non-teacher trained parent could understand. All parents want to know is what their child can do and in what areas they need assistance in for the future. If they cannot decipher what that actually is then your report is pointless. Despite being a trained teacher, one year I actually had trouble understanding one of my daughter's reports!

- Be concise. You do not have room for long-winded descriptions. Keep your comments factual and brief. Reread your comments and look at where you can cut words. Are there any superfluous ones? If you remove them and/or rearrange the sentence is the integrity of your comment maintained?

- Focus on the major curriculum areas. There's not too much point in commenting on the topic of symmetry that would take two lessons at most in the entire semester. Parents want to know how their child is going in the major areas of literacy and numeracy - reading, writing, spelling, the four mathematical processes, place value etc.

- No more than two connected ideas per sentence. Add in more and your sentence becomes too long winded and hard to follow

- Phrase comments positively. Whilst being realistic about the children we assess, we also need to be kind. Parents need to know exactly what their child is like in the classroom but we don't have to be negative or mean about how we convey that. A few years ago I taught a senior class that was a nightmare. Every day was a struggle to go to work to face many difficult boys. Here is an excerpt from a report of one of those young boys. 'He is an outgoing member of our class and keen to take on leadership positions.' What I meant was he is loud, never shuts up and is disruptive. He's keen to be a leader for the social status but has no hope in hell. 'Once settled to his task he works efficiently and produces work of a high standard.' It takes forever for him to settle and he's wasting his high intelligence on evil pursuits! 'To do this he frequently needs to work away from other students.' Far, far away...

- Be specific. This is an excerpt from a recent report I wrote: 'The Term Three topic of Social Justice saw Xxx investigate the experiences of migrants on arrival in Australia and the impact of immigration on Australian culture. Working with a partner he completed a good immigration research project on the experiences of Vietnamese migrants using Explain Everything.' I stated what the term three topic was and a little about what was taught. Then I was very specific about how this student responded to the topic and the platform he chose

» The numerical marks must match your comments. If a child is quite behind, or advanced, and you show this in your mark, you must reflect this in your written comments. Conversely, do not write about the child being ahead or behind and then mark them at level. Do a cross check

» Use formal language. Substituting 'kids' for students, pupils or class is not appropriate

» Always finish with a positive comment. This leaves a nice feeling with parents, especially if their child's report was challenging to read emotionally. "I look forward to working on strategies together for the remainder of the year" or "It has been a pleasure to teach Xxx this year and I wish her all the best for Grade Six."

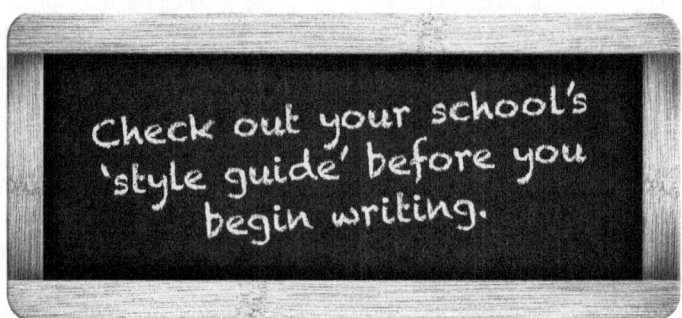

Siblings

Sometimes you will have siblings in your class. Your reports need to be worded quite differently, (they should be anyway as they are individuals), so keep the copy and paste to a minimum here. One year I had fraternal twins in Grade Six. They were both incredibly intelligent and focussed. When writing their mid year and end of year reports, it was so difficult to make them different as they were so similar! A thesaurus will be very helpful in this situation, to say the same thing in a creatively different way.

If your team share a bank of comments it is worth checking with the teachers who have siblings with those in your class. You don't want to send home very similar reports from different teachers.

Disabilities

In your report you should refer to the fact that the child has a specialised learning plan and works closely with the aide. The purpose of this is partly a legality - a future investigation into whether the school has attempted to meet the needs of the integrated child is always a possibility. This is the sentence I use, 'An Individual Learning Plan (I.L.P.) was developed to target his specific learning needs.' You would need to adjust the sentence to reflect the official acronym you are required to use. You could also be more explicit, 'An Individual Learning Plan (I.L.P.) was developed to target his specific numeracy needs.'

Another great phrase to use is '**with support** can complete formal algorithms.' I love this comment as it conveys so much – independently the child cannot do it and they require support to complete tasks. This may be due to behavioural or intellectual issues. Another one to use is '**when focussed** can demonstrate his knowledge of place value.'

Extension

Most parents these days seem to think their child is gifted. I've never taught any truly gifted children but quite a few highly intelligent students. You will be differentiating the curriculum already so it will be easy for you to comment in their report how you are extending them. (See Chapter 9 on Differentiation for tips). Make sure it is clear how you are meeting their needs.

E.A.L. or E.S.L. (or whatever acronym the department is using this week)

Before you began writing you should've established who in your class requires a specialist English as an Additional Language report. Generally, until E.A.L. students are on level they require a different report format.

The language you use in E.A.L. reports needs to be non-teacher speak to the max! Use basic text and simple concepts. It's very difficult for parents to read and understand a language that is not their primary one, so be considerate and don't make it any harder for them than it already is.

Future Comments

This is the section where you write about what either the school will do for the student, what the student needs to work on, or how the parent can help at home. Years ago I wrote these in paragraphs but found it hard to cohesively write about disjointed concepts. Luckily my leadership team decided using dot points was okay and I have found this much easier. If you are clever, you can use this section to convey more to the parents about what their child cannot do currently.

Clarify the punctuation requirements for dot points, i.e., will you use capitals at the start, or full stops at the end of each point? Also clarify the format requirements, i.e., should you start each point with a verb or in another way for consistency?

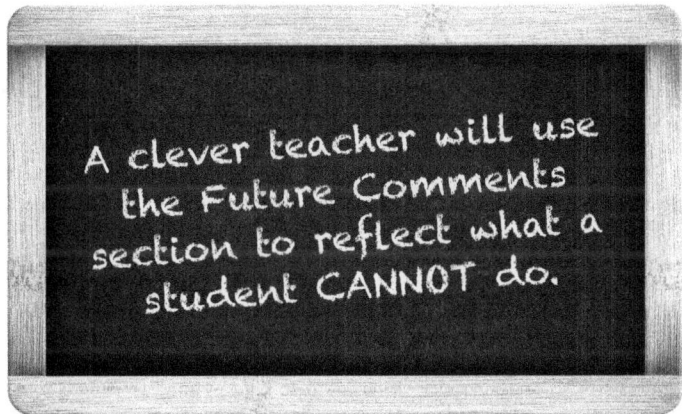

Here are some examples:

- » **Seeking clarification immediately when unsure.**
  The child just sits there when they are stuck and wastes time

- » **Choosing carefully who to sit next to or work with in group tasks.**
  She gets distracted (and distracts others) working with certain people and chooses the wrong students to work with

- » **Regularly using adjectives, metaphors and similes in all genres of writing.**
  He doesn't do this much

- » **Being diligent about handing in homework and assignments on due dates.**
  Poor time manager or lazy. Needs more support from home

After Writing

If you teach writing you will know that editing comes before proofreading. There's no point proofreading work that ends up being slashed or changed. It's a good idea to go through this process at least twice - once on screen and once with a printed version. You pick up different errors when you read it in alternative mediums.

Editing

Editing begins when you have finished your first draft. It's the process of improving the content. To do this well it's ideal to get some space from it first. Coming back to what you have written, at least a day after completion, helps you get some perspective on it.

When you edit, look for:

» Have you stated what the student CAN do or have you added in some comments about where their future focus should be? If so, cut and paste them to the 'Futures' section

» Have you used teacher speak or are comments fairly simple to understand? Reword any teacher speak phrases. If you are unsure, ask someone who is not a teacher to read it and see if they know what you mean

» Have you been concise or are you a bit long winded? Slash any superfluous words or condense sentences

» Have you said the same thing twice, just in different ways? If so, choose the better worded comment and remove the other

» Have you focussed on major curriculum areas? Are there enough comments on literacy and numeracy?

» Do your sentences have only two connected ideas? Any more and they are hard for the reader to process easily. Edit any that have more than two ideas

» Are your comments phrased positively? When you reread, do you get the sense parents would be okay with how you have worded comments? If in any doubt, reword and get a friend to read to check

» Is the report personalised? Would the parent get a strong sense that you know their child well?

» Have you referred to specific assignments or presentations that the child completed?

» Do the numerical marks that you assigned match your comments? Watch out for this mistake. If you assign a child a low numerical mark your comment needs to reflect this. Same for a student who is advanced

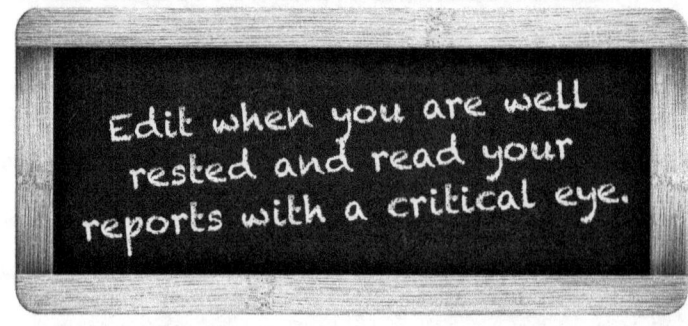

Proofreading

As equally important as editing, proofreading is the final polish before you are ready to print. After editing thoroughly your content is complete. Now you need to look at spelling, grammar and punctuation. When you pass your reports onto leadership or your team to read through, there should be only very minor corrections required. Parents are very quick to comment or complain if their child's teacher makes easily correctable errors.

Check for these things:

- Did you spell the child's name correctly? All the way through the report?
- When you cut and pasted some comments, did you change the student's name to the correct one? A friend showed me her son's Year Seven report. Half way through the comments the teacher switched to using his brother's name. Not very professional!
- Do you have capitals in all the right places? That is, the start of sentences and proper nouns. Capitals are also needed for subject names such as Mathematics, English and Science. Capitals are also needed for Semester One or Term One. They are not needed if you use the word mathematical
- Have you used the correct punctuation throughout?
- Did you just rely on a spell checker or did you read through yourself? Spell checkers are not fool proof
- Did you vary your sentence beginnings?
- Have you used the child's name too much? Alternate by using the pronouns 'he' or 'she'
- Are acronyms spelt out correctly the first time? For example, use the acronym E.A.L. but the first time you use it spell it out. English as an Additional Language (E.A.L.)
- Have you used the word for numbers? Semester One is the correct way to write it, not 1
- Did you read the report slowly and read every word?
- Homophones! Don't be tricked up by their/they're/there or other common ones
- Did you use the word practice or practise? Practice is a noun, whilst practise is a verb
- Did you use speech marks anywhere? Sure hope you didn't! You would have no need to quote what anyone has said in a report. Use inverted commas instead if you need to highlight a word
- Are there any double spaces between words? Check you have the uniform single space between words. This may be easier to pick up by using a paper copy
- Did you use the symbol &? Use the whole word, and, instead. This applies to all symbols

Parents can be critical of sloppy punctuation errors in reports. Don't give them an opportunity to complain.

Final Word

School reports are a legal document. This means that sometime in the future it may be used as evidence in court or legal proceedings. The reasons for this are varied and impossible to guess. However, it is imperative that what you write and the numerical mark you assign is accurate AND you have evidence to back it up. Areas that you don't test for, such as Personal Learning, rely on teacher judgement. This is perfectly acceptable. A child's organisation, or lack of, will be reflected in perhaps their poor time management, and if this is a concern you would refer to it. Evidence, if required, may be obtainable from other assessable areas.

List your school's specific reporting requirements here.

Parent Teacher Interviews

Chapter Overview

» Before Interviews
  – Preparation
  – Space

» During interviews
  – Getting ready
  – Interpreters
  – How to conduct an interview
  – Problem parents

» After interviews

Parent/teacher interviews are vital for building positive relationships between parents and teachers, and achieving the best educational outcomes for children. Most of the time these meetings are an enjoyable and reflective time for all involved and you should be able to look forward to them, providing you have done your homework beforehand.

All schools operate with slightly different systems. Some are early in the school year, some mid year only, some mid and end or even termly. No matter where, when or what school, there's a few key strategies that you can always rely on for positive interviews with families.

You will need to be guided by your mentor and school about the exact purpose for each set of interviews. This will form the basis for how you conduct and plan these meetings. At my children's secondary school I am allocated a generous FIVE minutes to meet with each teacher. That's if I'm able to actually book an interview in a time I am available. Primary schools are usually kinder and allocate between ten minutes and half an hour.

Before Interviews

Speak to your mentor or leadership about how your school conducts the interviews and what you are expected to contribute. It's important not to assume you know the purpose and structure, especially if you've already taught at another school.

Find out:

- Who is expected to be present?
- If the child is present, how do you involve them?
- How does the booking system work?
- How long are the interviews?
- How do you wind up the interviews? (Bell or self timed?)
- Do you follow up parents who haven't booked? How do you do that?
- What is the purpose of the interviews?
- Do students complete a self-evaluation or reflection activity prior?
- Is the student evaluation made available for parents to take home?
- What work samples should you show?
- How do I find out if an interpreter is needed?
- If an interpreter is required, who does the booking?
- Do reports go home before or after interviews?
- What is the procedure if you urgently require help during a difficult parent interview?
- What is the procedure for parents who are divorced/separated?
- How do you terminate an interview due to aggressive parental behaviour?

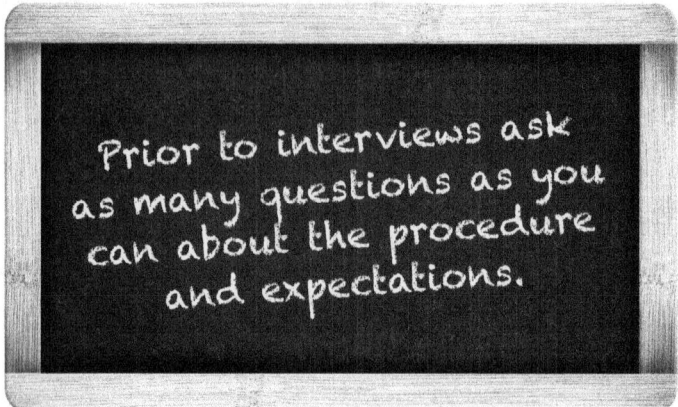

Prior to interviews ask as many questions as you can about the procedure and expectations.

Preparation

Before interviews you will need to think about what will be discussed about each child. In the weeks leading up to the interviews, begin to make brief notes about your students and list a couple of positive observations and a couple of areas of concern. Organise these notes so that they are in the order you will be seeing families.

Some schools like students to complete a self-reflection or evaluation activity prior to the interview. Determine the purpose of these with your mentor so that you ensure you utilise them correctly. These may be used as conversation starters or for agreements to be made about the way forward for the student.

Gather together any supporting evidence or resources that you may need to use. This may be homework, posters, tests or projects the child has completed. The purpose of this is to illustrate your point, if necessary, about why you marked the student as you did. Ensure also that you have quick and easy access to curriculum documents. I have only had to refer to these once, when a parent questioned my assessment. Luckily all my documentation was able to back me up!

Sometimes interviews are scheduled in the afternoon and evening, after you have taught all day. This is a little unfair but just the way it goes. Or, you work until 8pm and then start teaching again the next morning. Planning a couple of easier days in the classroom, curriculum wise, is a good idea.

Finally, go through the above dot point list to make sure everything is accounted for. The better prepared you are, the easier and more smoothly the interviews will run.

Space

What space will you be using for the interviews? Think about how you will set up furniture so that it's not too formal, yet at the same time everyone feels comfortable. I like to use a table, not the teacher's desk, because I need a few resources close by and because it's more friendly. Sitting at an angle to the table with the families means you are not too distant or threatening. Aim for warm and welcoming.

Prepare adequate notes and your classroom.

During Interviews

Getting ready

- Set up the room layout how you have planned
- Close to hand have tissues, water, your laptop, curriculum documents, supporting evidence, note paper, pen and possibly a timer
- Set up the waiting area outside the classroom with some chairs and a published list of interview times
- Eat! Being hungry is a big distraction
- Visit the toilet
- If you have a slight headache at all, have some painkillers!
- Your notes on each child should be at hand and in interview order

The Essential Teacher's Guide

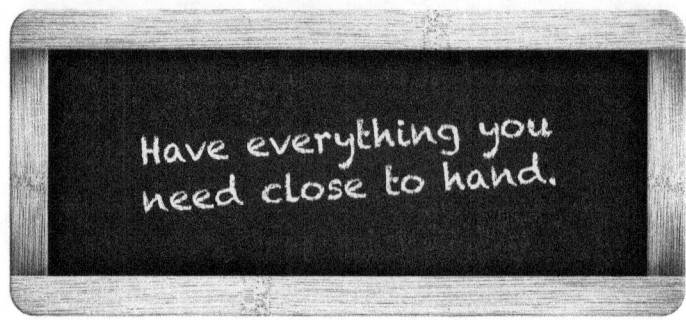

Interpreters

Using an interpreter, especially if you haven't used one before, can be an interesting experience. Ideally, the interpreter should sit next to the family. When you speak to the family maintain eye contact with them, not the interpreter. They are a conduit to the family; the interview is not with them.

It's hard to know if your message is being conveyed properly, however you will just have to learn to trust. If you have any requests that the family need to follow up, perhaps you could ask the interpreter to jot down some notes in their language. Use the opportunity of having an interpreter present to get any forms completed. Families where English is not the primary language often have trouble reading and understanding these.

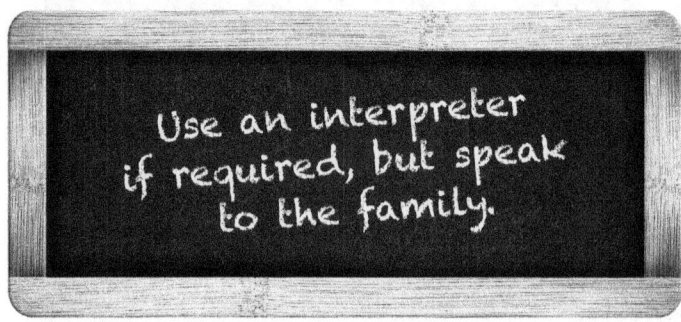

How To Conduct An Interview

Some schools request that children attend three way conferences. This has been my experience. I hated the whole idea at first and it took me a little while to get used to how to conduct a conference with a child present. I was worried that if I had something negative to share then it would be too tricky to do in front of the child. The purpose of three way conferences is to acknowledge that learning is a three way partnership between the child, parents and school. It's to discuss achievements and challenges and for all three parties to take some responsibility for this.

When the child is present, make them the focus of the conference and direct your conversation mainly towards them. Begin by sharing something you have enjoyed about having them in the classroom. This sets a positive tone. Even the most difficult of students have something you can praise. After this ask them to share with you what they think they are good at or do well in the classroom. If they say P.E. or Visual Art, agree but refocus them towards their main areas of learning. Children are very good at self-assessment and areas they suggest they do well in should be the same as your assessment too. Continue the conversation by praising their suggestions, agreeing if appropriate and then adding in some they may have forgotten. You can spend some time expanding on these; all parents love to hear their child encouraged and praised.

The next section of the conference is to ask the child to share with you areas they could work harder in or are finding difficult. Follow the same procedure as for the positive things. Agree (or not) with their suggestions, add in some of your own and expand upon them. At this stage, more of a discussion should begin to occur between the parents and yourself, delving into the areas of concern.

Finally, for the last part of the interview you can ask parents if they have any questions or concerns. Often this is really just about reassurance that their child is on track. If it looks like their concerns need deeper discussion, apologise that there's not enough time to address them now, and make a time in the next few days to have another meeting.

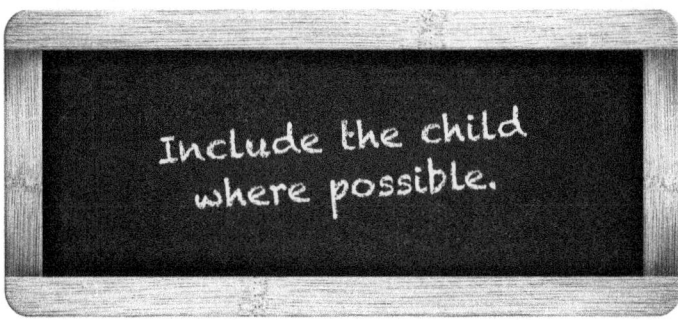

Another strategy to conduct interviews may be to begin by flipping through their portfolio or a workbook together and asking them to point out pieces they are particularly proud of and ask them why.

When the child is not present for the conference, you can run it in a similar way. Share with the parents areas for celebration and follow this with areas of concern. Make sure you are prepared with suggestions for how you will be able to assist their child with these problems areas and also how THEY can assist at home.

Never compare children or siblings. The interview is purely about the child you currently teach in your class. Something else to be aware of is to not show the work of other students to compare in any way. Sometimes it would be easy to illustrate your point about how far behind the student is by showing the work of a student at level. You need to rely on the curriculum here to detail the expected level, not comparison.

Sometimes during interviews a parent will draw to your attention an issue that may need following up. It's important to jot this down because back to back interviews for twenty-five children will leave you glazed and exhausted. There's little chance you might remember to follow it up. A parent may highlight some quiet bullying, friendship issues or possible referrals for you to make.

As you are conducting interviews, take great care to avoid families seeing confidential information about students that are not their own. Turn over reports or cover work samples.

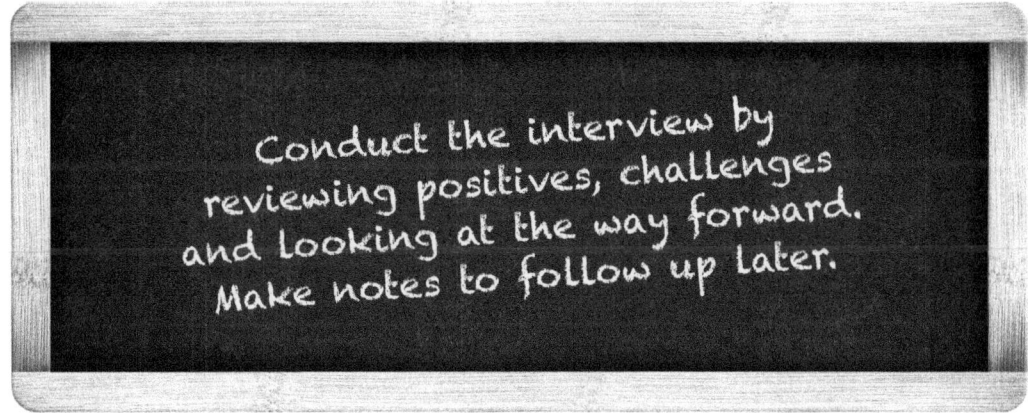

Problem Parents

In my experience, each set of interviews brings one parent that causes you grief. It's not always the ones you expect either.

Separated or divorced parents don't always interact healthily and you need to be prepared for this. You should not be expected to conduct two separate interviews for the one child. (Check with your school's policy). Either the parents come together or only one attends the interview. If you are worried it could get fiery, which is possible if blaming occurs, ask a third party to attend, such as the principal. Some interviews I have conducted with divorced parents have been wonderful and it was clear they were working with the child's best interests at heart. Once I even had the biological parents AND the stepparents attend together, very harmoniously. Sadly, divorced parents do not always have their child's best interests as the focus. I have seen nagging, blaming and niggling between parents. If you are witness to this, don't get caught up in their interactions, even if they request you to side with one of them. Just respectfully try to get the focus back on their child and decline to comment on anything other than that.

Some parents, usually those who you have not seen at all throughout the year, suddenly get angry with their child's lack of progress. Rather than admitting that their lack of support may be to blame, they turn that anger on the most convenient scapegoat - you.

The best way to handle parents who are angry or making accusations is to begin by acknowledging their frustration. "I can see you are frustrated/angry." Then show some empathy. "I'm sorry you feel that way." Finally, propose a mutually agreeable plan that indicates you both have a responsibility. "How can we work together to improve..." Jot down the agreed plan and restate the part each adult will contribute towards.

Interestingly, the most difficult interviews I have experienced are those where the parent/s are teachers. They always come from left field, as some part of me just expects them to understand how hard it is to conduct conferences with difficult parents. Surely they should be sympathetic! When I have thought about it further, I realised that they are more equipped than non-teaching parents to know what should and shouldn't be happening and so come at the interview from a more educated standpoint. It is still no excuse for rudeness or attacks however. If you have prepared well for the interviews and your written report is accurate, you should feel justified in your assessments. Even if you know you have done the right thing, it can still leave you shaken.

If you ever experience an interview with a difficult parent, it's kind to warn the teacher who has that child in their class the following year. Forewarned is forearmed! When worried about how a parent may behave in a conference, it is perfectly legitimate to request someone from leadership, your mentor, or a team member sit in on the conference to support you and back you up.

After a harrowing experience it's helpful to jot down your recollection of the interaction as soon as possible afterwards. Doing this helps you to analyse the conversation and reflect on how you could've possibly handled it better or to cover yourself if the parent makes a complaint. Talk to your mentor and leadership so they are informed and warned, and so that you can have some support.

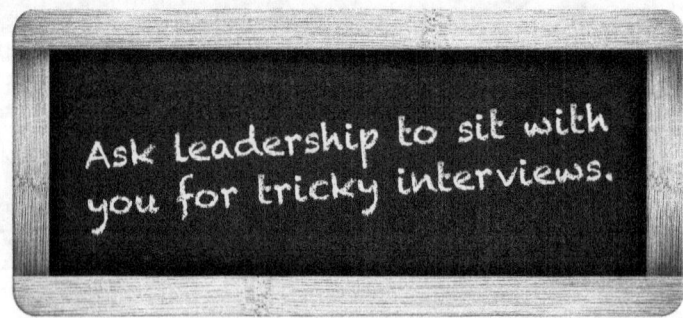

After Interviews

Phew! When interviews conclude I usually feel exhausted, relieved and happy. Overall they are a good experience, just draining when you have to concentrate for so long. If you finish in the evening, just leave everything where it is and go home. The students can help you move furniture back in the morning.

In the day or two after interviews, begin to work through the list you made when chatting with parents. It's really important that you follow everything up. If you agreed upon a plan for the remaining term or year, document it and send a copy home to the parents. Speak to children that concerns were raised about. Adjust the seating arrangements of students if required. Begin the process of referral for testing. Plan more specifically for some students. No matter what you said you would follow up or change, please inform the parents that you have done it. It only takes a minute to send home a note or to call them. It is really appreciated.

Any documentation that comes out of the interviews, and that you deem significant or important, should be placed in the child's file for future reference. Occasionally teachers need to chase up things that may take awhile. Diarise a reminder at an appropriate time in the future to prompt you if necessary.

Casual Relief Teaching

Chapter Overview

- How to get work
- Join an agency
- Direct contact with a school
- How to be a good C.R.T.
- How to be a crap C.R.T.
- Preparing your classroom for a C.R.T.

How To Get Work

The thought of being a Casual Relief Teacher (C.R.T.) used to fill me with dread and horror. I'd heard so many bad stories over the years from my C.R.T. mum. I was lucky enough to secure a full time job straight after graduation so didn't have to face that prospect. I've worked with many C.R.T.s over the years, particularly when I was team teaching, so have experienced the good, bad and ugly! The good ones are worth their weight in gold and will get constant work. Recently I have had the opportunity, by choice, to undertake C.R.T., and I have to say that I LOVE it!

Finding yourself needing to work as a C.R.T. in your first year or two out can be disheartening if it wasn't your choice. (Check out Chapters 1 and 2 on Applications and Interviews for tips and advice). Doing even a term of casual work really helps to hone and improve your skills, so try to look at it as an advantage. You will be exposed to different styles of teaching, different types of schools and a vast variety of student types and behaviours. Using this experience in your applications for more permanent work is a positive.

Join An Agency

There are a few agencies in each state or nationwide. Check out their websites and work out how to contact them. Some agencies will be better than others, so ask your peers for any feedback. They all have different formats for how they contact you to book a job. Going through an agency has pros and cons.

PROS

- » You don't have to find the work for yourself
- » You don't have to fill in tax forms at each school
- » Some offer guaranteed work
- » For tax purposes you only have one employer
- » Exposure to a wide range of school types and levels is a great opportunity
- » Some agencies offer in house professional development
- » Agencies don't like to book for part days so you will get a full day's work when you are booked

CONS

- » Possibly long commute times
- » An inability to form a long relationship with a school
- » Less control over schools and classes you are prepared to teach
- » The agency takes a cut of your day's pay. More if you are offered guaranteed work every day

List your local agencies here.

Direct Contact With a School

To gain employment as a C.R.T. directly with a school you will need to drop in with your C.V. and ask to speak to the teacher who employs the relievers.

PROS

- You choose the schools and areas you'd like to work in
- The opportunity to build up an ongoing relationship with a school
- It's possible to decide not to return to a particular school or grade, based on your experience
- If a job becomes available at the schools you relieve at then your chances of being the successful applicant rise just that little bit
- With often little to separate applicants on paper, knowing how you teach and interact within the school will get you noticed. It won't guarantee you a job due to Merit and Equity, but may increase your chances just that little bit. Gaining permanent employment really is about who you know
- Working in a school as a C.R.T. that you'd like to gain an ongoing job in means you get to informally interview them too
- First you may need to put your name down at many schools to get your foot in the door, but as you start to get a steady stream of work you might like to narrow this down a little
- When schools get to know you they will call you more regularly, especially if you are a good C.R.T. When this occurs you should regularly email the person who books you to let them know your availability. This is appreciated, as they know not to call you if you are pre-booked and it saves them time

CONS

- You will not get guaranteed work every day
- For each new school you work at you will be required to fill in employment and taxation forms. Boo to that!
- If you are not good at self promotion you may find it a bit difficult to push yourself forward in order to get booked
- Depending on how you look at it, being booked for half days through direct contact with a school could be either a pro or a con. A negative if you really need the money and a positive if you want some extra time to yourself. I love half days as a C.R.T. - I feel like I can fit so much more into my day!

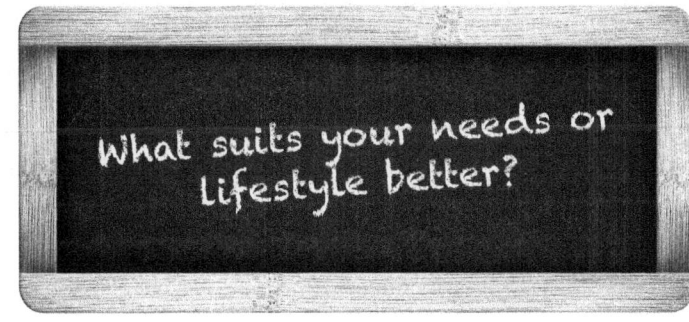

How To Be a Good C.R.T.

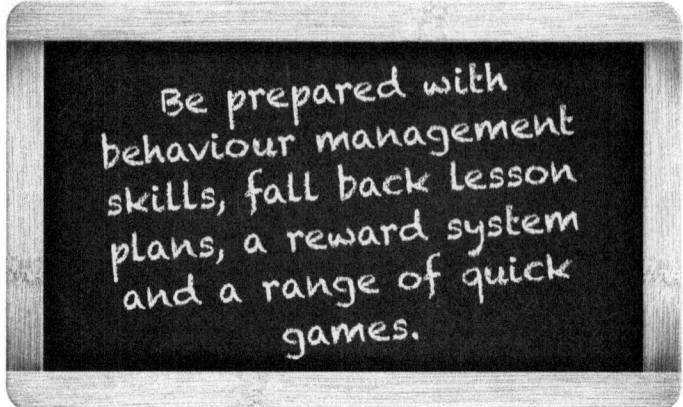

Be prepared with behaviour management skills, fall back lesson plans, a reward system and a range of quick games.

» This is rather nebulous, but all children I have spoken to about what they thought makes a good C.R.T. described a strong presence. Variously, this was defined as not airy, engaging, firm, fair, able to command attention and clued in to kids who will act up

» Look at every job as an opportunity for learning and making contacts

» Arrive early enough (where possible) to go over the work plan and school procedures

» Be enthusiastic and cheerful. Bounce into that school and that enthusiasm will rub off on your class for the day

» You only have a short time in the school or classroom. Make it worthwhile

» Introduce yourself to the class and to staff

» State your expectations to the class from the start of the day. Their teacher will have different expectations to you, and they will tell you that, but just be firm and fair whilst requesting that today, this is how they will do it

» Spend some time getting to know them by asking children to share one thing or some news as you mark the roll

» Share about yourself too, to make connections and help children feel comfortable with who is in charge of their class for the day

» Tell the class you have heard they are the best/favourite class in the school and you were so excited to learn you were teaching them for the day

» Inform the children that their teacher left them a note requesting you give feedback to him/her about their behaviour

» Be kind and encouraging throughout the day. A C.R.T. I had when I was in Grade 6 told me I'd never amount to anything more than a dunny cleaner. His purpose?

» Stickers and stamps. Stickers and stamps. Stickers and stamps. Get it? Always have these packed in your bag and give them out liberally

» Stickers and stamps don't work for senior students. Suss out the reward program the class or level have in place and use it

» Devise your own reward program for the day, especially if none is evident in the classroom. Make it short term for juniors and longer for seniors. For example, every time you think children are well behaved, focussed, cooperative etc., add a tick to the board. When they are the opposite, take off a tick. Some possible rewards might be to eat snack or lunch a little early, to eat outside, five minutes play on equipment, an inside or an outside game. Make it clear when you are adding or subtracting ticks and why

- » Have a good list of quick games to play with minimal equipment that you can cart around in your bag at all times, suitable for all age levels. (See chapter on Five Minute Fillers for ideas)

- » Prepare some quick go to lessons for filling gaps when a program is lacking. Make these non-dependent on resources and age appropriate. Design activities are always a good option as these don't rely on sequential knowledge children may not have as yet

- » Get the heads up from any other team members on children to watch out for and how to manage them

- » Manage the class yourself - don't resort to sending kids out for misbehaviour, unless it is dangerous or really, really atrocious. Besides, if you want to teach in your own classroom, this is a perfect opportunity to learn some behaviour management skills

- » Chat to other staff in the staffroom. Be friendly and get to know people as you are laying the groundwork for a possible job if one arises. And if you don't want a job there it's still polite to be friendly

- » Offer to do extra yard duty if someone is missing

- » Leave a detailed note for the classroom teacher. They want to know what was and wasn't covered and any behavioural issues for the day. This is especially important if parents or teachers want to follow up a problem that occurred when the C.R.T. was in the classroom

- » Rove. Circulating around the room whilst children are working independently is a fabulous way to keep them on task, minimise behavioural problems and for you to make connections

- » Thank the team for any support and thank the assistant principal for hiring you for the day.

- » Join groups on social media specifically set up to support C.R.T.s

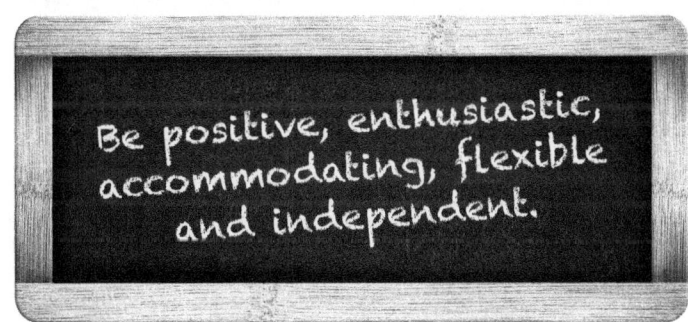

How To Be a Crap C.R.T.

(Which can translate to a crap permanent teacher too). This section was included because some people need it spelled out. Now that it's out there, you have no excuse!

- Panic. When you panic your brain shuts down and you can't think clearly. Keep a calm and cool head so you can be creative

- Have excessive anxiety over what to do and project it onto other teachers. You are a qualified professional and as such need to have your house in order. Anxiety and C.R.T.s are not a good mix. If you get overly anxious, perhaps this isn't a good casual job for you

- Bribe with lollies. Many schools have healthy eating policies now where lollies are banned. Besides, your skills need to be better than this

- Arrive late. Sometimes if you get a late call or stuck in traffic it's unavoidable. Arriving too close to the bell doesn't give you time to read and understand the plan properly (if one is left) or to come up with lesson plans if needed. Other teachers don't want to be bothered ten minutes before bell time with your questions. Allow at least thirty minutes

- Don't follow the plan left for you. Curriculum requirements are massive in the twenty first century. There's little time to catch up missed lessons. Many topics are sequential and the next concept will be reliant on this being taught

- Send misbehaving kids to other teachers or to the office (unless it's severe)

- Play games all day or too often. Lots of fun, the kids will think you're ace. Other teachers clue in very quickly to what is happening and you won't be asked back

- Be fooled by students into thinking games, behaviours or activities are the norm when they are not. In primary school during the early eighties my Grade 6 class managed to convince a gullible C.R.T. that every Friday our teacher bought us hot chips from the local shops. Hot chips were had by all!

- Come unprepared. You're asking for a difficult day if you have no fall-back lessons, games or behaviour management techniques ready to implement

- Be inflexible or stressed by changes. What happens from hour to hour can totally change from the plan. You need to learn to run with it

- Don't use initiative. Thought of a good add-on to a teacher's plan? Use it. Share your ideas with the team if appropriate

- Shirk your duties. Make sure you turn up for the yard duty on time

- Have students going bananas due to lack of behaviour management and control. Teachers in your area will discover very quickly if you cannot manage the class effectively. They will report that to the leadership team and you won't be asked back

- Be grumpy. Seems silly to have to point this out but grumpy C.R.T.s are out there. You cannot expect to have engaged and enthusiastic learners when you are grumpy. Or to be asked back

- Stay seated at the desk or up the front. Seriously?

- Need your hand held excessively. A C.R.T. I worked with recently seemed totally incapable of reading and understanding a work plan left for them and kept asking copious questions. There will always be things on a plan you don't quite follow and should ask about, but a couple of questions per lesson should suffice. Students can point you in the direction of supplies

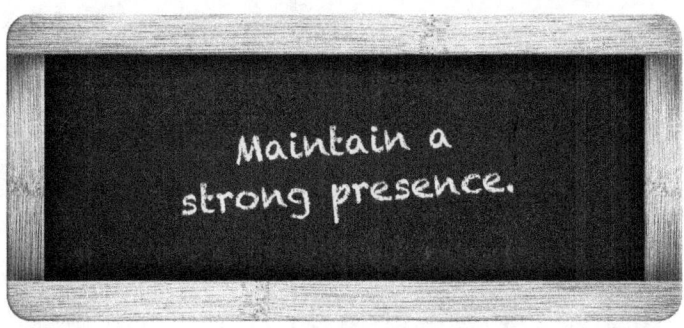

Maintain a strong presence.

Preparing Your Classroom For a C.R.T.

Whenever a relief teacher is booked to work in your classroom the main priority is that they can find the plan and resources as required. When you know you will be absent leave a detailed plan on your desk for them to follow, along with extra notes explaining your plan if necessary. The more you explain the smoother it will run for them, therefore fewer problems for you to deal with on your return. Photocopy all resources required and get out all other items needed such as dice or books. Have these all easily accessible for the C.R.T. The roll should be on your desk, or in a really obvious spot. Please leave notes on children with specific learning or behavioural needs.

Occasionally you unexpectedly need to take a day off and your classroom won't be as prepared as you'd like. You must send through a plan and notes via email to your team leader or the assistant principal for them to pass on to the C.R.T. It's good practice to have all your resources prepared the night before, labelled and ready to go for yourself, so if you are absent it will all be there ready for the substitute. Doing this also puts less pressure on your team to chase around and find things or photocopy items when they need to be doing their own preparation.

Ask your students for feedback on the C.R.T.s they have. This is a good indicator of their quality and ability. Over time you will get to know the teachers you want to invite back, who manage the class well and fit in well with your school. When you have a new C.R.T. in your class, or work with one in your level that you thought was great, please feed that back to the teacher who hires them. Also let them know the useless ones to avoid. Unless they get feedback they just won't know who to rebook and who to black ban!

Specialists

Chapter Overview

- » Pros
- » Cons
- » Beginning of the year
- » Inclusion
- » Reporting

Specialists are a vital part of the education process for a variety of reasons. Primary school teachers with generalist qualifications are able to teach any specialist area. You may find yourself working as a specialist in your first few years of teaching either by choice or necessity. Whatever the reason, it's imperative to embrace the importance and relevance of educating children in this niche area.

Pros

Independence: Whilst you are part of the specialist 'team', each area is quite diverse and you will usually not need to plan together. This allows you to plan at a time that suits you best and perhaps also negates the need for a meeting. That's always a good thing!

The independence allows for the spotlight on you to prove your capabilities. You get all the credit for what you do, for example, a production or artistic pieces, whereas it is harder for a classroom teacher to shine unless a mentor is singing your praises.

Whilst you work independently, it enables you to relate to all teachers in the staff room as you get to know their students' quirks and capabilities. Teachers love to share about their class! This is a good way to build relationships amongst staff.

Curriculum flexibility: Generally, curriculum documents for specialist domains are quite broad in the primary school setting. There are not a lot of benchmarks to be met or specifically reported upon, so you have some freedom in your planning. It doesn't mean you can do whatever you want however, there are still curriculum documents to use as your foundation for planning.

Less responsibility: As you don't have your own class group, you are not ultimately responsible for their literacy and numeracy or ongoing wellbeing. No parent meetings or phone calls!

Enjoyment: It's a rare child that doesn't enjoy going to specialists. As you only have one lesson per week with each class (usually), it's easier to make your lessons engaging and entertaining. Students are always disappointed when they have to miss out on Art or P.E. Make sure you channel that enthusiasm into worthwhile activities and lessons.

Behaviour Management: when you have your own class it is easy to develop and maintain behavioural expectations and routines. Having a new class every hour means you need to work harder on your behavioural management skills as each group of children has different needs and are different age groups. If you ever teach your own class you will have an awesome set of management techniques!

You will be exposed to a massive range of behaviours that will require you to adapt your management and teaching. A real bonus is that if a specific child is particularly challenging or hard to manage then you only have to teach them for one hour a week! You get to hand them back to the classroom teacher who has the headache of ongoing management and parental contact.

Reporting: Whilst you may have to report on ALL children in the school, the process for collecting data and observations is much simpler, as is the actual reporting process. Depending on your school, you might only have to write a generic paragraph for each level about topics covered and then a few sentences on each child's achievements. There is recognition that a fair bit of repetition is necessary.

Planning: You may only need to plan FOUR lessons a week. FOUR! (Prep, 1/2, 3/4, 5/6). How awesome is that? A classroom teacher may need to plan upwards of twenty, depending on a number of factors. Planning so few lessons means you can really focus on ticking all the boxes for a stimulating, engaging and differentiated program.

It may be possible to plan your term in advance, or perhaps half a term, so that throughout the teaching weeks you have more time to take reporting notes, organise resources, or do any of the other million responsibilities teachers seem to have.

Being able to repeat your lesson several times to a year level gives you the opportunity to really hone your lesson planning. You will be able to reflect on why some classes got more out of your lesson than others.

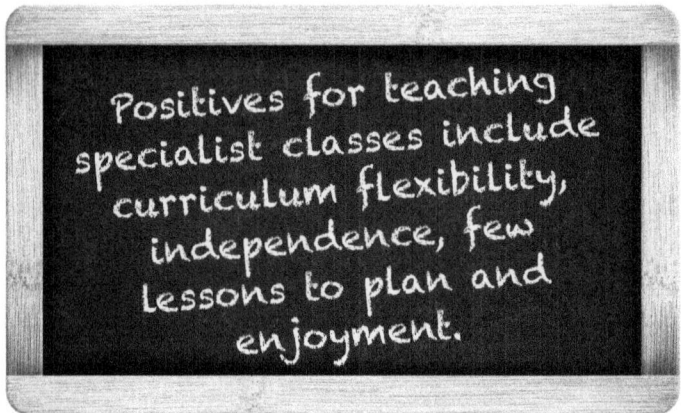

Positives for teaching specialist classes include curriculum flexibility, independence, few lessons to plan and enjoyment.

Cons

Independence: Being free from a team of teachers doesn't work for everyone. It might be difficult for you to operate in isolation without the support of other adults and experienced teachers. You may feel like you need more guidance than is possible, as you may be the only teacher in that area at the school. A suggestion is to make contact, or network with, teachers in your specialty area from other local schools.

Curriculum flexibility: Having really broad or vague curriculum documents can make it difficult to pin down what you will actually teach. It can be overwhelming as a new teacher to determine what to teach and you may require more direction. If possible, ask previous teachers of a specialist area for their planning documents or contact other local schools.

Less responsibility: Hmmm. Can't actually think of any cons here!

Enjoyment: It can be hard to enjoy teaching a specialist role if you really want to be a classroom teacher or the specialist position is Art and you have no creative bones in your body. If this is the case, look at what you can learn throughout the year to take with you when you achieve your desired position. You will be developing valuable and transferrable skills as a specialist.

If children don't appear to enjoy your class then you need to reflect on why. Teaching a specialist area makes it relatively easy to prepare enjoyable lessons. Ask any child what their favourite lesson at school is and 90% of the time they will respond with Art or P.E. Try and capitalise on this!

Getting to know the students well means you can foster deeper connections and often share some jokes together. See Chapter 3 on Enjoying Teaching for more tips.

Behaviour management: Difficult children to manage may require you to speak to their classroom teacher for tips and ideas on the best way to get the most out of them. Some students with behavioural issues can worsen during specialist time, as it is a change of teacher and in their normal routine. Keeping them contained and as occupied as possible may be challenging. See chapter on Behaviour Management for ideas.

Reporting: Data collection is fairly important as you can never remember every child's abilities or output. Classes in P.E. or Performing Arts usually do not have finished products that are easily graded. In Visual Arts or LOTE it is easier to produce a sample of work if requested by parents or leadership.

Reporting in specialist areas requires you to be organised and diligent with your note taking so that come time to write your comments you are well resourced. See Chapter 22, Report Writing for ideas.

Planning: Only planning a few lessons a week may mean you are a tad intellectually bored. If this is the case, you have plenty of opportunity to self reflect. What am I doing well? What areas do I need to improve in? How will I be able to improve?

Repeating lessons so many times throughout the day can also cause boredom. A clever colleague worked out a way to avoid this:

Middle K	Middle S
Week 1-3 dance	Week 1-3 drama
Week 4-6 drama	Week 4-6 dance

This is not always possible to do, especially if you require a lot of resources.

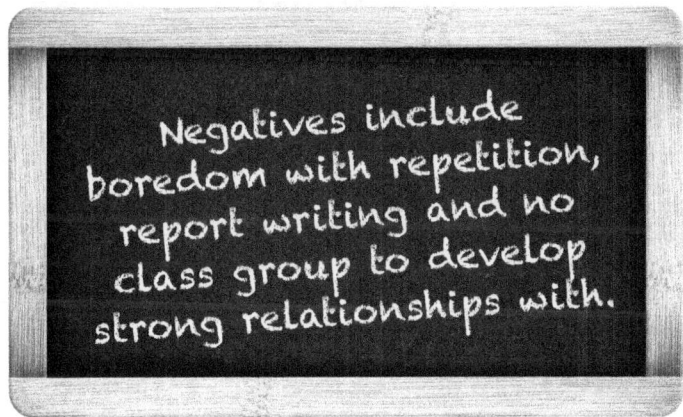

Beginning Of The Year

Names

Taking a specialist class means you have a lot of names to remember. You can tackle this by playing name games at the start of a lesson or two, or having name tags prepared for use in the first few weeks.

Another way to remember names is to use an app on your iPad and to take a picture of each child in the first week. This is quite time consuming, but absolutely worth it.

Behaviour management becomes so much easier when you know each child's name. When you get to the point where you think you should know all names but don't, you can create a game out of your mistakes. Every time you use the wrong name, or have a mental blank, reward that child in some way. Give out house points, coveted roles, a sticker, some free time etc.

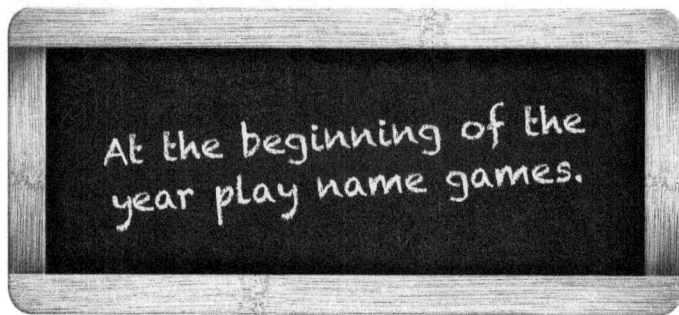

Class Expectations

Taking a specialist class means you teach every class grouping in the school. Each of these classes have teachers who have their own set of expectations, rules and ways to gain children's attention. At the start of the year it's important to make clear your own rules for the area you teach. Some may need to be around safety if you are using dangerous equipment or chemicals.

Whatever rules and expectations you settle upon, it's key to keep them consistent. **All classes should:**

- Enter and exit your work space respectfully
- Sit in a designated space for the whole class lesson or instruction
- Sit quietly and pay attention to your explanations
- Know where equipment and resources are stored
- Know whether they are allowed to access equipment and resources without your permission
- Know and understand any safety guidelines
- Be respectful of all student's work
- Know appropriate working noise levels
- Stop work and pay attention immediately upon your signal
- Pack up quickly and neatly

Many of these guidelines will need to be modelled, sometimes repeatedly. They will learn very quickly to follow the rules, especially if you sit them out of something they are keen to do when they are being disrespectful of your space and rules.

You will also need to check whether a class is delivered to your room by their teacher, or if you need to collect and drop off. See Chapter 5 on Classroom Management for more information.

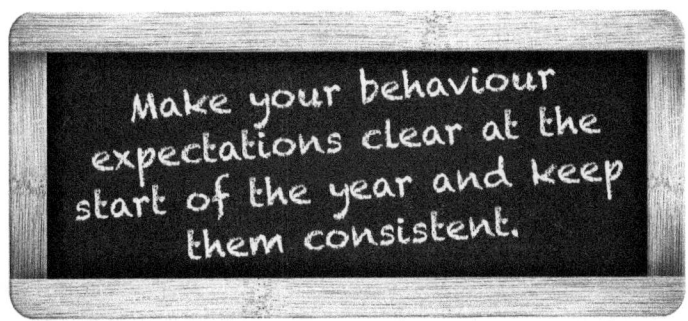

Organisation

It doesn't matter if you are a specialist or a general classroom teacher; you need to be organised. Being well organised ensures you have laid the foundations to be a great teacher. Planning on both a macro and micro level is essential.

MACRO ORGANISATION

- Organise folders (digital and hard) by year level
- File any term or lesson plans
- Attach or file any resource documents
- Insert class lists into year level folders
- File in these folders any communication notes with teachers/students
- Start a folder for your roll (for the entire school). Include any behaviour management or medical plans
- Determine children with integration aides and ascertain if they will be attending your class with the student
- Ask aides and teachers how best to cater for the specific needs of integrated children
- Prepare lists of resources and their locations so you know what you have and where it is stored
- Plan a term overview
- Plan a few weeks in advance to allow you to source resources (important for Visual or Performing Arts)
- Select a note taking app or note taking method before the year starts for ongoing report comments
- Read through the state or national curriculum documents carefully
- If you have captains for your specialist area find out how they are appointed and how you will utilise them
- Diarise important dates such as whole school sporting events or exhibitions. These occasions can be much busier than normal weeks so being organised is essential
- Plan backwards from these events by using a timeline so you manage your time well
- Plan appropriate and engaging activities that children can do if they finish early

MICRO ORGANISATION

» At the start of the day, look over your lesson plans. Read them carefully. Do they make sense? Is the lesson purpose clearly stated?

» Get out all the resources you will need and have them either set up or close to hand

» Check internet connection

» Cue up any music

» Check interactive whiteboard connectivity if needed

» Charge any devices needed

» Check the weather. Do you need to move your lesson inside or to another venue?

» Look over the classroom space. Are there any items needing moving or securing?

» Is the classroom set up appropriately for your lesson?

» Have your lesson plan and roll close to your teaching space

» Review the class list. Are there any children you need to be mindful of?

» Delegate small jobs to your captains - cleaning glue pots, tidying sports shed, taking down displays

» What will the children do who finish early?

» Are all children going to be occupied for most of the lesson?

For more ideas regarding organisation see Chapter 6 on Resource Organisation

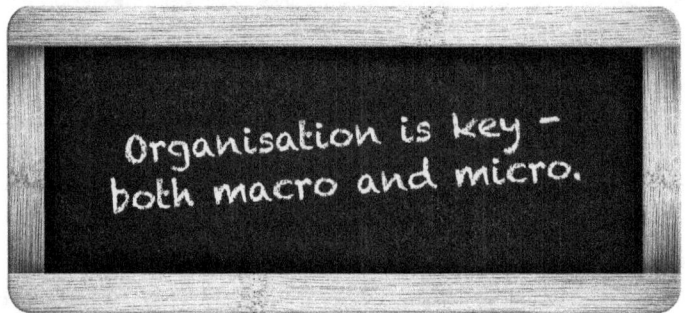

Organisation is key - both macro and micro.

Reporting

Reporting on specialist areas has the capacity to become quite onerous, however there are ways to avoid a time consuming stress out!

» Before the year commences source an easy to use note-taking app for a tablet device. Tablets are portable, efficient and functional and are preferable to hand writing notes

» If you elect to go the hand written route, organise yourself with specific folders for each level, label them and always have them close to hand

» Before you begin a unit of work, determine the skills being assessed. Write appropriate 'reporter speak' sentences that you can copy and paste next to a child's name. For example, 'Xxx displays excellent technical skills using paint as a medium.'

» For every area of the curriculum assessed, write a generic sentence that can be used as a blurb for all students in that year level

- » Get a colleague with excellent proofreading skills to read through your generic paragraph blurbs BEFORE you copy & paste them into reports. It's much easier to correct the one paragraph than ninety!
- » Check carefully you have used the correct pronouns of he or she
- » Imagine how hard it would be to write reports if you don't know everyone's name. That's why name games at the start of the year are so important. If you are really stuck, ask for a copy of the class photo to use to remind you

For more tips on report writing, see Chapter 22.

Inclusion

In the specialist classroom you will encounter all the children in the school with disabilities. Inclusion is a human right for all and includes availability of opportunity, acceptance of disability and an absence of bias, prejudice or inequality. You need to be proactive in identifying barriers and obstacles learners face in the specialist class to a quality education, as well as removing these barriers.

- » Talk to any integration aides about how best to adjust your program to include children with special needs
- » Find out if aides will attend your specialist class
- » Not all children with disabilities will have aides. Speak to their teachers about their specific needs and how best to be inclusive
- » Once you get to know who requires assistance to be included in your program, your lesson plans should reflect this. Clearly detail how Xxx can approach, or be included in, the day's task or activity
- » Reflect on the success of inclusion. Do you need to make adjustments?

See the Chapters 9 through 11 on Differentiation, Aides and Disabilities for further ideas.

Templates

The following templates are available for you to download from my website, www.survivingandthriving.com.au/templates. They are not definitive; that is, feel free to adjust them to meet your own specific needs. I'd love to hear how you adjust them to make them better. You can contact me via twitter @teacherthrive, my website, Facebook https://www.facebook.com/survivingandthrivingteaching or through email nadine@survivingandthriving.com.au

Beginning of the year templates:

Get To Know You Game: One per child and they cannot ask the same student a question as they play.

Photo Hunt: Put students into groups and they must use an iPad or similar to take pictures of each item on the list.

T-Shirt: Personalise the T-Shirt with words or drawings.

Literacy:

Middle and Senior Reading Log: For use both at home and in the classroom. Teacher decides if either a parent or teacher should sign.

Junior Reading Log: For use both at home and in the classroom. Even Preps can use this log.

Classroom management:

Toilet Visits: A behaviour management system to encourage children to not visit the toilet during the classroom.

Toilet Rules: A poster with some guidelines for visiting the toilet during class time.

Table Torture: A system to change seating plans at desks approximately once per week. Desks need to be numbered (I use a permanent marker but you could use contact to stick on numbers). Children line up in front of you, you flash the card number to them and they move their supplies to that desk number.

Free Choice Time Chart: A behaviour management system. Teacher adds or subtracts minutes throughout the week based on a child's behaviour or effort. Friday afternoon 'free' time is then allocated by the number of minutes each child has accrued. Teacher chooses how many minutes the class starts with each week.

Free Choice Time PPT: A guideline for appropriate activities for Free Time. Personalise this to suit your classroom situation.

Free Choice Time Poster: A guideline for appropriate activities for Free Time. Personalise this to suit your classroom situation.

Bonus Minutes: A chart to encourage children to bring specific items to school or complete tasks. Add these bonus minutes to the Free Choice Time Chart at the end of the week.

Free Choice Time Rules: A poster outlining appropriate behaviours during Free Time. Personalise to your own classroom.

Homework:

Homework Completed: A term template for the teacher to complete for each student in the class. This makes it easy to see who has and hasn't completed homework or it if was late. Allows you to see patterns and inform you for report writing or parent teacher interviews.

Homework Handed In: Children sign the appropriate column, based on when they returned their homework. Display on a wall. Handing in homework a day or two after assignment should attract bonus minutes. At a glance you can see who has and hasn't handed in homework.

Homework Excuse: A letter that children complete, stating their reason for not completing homework. Keep a folder on display in the room with copies of this template. Space for teacher to comment and you choose whether or not to send home for the parent to view and/or sign.

I'm sorry…: Front cover poster for the Homework Excuse letter folder.

Parent communication:

Christmas Party Letter: A unique way to run your end of year Christmas party.

Sample Class Party Letter: Inform parents about a class party and the requirements.

Sample Parent Helpers Letter: Sample letter to parents outlining expectations and a timetable for assisting in the classroom.

Reading at Home With Your Child: Information for parents of junior students on how to help their child read at home.

Take Home Reading: 3 ways and check- a visual poster to send home outlining how parents can help their child read at home.

Planning:

Sample Week Overview 1

Sample Week Overview 2

Sample Weekly Timetable

Sample Term Overview

ACKNOWLEDGEMENTS

I am very lucky indeed to have a huge list of people I need to acknowledge. Many people contributed to this book in numerous ways - ideas, tech support, publishing support, friendship, reading and encouragement.

Firstly, to my incredibly supportive husband, Peter. So very brave of you to support and encourage my dream. My extraordinary website and stunning book design is thanks to his talents. Check him out at www.burstcreative.com.au. (Unashamed plug!) I really appreciate the millions of ways you support me. xoxo

I hit the jackpot with my two gorgeous daughters, Chelsea and Jaslyn. I'm very proud of the young women you have grown into and am very excited about what the future holds for you both. Your support and enthusiasm for my new projects is appreciated. The soundtracks I wrote this book to were courtesy of the eternal loop they seemed to be on in your bedrooms throughout 2014 - Les Miserables and Grease. And Chels, thanks for your B.O. chant in the Student Hygiene chapter.

Mentor extraordinaire, Deb Simpson. Deb has taught my children, was my supervising teacher on rounds, team taught with me for two years, was my team leader for four years and became a good friend. Thank you for all your encouragement and support of my teaching career, for fun dinners out, and for many, many laughs.

Mel Dykstra diligently read EVERY chapter and made many wise suggestions. I used them all! A brilliant woman, who was born to teach. If every teacher had the diligence, ideas and enthusiasm that you have, all students would thrive. Thank you so much for your friendship and love.

Jane Searle, full stop. I am blessed beyond measure to have a friend who gets me, to talk about psychotherapy with and live life alongside. Thank you for being you! When my laptop died on Christmas Eve and I discovered my wireless back up hadn't worked since April (argghhh!!), Jane immediately offered to help me retype my whole book from the print outs. Thanks for enthusiastically workshopping many ideas with me and I look forward to seeing where our ideas take us!

All the cartoon images throughout were digitally created by the talented Frances Eddy and Peter King, of Burst Creative. Thanks for putting up with my constant changes and perfectionism! I appreciate your attention to detail with the typesetting job too!

To all my friends and colleagues who read a chapter or two along the way or contributed to this book with ideas or assistance - Marg Kittelty, Karina Bruce, Meg Moore, Amanda Callahan, Sarah Buckingham, Joel Parsons, Kirralee Lewis (love, love, love you!), Trevor Dykstra, Sharon Witt, Sarah Marrinan and Karen Alea Ford. A great big thank you!

To the formatter, Carol Dick, thanks for your enthusiasm and support of this project.

To all the proofreaders and early readers for feedback, my heartfelt appreciation!

To all the past and present Eastwood Primary School staff. Thank you for education, employment, friendship and Friday afternoon drinks! This school has been my community for over fifteen years and I cannot imagine not working there in some capacity. My front yard is always open for emergency evacuations!

Finally, to Darcy, my beautiful red and white Border Collie. Thanks for your paw on my knee as I typed and for the exercise we had together when I needed to stretch my legs.

Out Soon!

Surviving and Thriving:
Educating Children With Additional Needs
In The Mainstream Classroom

Out Soon!

Surviving and Thriving:
Parent's Guide
Assisting Your Child With Additional Needs
In The Mainstream Classroom

www.ingramcontent.com/pod-product-compliance
Lightning Source LLC
Chambersburg PA
CBHW060454300426
44113CB00016B/2591